D0596201

REBELS WIT ATTITUDE

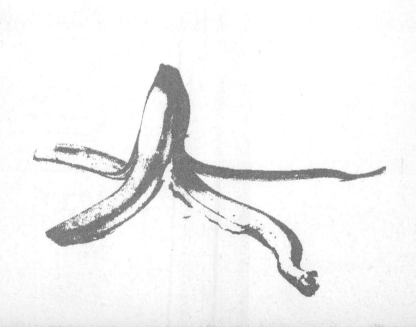

REBELS WIT ATTITUDE:
SUBVERSIVE ROCK HUMORISTS

IAIN ELLIS

For further essays from Iain Ellis on this topic,
please go to www.popmatters.com/whateveritis

Library of Congress Cataloging-in-Publication Data

Ellis, Iain.
  Rebels wit attitude : subversive rock humorists / Iain Ellis.
    p. cm.
  Includes bibliographical references and index.
  ISBN-13: 978-1-59376-206-3 (alk. paper)
  ISBN-10: 1-59376-206-2 (alk. paper)
  1. Rock music—History and criticism.
  2. Humor in music. I. Title.
ML3534.E43 2008
781.660973—dc22

                                        2008027013

Cover design by Gary Fogelson
Interior design by Pauline Neuwirth, Neuwirth & Associates, Inc.

Printed in the United States of America

Soft Skull Press
An Imprint of Counterpoint LLC
2117 Fourth Street
Suite D
Berkeley, CA 94710

www.softskull.com
www.counterpointpress.com

Distributed by Publishers Group West

10 9 8 7 6 5 4 3 2 1

Cheers to Kirby Fields and his vigilant red pen for bringing some sense to the sentences and some punk to the punctuation!!

—Iain Ellis

Contents

INTRODUCTION:

Subversion, Rock, Humor

> "A joke's a very serious thing."
> —Charles Churchill (1762)[1]

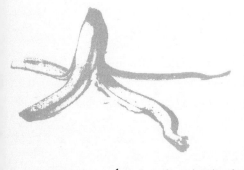

INVARIABLY UNDERESTIMATED and underappreciated, humor is often unfairly conflated with the light and the trivial. Yet, many strains of humor carry serious purposes, with their intent to subvert various institutional status quos. Whether Oscar Wilde or Dorothy Parker, the Marx Brothers or Richard Pryor, Chuck Berry or Missy Elliott, people in Western civilization have often expressed their discontents and desires through subversive humor. Such humor wields both a carrot and a stick, magnetically drawing interested audiences while simultaneously educating them with hard, raw truths. Mark Twain, for one, regarded his work as closer to a sermon than a comedy, the mirth quotient being of only supplementary import. In many respects, Twain is right. Often, the least significant impact a humorist has is to make us laugh. Whether it is Aristophanes scolding the Athenian authorities of ancient Greece for their democratic shortcomings or the Beastie Boys exposing hypocrisy in U.S. foreign policy, subversive humorists throughout history have performed the role of social rebels and representatives. French philosopher Henri Bergson called such comedians "disguised moralists" as they are often the sanctioned truth-tellers of our culture, the proud pied pipers of the cliché that many a true word is spoken in jest.[2]

There have been few artistic forms or periods that can boast such a plethora of subversive humorists as the rock & roll movement of the last half century. With its seeds of dissenting humor planted in blues, jazz, folk, and country, rock music rose to prominence in the United States during the mid-1950s; it has since become a primary force of expression and enjoyment in cultures all around the world. A youth-cultural core that exists at both the artistic and the audience levels has lent rock an inherently pre-adult exuberance and humor. Sometimes its humorists have been trivial, indulging in novelty or childlike silliness; other times they have been subversive social critics, recognizing wrongs, if not always providing solutions. More often than not, they have been combinations of the two, fusing youthful immaturity and rebellious instincts in ways that have given rock and rock humor their particular distinctions. Subversive rock humor has emerged as a formidable force of modern art, garnering rock music a reputation over its history as being a rebellious—sometimes dangerous—form of expression that can dismay the adult mainstream as it empowers the youth culture.

For over fifty years, rock music has been the principle outlet of youth rebellion, and though much has been made of these rock rebels, little analysis has been done of rebel-rock humor. This book will scrutinize this humor: what it consists of, how it manifests itself, who and what it is targeting, and how it ultimately functions and affects society. Just as literature and film critics of recent decades have begun to recognize and reassess their humorists within their respective canons—reevaluating their Mark Twains and their Charlie Chaplins—so, too, it is time to foreground the pervasive yet underappreciated role that humor has played in the history of rock, especially in relation to the historical trajectory of rock rebellion, which is itself the very spark plug of the modern youth counterculture.

Rock is a ubiquitous force of modern culture, its rebellion and dissent determining artistic trends, social realities, and consumption patterns. Like the court jesters of medieval times or such stand-up comedians as the late George Carlin and Chris Rock today, the most subversive rock humorists serve as the conscience of our culture. They chastise pretensions, satirize hypocrisy, and pour scorn on power, corruption, and lies. Of course, not all rock humor is subversive, nor do all subversive jests and gestures meet their intended ends. However, a survey of the musical landscape since the 1950s reveals an array of artists who have either foreshadowed or immediately contributed to an atmosphere of change through their humorous candor. Sometimes they have targeted specific social structures and mores, on occasion taking on the political system or its policies; other times they have bitten the hand that feeds, mocking the music industry itself; often they have looked closer to home, targeting other rockers (or themselves) or the conventions and aesthetics of a particular rock genre. Whether they have leveled their wit at these institutions or beyond, subversive rock humorists have invariably pinpointed establishments in their address, while drawing from a variety of weapons in their respective comedic arsenals.

Lyrics are the most obvious medium through which rock humor is expressed; however, this book's analysis will also address the subversive potential of image, style, performance, packaging, and musical content and expression. A guitar solo, hairstyle, or dance move (in context) may be just as subversive *and* humorous as a satirical or incisive lyric. The purpose of this book is to analyze all relevant aspects of key rock humorists, investigating the nature of their humor and how it has played an expressive and subversive role in the artists' oeuvres. Here, rock humorists must be distinguished from rockers who occasionally use humor. We must not conflate an occasional quip or stab at satire by a band like, say, Pearl Jam, with the sustained artistic humor of a comic zealot like Frank Zappa. Eddie Vedder may be amusing (at times), but his band's collective work does not qualify here as subversive humor.

The subversive rock humorist, like dissenting comedians from other arts through the ages, functions by virtue of an opposition, an antagonist, an antithesis. (S)he needs an environment of conflict and an organization to resist. Consequently, one discovers that the nature of humor, or the volume of its subversion, is intimately tied to broader contextual circumstances and conditions. Humor is defined by its cultural context and thus is accountable to society's *permission*. Topics such as sexual mores and social injustice may consistently be at the heart of humor, but the manifestation of that humor is intimately tied to what is socially acceptable at the time. Thus, the sexual innuendo humor of fifties rhythm & blues contrasts in degree to the provocative sexual explicitness of recent rap and hard rock output; both are subversive, but their expressions and receptions differ by virtue of their historical times and the social and expressive norms of those contexts. Subversive rock humor can, therefore, never be divorced from the forces that produce, determine, allow, or invite it.

SUBVERSIVE ROCK HUMOR'S DEFINING FEATURES

The history of rock humor—indeed, of rock music—is intimately connected both to the history of pre-rock popular music and to other art histories. However, though a part *of* these other genres, rock humor is also apart *from* them. It draws from the cultural past, but, in so doing, it creates something new and distinct; it may not have reinvented the wheel of humor, but it has certainly changed its trajectory. Thus, the satirical lyricism of Randy Newman may be inspired by Jonathan Swift, and Ice T's gritty street-speak may evoke the spirit of Raymond Chandler, but these literary antecedents are only distant relatives. We recognize vast differences in *the way* their respective genre-humors are articulated—their distinct languages, tones, and attitudes—as well as in the target audiences to whom they are addressed. Like the best party punch, rock humor mixes an amalgam of recognizable ingredients—then adds its own additives for the kids—to create an original concoction that both surprises and satisfies. Following are the ingredients for that punch, an overview of the distinct and defining features of rock humor that have fostered the genre's predisposition to subversion.

Youth Orientation

Produced and consumed largely within a demographic of youth or youth orientation, rock music operates in a pre-adult world; some would call it an environment of arrested adolescence. As such, rock—like youth itself—naturally inclines toward dissent. It functions like Huck Finn and Holden Caulfield: questioning authority, outing phonies, raging against accommodation and compromise. Humor historian Charles E. Schutz (not to be confused with the *Peanuts* guy) connects this youthful spirit to humor, saying, "He [the child] serves as a kind of preview revolutionary and gives us a glimpse of the critically realistic function of comedy."[3] Rock rebels are the "innocent" truth-tellers, outsiders expressing their "natural" distaste for any impositions upon their individualism. They are getting their kicks in (and just getting their kicks) prior to their subsequent social incorporation. Here, youth is both a literal and a metaphorical category. Literally, most performers and consumers of rock music are young, part of a demographic spanning ten- to thirty-year-olds. Rock champions this in its 1960s caution to "never trust anyone over thirty" or in Roger Daltrey's yelling, "I hope I die before I get old."[4] Nevertheless, youth is also a state of mind, not merely a numerical determination. Young-at-hearts like the New York Dolls, the Beastie Boys, and George Clinton continue to tap into the forces of youth rebellion and expression, ever drawing in new disciples from next generations. Their vibrant articulations of physical and verbal wit reveal that in rock humor as in rock music, youth must always be served.

Primal Emotions

Youths emit the screams of joy and pain that most adults learn to contain or privatize. These outbursts—in rock and elsewhere—are often raw and uncivil because young people act out, oblivious (or resistant) to the decorum that comes with maturity and social manners. Rock humor harnesses such primal emotions, theatrically parading, loudly antagonizing, or just spitting on constraints. It exceeds the reasoned and rehearsed humor of even the most rebellious practitioners of other arts. Stand-up comedians like Dave Chapelle and the late Bill Hicks have certainly tested proprieties in their presentations, but within rock such conventions are gleefully ignored or ridiculed through grotesque acts of uncontained energy, candor, and anarchy. For example, the much-shown 1970s performance of Iggy Pop, sweat glistening from his naked torso, slicing his skin with a broken microphone stand, is a sign of theatrical grotesquery not to be forgotten nor surpassed in its primal excess. Sam Kinison and Andy Kaufman may have pushed the limits of gesticulation comedy in their times, but even they never tapped into that level of base primitivism. Iggy-type expression symbolically undermines the staid behavioral patterns of most adult life, where emotions have been refined into a slumbering state. With extreme cases like Iggy Pop (or GG Allin, or Screamin' Jay Hawkins), we enter the danger zone of humor, one that is discomforting and invigorating, where the infantile id is given free rein to terrorize without constraint.

Id-iotic Outbursts

Freud theorized that during the socialization process, a child is taught to repress aggressive and sexual impulses in order to conform to the rules and expectations of the society. These feelings are thereby banished to the subconscious. However, they are not eradicated; they are, instead, only sublimated. The consequence, argues Freud, is that periodically such wild feelings will erupt, though in perhaps unfamiliar ways. In *Jokes and Their Relation to the Unconscious*, Freud suggests that humor provides a vicarious means of release, a way of shedding internalized emotions.[5] It is because these emotions have been deemed socially dangerous that they were suppressed in the first place. It is no coincidence that sex and violence are two of the most common features of rock humor; these are the primary forbidden feelings we repress as infants. When these taboos are filtered through the extensions and exaggerations of rock's primal outbursts, humor is born that is extreme—or hyper—in nature.

The noisy scream of the young child becomes the noisier scream of the rock humorist; the public displays of sexual discovery we see in an infant become perverse excesses of degeneracy in the artistic hands of the rock humorist. And what the adult world condemns and censors as obscene and disgusting in infancy contributes to the very process that produces subsequent rock grotesque. Hyperactive rebel-humor is particularly apparent in the rock provocateurs of mid-1950s rock & roll, when the form was first bursting into full bloom. Little Richard, for example, was a shock to the senses of mainstream America in 1955, and not only because he was homosexual and black. His untamed performances, sexual body moves, and pre-verbal (or extra-verbal) sonic babble were the representative embodiments of the child's id during psychosexual development. A comparable hyper-humor of phallic sexuality, coded scatological utterances, and aggressive abandon is equally evident in Richard's rock & roll peers: Jerry Lee Lewis, Screamin' Jay Hawkins, Bo Diddley, and Gene Vincent.

Dumb Wit

This "critical" tag is intended to be as ironic as the way in which it is employed by rock performers. Connected to the above Freudian theory, dumb humor broadly showcases defiance to the norms of the adult superego. It does so by mining regression, theatrically acting out any number of dumb articulations. The genre of bubblegum pop, which enjoyed its heyday in the late 1960s and early 1970s, symbolizes quintessential dumb rock. Its infantile vocabulary and joyous delivery betray not an ounce of shame or embarrassment;

that is because the humor is far from accidental or "innocent." In an era when many rock musicians went to college, art rockers like Emerson, Lake and Palmer and Yes aspired to "adult" criteria, crafting semi-symphonies for discerning "grown-ups." In response, bubblegum sought to burst (pop?) art rock pretensions with its own "anti-art" excesses of innocent play and calculated silliness. Rolling off the production lines were songs with such childish-gibberish titles as "Yummy Yummy Yummy" (1968), "Goody Goody Gumdrops" (1968), and "Gimme Gimme Good Lovin'" (1968), by Ohio Express, 1910 Fruitgum Company, and Crazy Elephant, respectively. Actually, these bands were merely fronts for the writer-producer team of Jerry Kasenetz, Jeff Katz, and Neil Bogart, whose Svengali-like operations only further deconstructed art rock's notions of the individual and revered creative artist.

The site of subversion here is rock culture itself, and bubblegum's mission was to undermine those who would attempt to dislodge rock music from its primary roots (youth culture) and essential character (dumb humor). It is not surprising that other advocates of roots-rock dumb humor would succeed bubblegum and continue to intercept the intellectual interlopers. As art rock reached its zenith of classical complexity in the mid-1970s, punk upstarts the Ramones harnessed their three-chord barrage, cartoon lyrics, and dropout image to scornfully undercut the then-dominant pomp-rock of such epics of the day as *Dark Side of the Moon* (1973) and *Tubular Bells* (1973). Both the Ramones and bubblegum pop have received heightened critical praise in recent decades as postmodern art has gained credence. One longtime supporter of bubblegum, proto-punk journalist Lester Bangs, has paid tribute to its antics, speaking of the genre as crusading for that "one tender spot deep in the heart of rock and roll which should never grow up and never will."[6]

Subcultural

Rock's dumb humor and images have provided the subcultural glue for dissolute youth over the past half century. A haven for marginalized and outsider youth, rock music has historically offered a welcome mat where parents, schools, and other cultural institutions have not. Subcultures, like youth gangs, serve as surrogate families, giving identity to the ostracized and granting purpose to the alienated. Because outcasts are often defined as such by virtue of their resistance to social institutions' accepted behaviors, subcultures function to consolidate dissenters, coalescing a resistant demeanor into a loosely constructed subversive collective.

In sartorial style, (body) language, and behavior, subcultures are, as Dick Hebdige comments in his book *Subculture: The Meaning of Style*, "spectacular" to the mainstream culture. From the perspective of the participating practitioners and creators themselves, subcultural displays provide a unified sign language that insults and undermines the mainstream culture. Antagonism is the key to their ironic gestures and grotesque exaggerations. Consider the zoot suits of 1940s hipsters, their winged lapels, baggy trousers, and shocking colors re-dressing the conservative expectations of public identity, or Jerry Lee Lewis, his rockabilly quiff sweat-soaked, hanging just so with disheveled abandon, the rocker-as-rebel hood returning from a street fight. These are but a couple of the images that portray subcultures' proud and oppositional wit, one that binds within and subverts without.

Seekers and Trailblazers

Subversives—like revolutionaries—are defined by their intents, not by their achievements. To be a subversive is to desire to subvert; through undermining, attention is called to circumstances, caution is proclaimed, admonishment is administered. Subversives recognize wrongs, though they may not have much to offer in the way of alternative "rights." The latter is the other side of subversion, the politically prescriptive side, and it is rare for the rebel-humorist to programmatically venture there. Subversion within rock music is in the *acting out*, not in a rational advocacy of answers.

Subversive rock humorists are trailblazers, spotlights in hand, unveiling repression with a visceral spontaneity. And they are often ahead of the rest of the culture in doing so. What other art forms challenged racial segregation as courageously as jazz, rhythm & blues, and rock & roll in the 1950s (and before)? Where else did one witness such dramatic representations of the "new woman"—strong, feisty, self-reliant, sexual—as in the female (and mostly black) singers of those insurgent genres during the same time period? Big Mama Thornton, Ethel Waters, and Ruth Brown were the trailblazers of a proud proto-feminism in its early formation, just as Madonna, Kim Gordon, and Missy Elliott have been in the "post"-feminist era. Armed with their protective wit and courageous tenacity, these artists have been forerunners of cultural change, striking and uniting with satirical stabs on behalf of progressive social action.

Many times subversive rock humorists have captured the general sentiments of a time period, sometimes ahead of time. The challenges made to institutional racism by jazz bands and folk singers of the 1920s and 1930s, and later by rock & rollers in the mid-1950s, not only prefigured but also created the sparks that lit the fuses of subsequent desegregation and social change. Trailblazers ride ahead of the pack; what they have to say is often uncomfortable and unwelcome to the conservative mainstream; in such situations, humor plays a *critical* permissive role; it provides a pass, a cushion of lenience for controversial sentiments that might otherwise be silenced.

Perhaps because young people feel that they have less to lose than adults by trailblazing—or perhaps because of youth's irresponsible recklessness—rock has historically proven itself to be the art form most willing to take the most comedic risks. As a result, it has often had to pay a social price for its envelope-pushing, for the history of rock is also a history of pervasive censure and censorship. Despite this, trailblazers beget more trailblazers, and the prescriptive interventions of groups like the Parents Music Resource Center (PMRC) often amount to little more than red rags to bulls, their stickers of shame worn like magnetic badges of honor by dissenting youths hungry for more edgy cultural art. Today, the legacy of rock's trailblazing humor is that any young person growing up who feels social victimization—whether it be because (s)he is homosexual, black, female, poor, or just young— knows that rock offers a forum to join the like-minded in a broad army willing to wield its weapons (of humor) against all forms of insensitivity or oppression.

Three Chords and an Attitude

Rock music is an "anyone can do it" art form; as a participant in rock bands for over two decades, this is something I can personally attest to. Its demands on technical prowess are minimal at most, something I can also speak to. Of course, scholars and practitioners of blues, jazz, and art rock will justly argue that much of the music loosely captured under the rock rubric involves extensive training and skilled expertise, and though this is certainly true, such excellence is not a prerequisite to trying your hand at the rock game. For every Jimi Hendrix and Rick Wakeman there are multiple Johnny Ramone and Sid Vicious sound-alikes out there, sharing their limited (minimalist?) musical chops with nonjudgmental audiences. For playing rock music does not *require* technical excellence, nor do listeners demand it. The rich recent history of alternative and independent rock speaks eloquently to this proud DIY attitude.

Such anti-elitist attitudes have significant implications, not only for rock music as a distinct practice, but for the type of humor it expresses. First, to jump onstage or into a studio might require courage and a command of three chords, but it rarely calls for specialized schooling. Thus, for those less academically inclined, rock music serves as a creative refuge and outlet. For the millions of children who grow up being told that they are stupid and useless by virtue of their poor school records, rock provides a place to produce their own type of records, as well as a haven to express the frustrations, alienation, and (self-)loathing they have accumulated as a consequence of such upbringing. And once established in the rock school of life, such kids find empathetic peers, similarly pissed off at the world, ready and eager to vent their spleens as victims no more. Not surprisingly, rock magnetizes the marginalized and those socially inclined to rebel against their adult-guided fates. These youth outsiders form loose coalitions, create their own organic intellectuals on the basis of their own criteria, and rage with the passions of their generation.

When expressed as humor, sarcasm and satire are common styles for their pent-up frustrations. The fusion of aggression and humor presents an equation that speaks to entire genres of music. Rockabilly, punk, and heavy metal performers, for instance, sport antagonistic wits that course through their every bulging vein. The Cramps, the Descendents, and Andrew W.K. appear to be saying to every parent, schoolmaster, or employer who ever put them down: "So you think I'm idiotic and worthless; well, I'll show you idiotic and worthless." Rock's parodies of dumbness (or dumb parodies) are but mirrors held up to a mainstream culture responsible for perpetrating the dispirited disconnection of alienated youth.

Here and Now

Rock music has a short history, and an even shorter *sense* of history. Literature and the fine arts may make thematic connections that speak over time, connecting the present to an analogous past through allusions and parallel gestures, but rock music is more a practice of the immediate present. Even when old genres are dug up and dusted off for reuse—as they periodically always are—the revivalist rockers act as though those styles were their own original contributions to the form. A lineup of such guilty plagiarists of recent years—all hiding history behind their hipster fronts— might include the Killers, the Hold Steady, and the Scissor Sisters. Through cunning and comedic sleight of hand, plus the realization that the new generation of kids could not care less about the music of yesterday, these artists are able to perpetuate an eternal present in rock's consciousness.

Sometimes, conversely, the tense presence of rock's present tense is a vital feature of the form's expressive power. Asked about rap's graphic portrayals of inner-city urban life, Public Enemy's

Chuck D responded by calling his band's (and genre's) lyrics "The black CNN." This comment not only reflects the "now" of rock expression, but also the fact that it is often a shocking "now" we rarely see portrayed through other cultural outlets. The immediacy of rock music is part of its visceral rawness, often manifesting itself in an inarticulate rush of words that bespeak urgency over reflection, communication over eloquence. Surveying its history, we witness rock's power to capture momentary time in a bottle. When recalling President Reagan's insensitive visit to a Nazi SS graveyard while in Germany in the mid-1980s, I think of the Ramones' mocking "Bonzo Goes to Bitburg," released just after in 1985. Some might dismiss such an off-the-cuff lyrical newsflash as unreflective and lacking context, but rock lives in the here and now and its fans connect—and relate to—the social immediacy of topical humor.

Jacks-of-All-Trades

Though other art forms show their adaptability to various types of comedy, rock music's sensory range allows for a particular diversity of humorous styles. Satire, (self-)parody, irony, whimsy, cartoon, grotesque, and absurdism are just some of the humor techniques that have emerged from the lyrics, performances, sounds, artworks, and images of rock expression. Few other art forms express themselves with such diversity.

Subversive rock humorists are multi-humorists, expressing their purpose through an amalgamated collection of outlets. Take Nirvana, for example, whose social satire brought the band critical acclaim as one of the most pointed practitioners of grunge rock subversion. Their lyrics plumb the dark basements of black humor and sarcasm; Kurt Cobain's disinterested vocal exudes dismissive mockery; the band's performance style is one of grotesque provocative assault; their bare-bones punk-metal riffs parody artistic excellence; their shock-image album covers ridicule art and society's concepts of beauty and challenge mainstream culture's tolerance of the unacceptable; and their clothes, ripped and ragged, present mocking mirrors of a desperate and alienated youth to a middle-class adult mainstream that builds high fences to keep such undesirables beyond its purview. Satirists on multiple fronts, Nirvana exude a collage humor of disparate ingredients that serve in unison to undermine a society that systematically turns its back on, or suppresses, who and what they represent.

Artistic Debts and Futures

Rock humor was not born in a void as an original entity. It developed from various proto-rock music genres and from a cast of other art forms and histories. Variously, it showcases the linguistic flair of poetry, the theatrics of drama, the audience interaction of stand-up comedy, and the graphic displays of visual art. Indeed, as Simon Frith and Howard Horne have documented in their book *Art Into Pop*, the fine arts have been a consistent influence (at levels of both theory and praxis) on the many ex-art-school boys and girls who switched ships to rock music after their college years. The subversive wit of art movements like surrealism, dada, pop art, and situationism is indelibly imprinted on the work of many of the more heady rock humorists. Rock humor is often the result of this synthesis and recontextualization of other artistic humors, mixed and matched to form a coalition of humorous facets that produce a new style and substance.

The eclecticism of rock humor gives the form much diversity and potential future directions. From outside to in, we see that the trajectory of rock history takes us from external concerns to in-house matters, from the exploratory inventions of late 1960s modernists to recent postmodernists who look backward in venturing forward. Ironically, today's rock music is *not* your parents' rock music, by virtue of the very fact that it often sounds so much like it. The technological revolution has altered rock beyond recognition; it has created a present and future situation where the "anyone can do it" ideal is increasingly being substituted by "everyone will do it." New generations of youth are growing up as information strategists, masters of their own mixes, postmodern creators. Roland Barthes's comment that "the death of the author is the birth of the reader" was more prescient than he could ever have imagined.[7] The breakdown of the age-old artistic roles of producer and receiver might close the book on traditional concepts of art and the artist. However, changes will also create fresh spaces for more universal engagement in the expressive communicative process, what will soon be recognized as the art of our times. Whether humor and humorists will also morph and multiply remains to be seen, though different contexts and meanings will surely be created by the new social dynamics, expressions, and targets of subversive humor that are developing in currently unforeseeable directions.

SUBVERSIVE ROCK HUMORISTS: WHO? WHERE? WHEN? WHY?

Those readers who headed straight to the contents page may be wondering, "Where's the Beatles? The Kinks? The Smiths? Art Brut?" Likewise, lovers of Scandinavian subversive humorists may be perplexed by the conspicuous absence of the Hives, the Cardigans, and Junior Senior. Well, obviously, subversive rock humor is not the sole preserve of the United States, and many of the most radical rock humorists have emanated from beyond its shores. However, humor is a phenomenon determined by national character and identity as much as it is universal, produced by native historical forces as much as by autonomous individuals; thus, geographical parameters have been deemed both appropriate and necessary here. Although references are made throughout this text to non-U.S. humorists who have influenced the trajectory of America's subversive rock history, those artists—particularly the Brits—are deserving of their own study, one couched within their own historical contexts and determinants. Therefore, the story here is largely an American one and its all-American lineup of critical profiles reflects that focus.

The chapters within this American-b(i)ased book on subversive rock humorists are divided by decade; each decade/chapter is then arranged to showcase the selected artists within their particular prime times. By scrutinizing each humorist independently and contextually, an individual's (or group's) aesthetic is thereby connected to the broader circumstances and relationships that have influenced its formation and nature. Each profile seeks to reveal larger cultural understandings, as do the accompanying and contextualizing preambles. These prefatory introductions always precede the profiles, and they serve multiple purposes: First, they offer sociohistorical contexts within the decade to the style of rock and the artists being addressed; second, they establish the genre of music and type of humor under discussion, as well as comparable humor from other arts that might coincide with that particular period and style; lastly, they allow for minor humorists of the genre, not developed with independent profiles, to be recognized and reflected upon in context, if only in brief. In the final chapter of the book, covering the present decade, more abbreviated profiles are integrated within the broader categorical sections, as these newer artists have yet to enjoy the kind of fleshed-out careers that would warrant developed, separate sections. Maybe in the second and third editions . . . !

From the 1950s to the present, a chronological approach is taken, the pertinent genres and relevant rock humorists captured during the heydays of their subversive humor; however, the chronology is also "loose," allowing me to account for the artists' careers before and after the decade in which I profile them. As each section is not reined in according to a rigid set of arbitrary time constraints, readers can either follow the general historical flow of the book or dip in and enjoy particular sections at will.

As for who satisfies the criteria for inclusion, primarily, artists must pass the test of the book subtitle's three key words: They must have a purpose to subvert an establishment; they must operate under the broad umbrella of the rock music culture; and they must express a recognizable humor throughout their work. Most importantly, artists must embody all three determinants simultaneously. Obviously, an anthological text such as this must be discriminating by necessity. Indeed, the aim here is less to be exhaustive and more to be selectively representative. Thus, sometimes artists are chosen to reveal a particular strain of rock humor; sometimes they are included for the pure potency of their subversive wit; sometimes popularity and success are significant and sometimes they are significantly not; sometimes the interests of cultural and musical diversity are key criteria and, again, sometimes they are not. Often times, quite frankly, if an artist tweaked my funny bone and I could sense subversion in the wit, (s)he qualified as a viable candidate for inclusion. No doubt some readers will question, disagree with, or balk at the choices made—whether on the grounds of inclusion or omission. If you are such a dissenter, then we will just have to agree to disagree on who qualifies; or alternatively, go and write your own bloody book!

THE FIFTIES:

Evolution to Revolution

DECADES DECEIVE as self-contained units. Just as many rock historians have mused over how the 1960s began in the 1950s, so the same can be said of the 1950s and the preceding decades. The escapist hedonism of swing and the jump blues—as practiced by Louis Jordan, Cab Calloway, and others—had initially served as comic relief music from the hardships of the Great Depression and World War II; these styles evolved, soon to morph with R&B, country, and other popular genres into what would be designated by the umbrella term "rock & roll" (or "rock 'n' roll") by the mid-fifties. Despite the prevalent "big bang" theory of rock & roll, this music was actually the result of the evolution of prior—mostly African American—forms.

Subversive musical humor had also thrived as part of the same evolutionary process; the ingredients one usually associates with the humor of mid-fifties rockers were already present beforehand: lyrical sexual innuendo, visual flair and flamboyance, and a "secret" youth subcultural identity that disturbed parental authorities while invariably eluding their full comprehension. These were the constituent features of swing as practiced by Jordan and Calloway, of jump blues as played by Wynonie Harris and Big Joe Turner, and of R&B, the main "race" music style that preceded rock & roll. Integrating visual and verbal humor into the rhythmic "physicality" of their respective genres, the trailblazing artists of pre-rock *played* within the sensitive territories of sex, race, and generation, testing the parameters of adult social permission just as Chuck Berry, Little Richard, and Elvis Presley would a few years later. And the only things louder and more offensive to parents than the messages and the music of these forerunners were the cut and colors of their clothes.

Nowadays, we take for granted how a rock star's image and dress intertwine to project subversive visual humor and meaning. We recognize that Gene Vincent's greased leather look parodied the stereotype of the fifties juvenile delinquent; how David Bowie's glitter glamour was a caricature "camp" sign of a seventies other-worldly and alien-ated identity; even how Kurt Cobain's ragged flannel shirts served as a clothes-line into feeling his sarcastic social rejections in the nineties. Similarly, within the swing, jump blues, and R&B scenes that flourished between the thirties and the early fifties, clothes were not only interesting and sharp, but they were consciously employed for the purposes of being message projectiles.

Central to the hepster cool of swing was the zoot suit, literally an exaggeration of a suit, with its wide jacket lapels and baggy pants, each outfit arriving in an array of many possible (and usually bright) colors; this would be set off—like the mélange of instruments in swing music—by clashing-colored shirts and *amplified* wide ties. Invariably the look would be topped off with a striking fedora tipped just so. Cab Calloway and Louis Jordan wore these clothes less for style than to comment ironically upon style; they signaled a proud, witty declaration of racial pride, confidence, and individuality—as well as a parody of social upward mobility. Their very excesses assaulted the mainstream establishment with sartorial sarcasm. Complementing this clothing, youth-specific dialect and dance further set the subculture in outrageous opposition to the adult world. Each of these facets of humor was simultaneously childlike *and* subversive, expressing the pent-up primal frustrations of youth and a concerted rebellion against the stultifying adult authorities who would (attempt and wish to) deny such feelings.

Not surprisingly, many adult citizens, particularly the bastions of authority, neither appreciated (nor often recognized) the rebellious humor of these expressions. What they saw was not freedom and creativity, but decadence and degradation; not inclusiveness and youth articulation, but racial miscegenation and "negro" primitivism. So-called "race music," for many, was not just an assault on mainstream middle-class values, but a call to arms on behalf of juvenile—and worse, black juvenile—delinquency. Concerned parents heard the sexual innuendo in the songs, saw the criminal types that hung around the dance clubs and their daughters, and stared aghast at those clothes! Such mainstream adult responses laid the sure foundations for what would thereafter be an ever-widening generation gap. Little did anyone know at the time, but swing, jump, and R&B—and their attendant youth subcultures—were setting the stages for the arrival of rock & roll.

FROM "RACE" MUSIC TO R&B TO ROCK & ROLL

Black popular music (and the white music inspired by it) of the early 1950s—whether called "race music" or, later, R&B—was regarded by mainstream culture (white and black) as a corrupting force. Parents heard "jungle" sounds and sexed-up lyrics, while their kids heard rebellion and excitement. By the time the forerunner forms were rechristened rock & roll in the mid-fifties, a generational tug-of-war was already underway for the hearts and minds of intoxicated youth. A back-and-forth struggle—played out through complaints, negotiations, and sometimes censorship—created tension at the heart of music developments throughout the decade. With the racial crossover trend in music propelling the civil rights movement and desegregation, and with the vast youth (sub)culture parading itself en masse in unprecedented numbers and strength, the stakes were high for the concerned and conservative adult world. From its side of the front lines, the subversive humor of the upstart youth performers was no laughing matter.

The forerunning R&B style was far from generic or homogenous. Under its broad rubric, jump, swing, doo-wop, shouters, and electric blues all competed for radio play and record company attention, while increasingly intrigued white youths picked up the sounds from the outskirts of their radio dials. Still, the eclectic R&B genre was highly marginalized in relation to a mainstream culture that prioritized access to white pop crooners like Frank Sinatra, Bing Crosby, and Doris Day. Left as crumbs to be picked up by independent record labels, R&B acts were plentiful but rigidly ghettoized in the popular music landscape. It was not until white artists—orchestrated by major record labels—began to cover black R&B songs that the genre emerged from the shadows. The consequences of this trend were multiple. White performers began to popularize black R&B, often by sanitizing the sound, cleaning up saucy and subversive lyrics, and putting a clean-cut white face on the record's sleeve. Such accommodation was tantamount to theft and clearly took advantage of the racist subordination black artists and their communities suffered. However, it also created a crossover effect where the music was now reaching white and black audiences, where high-distribution major labels were providing broad outreach, and where R&B-loving DJs were green-lighted to play the music they admired, even slipping in the original black versions when no one was looking and, they hoped, everyone was listening.

Celebrated instances of the crossover phenomenon included Elvis Presley's success with "Hound Dog" in 1956, originally a Big Mama Thornton recording, and the various Little Richard songs that teen crooner Pat Boone covered—some would say butchered—during the late 1950s. Bill Haley and His Comets' 1954 hit "Shake, Rattle, and Roll" was originally recorded by jump blues shouter Big Joe Turner. Whereas Haley's version of the song had a peppy bounce and a country-tinged party-celebration quality, Big Joe's was full of macho sexual innuendo and sexist shout-outs. What constituted Turner's braggadocio humor—reflecting an emasculated black man confronting white manners and civility—was stripped of all its subversive wit in the hands of Haley, who, essentially, bypassed the song's danger zones in the pursuit of innocuous fun. Although the phenomenon of whites covering and sanitizing African Americans' songs continued unabated throughout the 1950s, the trend was slowed by the stand taken by Alan Freed and other sympathetic DJs, who refused to play the cover versions in preference to the originals.

For the major record companies, putting a white face on black music made good business sense; white performers and white youth listeners gravitated to the material because it represented danger and the forbidden—in all their appeal. And these elements were intimately tied to the music's comedic expression. Lyrically, much 1950s R&B toyed with sexual titillation, using the same innuendo, wordplay, and suggestiveness it had been developing since 1920s blues and 1930s swing. But this was not just sex for sex's sake. Via the pens of the sexual provocateurs, the trickster humorist was engaged in a hide-and-seek game with the larger superstructure. Society's repression of sexuality was analogous to its suppression of racial minorities; indeed, it often merged the two "dangers" and—through its professional moralists—was always on the lookout for black R&B records to expurgate. Joe Turner's much-scrutinized recording of "Shake, Rattle, and Roll" in 1954 is, again, illustrative with its sexually "implicit" lines, "You make me roll my eyes, baby, make me grit my teeth," "You wear those dresses, the sun comes shining through," and "The devil in nylon hose." By the time the song had reached Bill Haley's recording in 1954, these sexually provocative "leerics" had been excised, yet the most outrageous innuendo, "I'm like a one-eyed cat peepin' in a seafood store," remained.[1] Some have suggested that this line outwitted the censors, while others have claimed that Haley kept it in because he himself was blind in one eye, thus sanitizing the meaning in the process!

The Drifters, with "Such a Night" and "Honey Love" in 1954, and Hank Ballard & the Midnighters, with "Work with Me Annie" from the same year, similarly tested limits and challenged their adversaries; these songs' veiled sexual humor "tricked" adult censors, who sensed subversion but were unable to fully decode or determine its in-club youth rhetoric. As with rap decades later, R&B double-speak was essentially a paradoxical signifier of power and powerlessness. Ostracized to the outskirts of society, black R&B artists were left alone to be outspoken, honest, and challenging. Their "leerics" symbolically gave the finger to a white establishment that would not let them "play in the game" anyway.

The dangerous attractions of early fifties R&B were by no means limited to lyrical content, either. Courting the Dionysian, musical styles and delivery were equally sexual and provocative. One only has to play any R&B song of the period next to a contemporaneous white pop song to highlight the contrasts. Black R&B fronted rhythm and beat, both sexual metaphors at the musical level. Accompanying this driving force, this pounding backdrop, were voices often untamed, celebrating abandon. Moreover, these voices implicitly ridiculed the uptight controls of anxious America; they shouted and taunted with a childlike recklessness at the national commandments of restraint and denial. These were the voices Jack Kerouac heard when he ventured into the ethnic sections of Denver in *On the Road* (1957), or that Norman Mailer celebrated in his controversial essay, "The White Negro" (1957).

Though the R&B satirists and provocateurs may have felt protected by their double entendres and ignored because of their marginal status, as their songs crossed over into white markets—whether via cover versions or as originals—and into the homes of "innocent" white youths, the establishment took note. Ice T would later refer to this development of black culture infiltrating Caucasian society as "home invasion," and just as his explicit rap music was largely ignored until it penetrated the white suburbs, so 1950s R&B soon incurred the kind of wrath and white backlash that one witnessed in relation to Ice T, 2 Live Crew, and NWA thirty-five years later. The R&B clampdown of the mid-1950s—again like rap music in the 1980s—saw Senate committees scrutinizing this "enemy within" as DJs scrambled to police themselves in preemptive maneuvers. Soon, songs were being cut from playlists or quietly cleaned up. Such defensive music industry reflexivity proved to be a placebo, though, as society soon discovered that the genie stubbornly refused to return to the bottle. Furthermore, emerging white rockers were joining the rebel-rock bandwagon. By the mid-1950s, the separation between white and black performers, music styles, and audiences had dramatically narrowed, and the old designations of "race" music were dismissed as archaic, as was the black-associated tag of "R&B." From 1955 on, the alternative term of rock & roll was applied to the new "beat" music exploding from both black and white sources.

Despite the largely valid generalization that the story of the emergence of rock & roll is the story of how the white boy coveted the blues, many black artists from around the nation also profited from the rock & roll insurgence of 1955. No longer did the likes of Chuck Berry, Fats Domino, Bo Diddley, and Little Richard have to labor in the ghettos of "race" music culture. Now called "rock & rollers" rather than "race" musicians or R&B acts, these black artists took center stage, enjoying the fruits of the developing musical crossovers and youth-race integrations. For them, humorous expression was much less incidental than it was for their white counterparts, and, as still-segregated minorities, more was at stake in relation to the choices they could and could not make. The results were diverse but always strategic in nature.

Chuck Berry

The influence of Chuck Berry upon developments in 1950s music cannot be overestimated. His trailblazing and influence on contemporaries, alongside his catalogue of musical manifestos to youth identity, make him the prime candidate for attribution as rock & roll's primary creator. Berry used the power of his lyrical wit to exploit the growing visibility of the boom-youths. His witty anthems to youth identity both captured the concerns and dreams of youth, while often quietly subverting those themes with subtle racial quirks and calls to youth dissent.

An American scribe in the geo-mythological tradition of Mark Twain and Walt Whitman, Chuck Berry ranks as one of rock's most literate lyric-laureates. Like these predecessors, Berry's American purview was one that encapsulated national scope and energies. His "everychild" narratives united the country's youth beneath the broad tent of rock & roll, providing the vocabulary and the spirit it craved as it rumbled against the old adult order(s). The clever humor that stoked the fires of Berry's lyrical landscapes was born of personal inspiration as well as mythical tradition. Beneath the apparent straightforward ease of his youth-propelled narrative tales were the heart and soul of a trickster employing self-conscious humor toward rebellious ends. Berry represented a fundamentally rooted American character: the patriotic dissenter. In prowess and (sense of) place—and again, like Twain and Whitman—Berry was a quintessential all-American maverick.

Nowhere was this artistic inclination more apparent than in his trickster-derived rhetorical codes. Historically a deep-rooted African mythos, the figure of the trickster applies his verbal skills in order to deceive and contest in the public terrain. "Signifying" trickster humor has often been deployed by African Americans as a method of pride and survival in the face of oppressive social forces. It embodies a playful approach achieved through adept linguistic signification, often spoken in two or more tongues. In African archetypal folklore, the Yoruba's trickster tale of the signifying monkey, Eshu, is oft-cited. It was a source incorporated by Cab Calloway in his 1947 song "The Jungle King," and Berry updated it for his 1958 cut "Jo Jo Gunne." Essentially, the story illustrates how, in a battle of wits, the wittiest rather than the strongest adversary prevails. Berry clearly understood that he could not win the war against America's racist white hegemony, but through allegory he could score points in a few skirmishes. However, to achieve such ends, he realized the necessity of playing in enemy territory as a successful crossover artist, applying his skills as a trickster humorist both to reach and to subvert mainstream terrain.

Arriving on the musical landscape in the early 1950s, Berry—dark-skinned, in his late twenties, and signed to the independent Chess label—did not appear as a likely candidate to be the revolutionary voice for middle-class, white, suburban youth culture. However, he soon used his apparent deficiencies to his advantage. His adult maturity gave him the shrewdness to imaginatively inhabit the world of youth, and his passion for both R&B and country & western music, rather than leaving him without a niche, blasted open a broader space for musical adventure. By seemingly fitting nowhere, Berry created a musical vision that had the capacity to reach everywhere. Coupled with an ambition to conquer and a willingness to compromise, Berry adeptly walked America's racial and cultural tightropes with trickster dexterity.

For any black artist attempting to cross over to mainstream audiences in the mid-1950s, race posed the primary hurdle. The challenge for Berry—and for contemporaries like Little Richard and Bo Diddley—was to create a style that would reach out to, and then draw in, unfamiliar audiences. The difficulty was to discern and connect to the perceivably alienated white youth demographic without estranging it in the process. Berry—like his contemporaries—found humor as the protector that would facilitate defiance, provocation, and appeal without scaring white listeners off.

In "Brown Eyed Handsome Man" (1956) he constructed a song using a double-speak that could cross over to mainstream audiences at the same time that it conveyed a devilish subtext that contested racial stereotypes and injustices. Although initially released as the B-side to "Too Much Monkey Business," "Handsome Man" stands both as one of Berry's most strident cuts of subversive humor and as a prototype of the black pride protest song. The "brown-eyed handsome man" (a sly synonym for "black handsome man") characters pop up in various guises and episodes within the song, mostly serving as objects of appeal for multiple (white) women of good social standing. Though protected by his comedic code (i.e., the misnomer "brown-eyed"), Berry hereby entered (through his subject) American society's no-go territories of miscegenation and social class transgression simultaneously.

The first verse presents a classic racist scenario whereby the "black man" is facing trumped-up charges; he has been "arrested on charges of unemployment," wryly informs the narrator. To the rescue comes an adoring judge's wife, who demands her husband "free that brown-eyed man." The song proceeds to other anecdotes and other women across time and races, including one mother who encourages her "beautiful daughter" to opt for a "brown-eyed handsome man" over a doctor or lawyer (code "white"). In another verse, "Milo Venus" loses both her arms in a wrestling match fought over the brown-eyed handsome man. And in the final verse, Berry waves the flag of racial pride with an allusion to fellow black trailblazer Jackie Robinson, the victorious brown-eyed handsome man who passes home plate. In the sweeping song, Berry's anecdotal brevity and wit pervade every verse, each skewering some sacred cow of racist white hegemony.[2]

Like most trickster humorists, Berry was acutely aware of prevailing social trends and he drew from their key symbols and codes when methodically satirizing them. His keen grasp of the post-1945 baby boom phenomenon was evident in his specific lyrical themes. Berry keyed in on particular symbols to capture the increasingly widening generation gap and to give voice to the concomitant youth yearnings for independent adventure and escape; one such symbol was the automobile. Thus, he wrote teen-centered car songs like "No Particular Place to Go" and "Maybelline," the latter released as his debut single in 1955. Detailing a lovers' car chase, "Maybelline" sees the speaker's V8 Ford racing against Maybelline's Coup de Ville. The verses detail the thrill of the ride, incorporating car-rhythm-alluding alliteration and classic Chuck puns (like "motor-vatin'") throughout the journey.[3] Through both style and substance, Berry's car songs wittily capture the youthful feelings of autonomy and daredevil abandonment that so scared the wits out of responsible parents.

Another symbol Berry employed to set youth in stark and combative opposition to adult institutions and culture was the new rock & roll form itself. "Roll Over Beethoven" (1956) was a sophisticated "diss" of white, adult, European-derived cultural sophistication, as well as a celebratory revel in the joys of rock &

roll. A revolutionary anthem, Berry sent out the clarion call to "tell Tchaikovsky the news" that there was a new sound in town and it was for youth-ears only. Inverting the then-pervasive perception of rock & roll as a dangerous plague on American youth, "Roll Over Beethoven" presents it instead as a sweet sickness, a "rockin' pneumonia" and "rollin' arthritis." As that metaphor extends, Berry broadens the humor, comparing rock & roll to a new cultural Noah's Ark as the kids dance their way into the new world, "rockin' in two by two." The physical release of rock & roll dancing is also set in sharp contrast to the adult stiffness of classical music, as the narrator alludes to the in-crowd with "Don't you step on my blue suede shoes," then shoots out two (e)motional similes: "You know she wiggles like a glow worm / Dance like a spinning top."[4] All this linguistic play and succinct satire is drilled out over a primal backbeat unprecedented in the popular music of the time.

"School Day" (1957) continued Berry's merciless tweaking of the raw nerves of the generation gap. Again, he selected a symbol to pursue his investigative humor; here, it was the institution of public education. The school was a ripe sign because, like the legal system in "Brown Eyed Handsome Man" and "Thirty Days," it constituted an establishment through which adults exercised restraint, control, and containment. Thus, in "School Day" (and later in "Sweet Little Sixteen" [1958]), Berry pits the liberationist world of rock & roll against the stultifying rules of school life. "Soon as three o'clock rolls around / You finally lay your burden down," narrates Pied Piper Berry, who then proceeds to guide his lyrical lens from school to "juke joint" (a subtle African American referent). The transformation from adult confines (the school) to youth freedom (the club) is captured with the instruction to "Drop the coin right into the slot" of the jukebox. However, it is the way Berry's voice lingers on the "D" of "drop" that creates the humorous suspense of transition. With its comic use of onomatopoeia, the "Ddd . . . rop" signifies the passing from one situation to another, the movement from the authority of the *outside* adult-ruled world to an *inside* youth-determined one.[5] The kid with the coin is essentially paying for a journey out of the real world and into a fantasy musical one, "dropping" out mentally, psychologically, emotionally (and physically) into a world of unfettered fun, freedom, and frolicking. And if the insurrectionary humor is not sufficiently apparent through the narrative and visual imagery, the song concludes with a rally around the manifesto slogan, "Hail, hail, rock 'n' roll / Deliver me from the days of old."[6]

Berry continued to produce similar youth-rock anthems throughout the late 1950s and into the early 1960s, but his career was largely derailed between 1962 and 1964 when he was sentenced to a prison term under the Mann Act, found guilty of transporting a young prostitute across state lines. In this instance, his predilection for youth and fun pushed the tolerance of the authorities too far. The British Invasion bands of the 1960s were supportive of Berry and, on his prison release, helped him resurrect a comeback, but he was never able to recapture his 1950s glory years. In 1972, though, he did receive an unexpected but welcome surprise with the success of "My Ding a Ling," a novelty number that reached the top of the charts on both sides of the Atlantic. Full of sexual double entendres, the song hardly matched the subversive weight of his earlier recordings, but it suggested that the ageing Berry was not through with provoking parental authorities with controversial material.

During his heyday in the mid-1950s, Chuck Berry was rock & roll's most subversive and sophisticated humorist; his influence and legacy are beyond measure and documentation. More than just a trailblazing African American artist, he was a trailblazing American artist, period. Wielding humor as his weapon and gifted with the imaginative scope of his nation, he charted and captured the tenor and ruptures of his time, for his time, in his time. And like those maverick American literary forebears Twain and Whitman, Chuck Berry paraded his stars and stripes nationally through an all-inclusive reach and ever-dissenting spirit.

Little Richard

Little Richard has never been bashful in proclaiming himself the "architect" or "originator" of rock & roll, and, like Chuck

Berry, his contributions to the form and its methods of humor are considerable. As dual creators of the mid-fifties rock & roll sound, Richard and Berry represent different sides of the same coin. Whereas Berry was the narrative documentarian of the era, capturing the nuances of the movement with satirical, naturalistic snapshots, Richard represented the mayhem within, exuding the spirit of the day with expressive inarticulateness. Berry was the rational wit on the outside looking in, but Richard was the irrational madman lurking inside and bursting forth. If Berry brought a certain "mature" mirth and understanding to the youth condition, Richard was the living embodiment of that condition: crazed, fiery, the infantile id set free.

Little Richard's humor had little to do with the lyrical flair and poetic insights we associate with Chuck Berry; conversely, it was rooted in irrationality, confusion, and silliness. At its core, Little Richard's was "dumb" humor, the unapologetic expression of a child lacking self-consciousness; it is no accident that this eternal child would keep his formative nickname of "Little." His humor integrated aspects of voice, sound, style, and physicality into a polysemic homology that pushed listeners beyond the realm of meaning, sending them to that zone of feelings where they were forced to—as David Byrne would put it—stop making sense.

Richard Wayne Penniman was born in Macon, Georgia, in 1935, to a family of faith and traditional virtue. A strict Seventh Day Adventist, Richard's father was less than amused by his son's penchant for makeup and flamboyant clothing during his preteen years. Outraged by his persistently wild antics, Richard's parents threw him out of their home at age thirteen, whence he set about surviving by performing with traveling minstrel shows and in an occasional drag show. By the early fifties he was an established R&B shouter, surviving the circuit but hardly distinguishing himself apart from it. It was at his initial recording sessions with independent R&B label Specialty that Little Richard's *voice* emerged. This session was fraught with frustration; Richard just could not capture the fiery exuberance of his stage performances on record. However, after tinkering with the (somewhat risqué) lyrics to a song called "Tutti Frutti," and after shifting the rehearsal to a local bar for relaxation purposes, a recording metamorphosis occurred such that the Little Richard we know today was born.

As with Chuck Berry's early songs, "Tutti Frutti" (1955) was an immediate shock to the senses, faster than any other popular song at the time—and way wilder. With its pounding New Orleans–style piano providing the backdrop of beat as sexual metaphor, Richard yelped, screamed, and trilled his way through the song like a man possessed; it is a wonder he had time to draw breath. Critic Langdon Winner recalls his "gleeful, bombastic voice" as gloriously over-the-top, a "comic madness" caricature of the most extreme R&B shouters.[7] Lyrically, an ambiguous line like "I got a gal named Sue, she knows just what to do" suggested sexuality, but overall it was the alliteration and rhymes in "Tutti Frutti" that encapsulated the spirit of the song.[8] "Little" sense was made, and the sonic speed of the words signified movement, abandon, and craziness—states of mind youth could viscerally feel, if not fully comprehend. In Charles White's biography *The Life and Times of Little Richard* (1984), H. B. Barnum, Richard's saxophonist, explained the youth connection that the music made in terms of the relief humor it provided: "It gave people who wanted to scream a chance to go ahead and scream instead of trying to be cool." Barnum saw the implications of this achievement in grand terms, suggesting that Little Richard's courageous leaps into the unknown and the unheard set in motion a crossover effect, where all barriers between groups—whether racial, sexual, or gender—could be broken down.[9]

Using carnival-like body gestures to subvert social norms and to transgress established rules, Little Richard kept his personal parade moving into the psyche of America's mainstream and marginalized youth. His appearances on TV shows and in early rock films like *The Girl Can't Help It* (1956) showcased the visuals of his gender-bending antics to those who had not witnessed his live shows. At a time when male gender roles and looks were clearly defined, distinguished, and delineated, codified by the image of the "gray flannel suit," Little Richard trampled on social expectations of masculinity and laughed at concepts of gendered decorum. With a six-inch pompadour, heavy mascara, baggy blouse, and billowing cape, Richard presented a shocking image of what we now recognize as "camp," but that at the time was just perceived as bizarre. For Richard, his look was a form of revenge, a type of trickster humor; it symbolically subsumed all of the abuse leveled at homosexual men, then mocked such assaults by exaggerating the features ascribed to them. As within carnival traditions, the more outrageously the look flaunted convention, the more subversive the body politics. Furthermore, and ironically, Richard was aware that the more "beyond sense" he looked, the more he would be accepted, or at least tolerated. He explained: "We decided that my image should be crazy and way out, so that the adults would think I was harmless."[10] James Miller, in *Flowers in the Dustbin* (1999), also recognized the protective and permissive nature of Richard's flamboyant physical humor, saying, "Being black and being gay, he was an outsider twice over. But by exaggerating his own freakishness, he could get across: he could evade the question of gender and hurdle the racial divide."[11] By being beyond comprehension, he put himself beyond rational objection.

The shock and excitement that Little Richard elicited was made all the more remarkable by the fact that his prime-time career spanned only two years, from 1955 to 1957. Yet, during that time he applied his range of humor to a small but rollicking collection of rock & roll classics. Following "Tutti Frutti," he released the boisterous and bizarre "Long Tall Sally" (1956). Perturbed that Pat Boone had garnered a bigger hit from "Tutti Frutti" than he had, Richard recorded this follow-up with break-neck rhythmic pace and an even greater crazy-quotient, hoping to outflank the stiff limitations of the cover-predator Boone. Lyrically, the song ventured into strange territories of sexuality that are both vague and mysterious, with speculation more than sense surrounding such lines as "Well, I saw Uncle John with bald headed Sally / He saw Aunt Mary coming and he ducked back in the alley."[12]

"Good Golly Miss Molly" (1958) has the alliterative play of "Tutti Frutti," as well as a large dose of double entendres. Here, Molly, who lives "at the house of blue light," "sure likes to ball." Playing with childish glossolalia, Richard describes how Molly "made me ting-a-ling-a-ling."[13] More meaningful than these in-song locker room trifles, though, is the voice that delivers them and the rhythms that propel them. The Little Richard experience is a visceral one, an exciting tightrope trip where childish gibberish combines with musical momentum to create a new sense of sense.

Retreating from the "sin" of rock & roll to the sanctity of the church in 1957, Little Richard's career all but dried up. His periodic comebacks stuttered and started, but were never sustained. Though he continued to reappear once in a while on TV talk shows or the nostalgia concert circuit, his brilliance was essentially bottled into two wild years in the mid-1950s. Despite his short-circuited career, the influence of Little Richard's work upon subsequent rock artists—particularly physical humorists—is broad-reaching and pervasive. Richard's voice, image, sound, and performance style echo through myriad genres of subsequent rock & roll, from American soul, funk, and rap to British glam and punk. Testimonials from contemporaries and successors offer us glimpses into his far-flung influence. Gene Vincent once conceded, "Jerry [Lee Lewis] and I both rate ourselves pretty wild performers, but neither of us could keep up the excitement that Richard generates."[14] Buddy Holly concurred, calling Little Richard "the wildest act in rock 'n' roll."[15] John Lennon reflected on his first listening of "Long Tall Sally," saying, "When I heard it, it was so great I couldn't speak."[16] Critic Langdon Winner, alluding to the childlike humor of Richard, opined, "Any list of rock immortals which does not include Little Richard near the top has gotten too sophisticated."[17] Or, as Richard himself once put it: "A-wop-bop-alu-bop-a-wop-bam-boom!"[18]

Bo Diddley

Another rock & roll originator, the late Bo Diddley brought ambitious innovations to the form that alluded back to pre-slavery African roots and extended forward to contemporary hip-hop culture. Like Chuck Berry and Little Richard, his expressive humor drew from an eclectic range of elements—sound, style, lyrics, performance—but within "gunslinger" Bo's arsenal, they all worked to serve the same master: rhythm. It is within and through Diddley's rhythmic mantras that we locate the potent humor of his street-corner signifying and pre-rap braggadocio.

Born Elias McDaniels (Bo Diddley was his nom de plume, meaning "funny storyteller" in Africa), he spent his early years in Mississippi absorbing the sounds of Southern folk-blues and gospel before the family migrated to Chicago. There, as a teenager, he began to mix his combined passions for roots music and street humor into a strange brew. By 1951 he was performing original songs at Chicago's comedy clubs, the only venues that would give him a time slot. There, Bo also crafted a comic showmanship to complement the humor of his lyrics. Set to music in the blues and R&B styles, his songs mostly consisted of tall tales full of sexual innuendo and puns. One, called "Dirty Mother Fuyer," became a crowd favorite and encouraged Diddley to be daring in pushing the comedic envelope.

Accompanied by his maracas player and hype-MC, Jerome Green, Diddley developed simple rhythmic songs around a distinct beat. Sometimes called the hambone (or patting juba), this "bomp ba-bomp, da-bomp . . . da-bomp-bomp" rhythm was familiar to most African American street kids who had grown up clapping and stomping it along to nursery rhymes and games. Its roots, though, extend more deeply, dating back through minstrel and vaudeville traditions and back even further still to traditional Yoruba drum patterns in Africa. Adopting this familiar and deep-rooted drum sound, Bo added guitar and maracas, not as counterpoints, but as supplements to the same rhythm. Moreover, his lyrics and vocal style stoked that same rhythmic fire, as the nursery rhyme form was transmuted into childlike raps of macho bravado and sexual conquest. The hot independent record label Chess—renowned for courting machismo R&B in the tradition of Big Joe Turner—was intrigued and soon added Bo Diddley to its roster.

His debut release in 1955 was a double-sided monster that presented a sound and aura never heard before. The A-side, "Bo Diddley," was a raucous introduction to the Bo-beat. As the rhythm chugs along like a slow train, Bo raps a strange nursery rhyme full of macho boasts and infantile jokes. "Bo Diddley caught a bear cat / To make his pretty baby a Sunday hat," narrates a deadpan Bo, supplementing his self-aggrandizement with the third-person perspective.[19] Meanwhile, a guitar floats over the rhythm with a distorted vibrato tone while the maracas bring a carnival spirit and communality to the whole trajectory. Collectively, these ingredients, in sync, present a weird yet catchy sound, both sinister and fun. The B-side, "I'm a Man," also showcases a paradoxical incongruity humor as funny images collide with discomforting ones. A grind-blues song, "I'm a Man" lays down a sexual groove over which Bo brags about his own sexual allure and powerful masculinity. "All you pretty women / Stand in line," he instructs before literally breaking down what he means: "I spell M-A-N . . . man."[20] Such ego excess and exaggeration were far from unique within the R&B field, but here there lurked additional danger. Bo's spoken-word delivery added threat to the absurd swagger; set against a primal backbeat, such songs teased white people's stereotypes of black primitivism, testing their deep-seated fears of a black planet. Whereas Chuck Berry and Little Richard softened or masked their subversions behind crossover strategies and accessible appeals, Bo Diddley did the opposite. What on the surface *could* have been broadly appealing was deconstructed into a danger zone via distortion, deadpan, and the doggedly "black" sound of it all. In the infancy of the civil rights movement, "I'm a Man" and other Bo-boasts can be seen and heard as the trailblazing forerunners of the James Brown–coined sentiment to "Say It Loud, I'm Black & I'm Proud."

Over a six-year span, from 1955 to 1961, Bo Diddley continued to tap into the same intoxicating sound, distributing his "Superman" iconography across various platters. "Who Do You Love?" (1956) is about—guess who? "I walk forty-seven miles of barbed wire / I use a cobra snake for a neck tie" are but two of many of the song's bizarre claims of superhuman machismo.[21] "Women here, women there / Women, women, women everywhere," he rhymes and rants in "Hey, Bo Diddley" (1957), reminding us again (if we had forgotten) of his name and that he is still "the man."[22]

Tapping into America's patriotic love of Western movies in the 1950s, Bo replaced the conventionally all-white casting of this genre and played the designated hero in his song "Bo Diddley's a Gunslinger" (1960); a few years later he would apply his strengths in the equally manly "Bo's a Lumberjack" (1963). In the silly "Say Man" (1959) he earned his only top-twenty hit. Like Chuck Berry's "My Ding-a-Ling," this was largely a novelty song loosely free-styled in the studio. It showcased Bo and Jerome Green in call-and-response mode, playing the dozens, trading standard "You're so ugly . . . " and "Your mama . . ." jibes.[23]

As much as Bo Diddley's lyrical and musical features define his subversive humor, one amusing incident from 1956 is also emblematic of its nature. Impressed by the look of Bo in his Coke-bottle glasses, sporting his furry custom-made square Gretsch guitar, Ed Sullivan decided to employ and exploit Diddley's striking image by having him perform, as a cover, the then-popular hit of the day "Sixteen Tons" on his live TV show. Decked out as Sullivan had requested and set up with large cue cards so that he could follow the lyrics, Bo instead ripped into his own "Bo Diddley." Afterward he quipped, "Man, maybe that was 'Sixteen Tons' on those cards, but all I saw was 'Bo Diddley.'"[24] Here, Bo's (black) pride, cynical bravado, strident independence, and refusal to be a co-opted "slave" to the system foreshadowed the rise of the civil rights and Black Power movements, as well as the era of hip-hop autonomy.

Not surprisingly, Bo Diddley's most visible (and audible) legacy is in the continuation of the Bo-beat. Whether heard in contemporaries like Buddy Holly and the Everly Brothers, British blues revivalists like the Rolling Stones and the Yardbirds, or punk/new wavers like the Clash and U2, the rumble of Bo's primitive Dionysian rhythms spans the length of rock history. But it is in Bo's proud identity and self-conscious boast humor where perhaps his most significant legacy lies. His superhero figure-of-fun persona was but a childlike mask for a subversive independence that few black artists or citizens dared assert within the midst of a white-powered America that preferred its "negroes" passive and emasculated. Behind the deceptive nursery rhymes and streetwise signifying of his songs, there was a larger purpose that "Bo knew," one that successors like James Brown, Gil Scott-Heron, and Chuck D would later inherit and learn.

WHITE BOYS WHO STOLE THE RHYTHM & BLUES

Rock & roll became the designated home for a multitude of musical styles that were around and about in the 1950s. New Orleans boogie-woogie, R&B's myriad forms, upbeat country & western, and the electric blues were among the youth-popular styles soon gathered under the umbrella of rock & roll. Its eclectic ingredients provided an amalgam of humor sources, styles, and motivations that revolved around the ubiquitous issues of sexuality, youth distinction, and racial identity. As differently as these matters were addressed by particular acts within rock & roll, they were all treated with an instinctive generational drive to rebel against adult standards.

The range of rock & roll in the 1950s was very much a by-product of geographical diversity among its artists. The migration of African Americans during the 1940s had made many Northern cities the loci of R&B and electric blues by the next decade, while many of the white rockabilly acts were from the Deep South and had learned their trade listening to and absorbing the black and white music that had surrounded them. What emerged when these various influences were put into the mixer were white artists who often sounded (somewhat) black (e.g., Elvis Presley) and black artists who often sounded (somewhat) white (e.g., Chuck Berry). Such mutations and melting pots created styles and humor of many hues, expressed in multiple ways.

The emergence of Elvis Presley from Mississippi into the mainstream in 1956 brought attention to the sonic concoctions emerging from Sam Phillips's Sun Studios in Memphis. His roster of white acts merging hillbilly sounds with R&B created a subgenre in "rockabilly." These performers—Presley, Jerry Lee Lewis, and Carl Perkins, among them—were white, Southern, working-class kids, disaffected, but inextricably tied to their conservative, fundamentalist, rural roots. However, their search for thrills and danger had led them to the blues, and, importantly, to the black parts of town where that music could be heard. There, they learned how the black hipsters dressed, danced, and moved; they were introduced to how they sang, played, and performed. Like sponges, they soaked up the spirit and the excitement of an unconstrained musical culture and parlayed it into their own creations. In the racial transference, however, changes occurred. Adopting black slang like "cats" and "bop" was in the spirit of reverential accommodation, but in courting black culture these white kids often forced into it their own excesses. Thus, Elvis's pelvic gyrations were his attempt to replicate the black dancing he had witnessed, but in transposition to his baggy trousers, the leg-shake took on the form of a humorous gesture of sexual play. Likewise, the "possessed" piano style of Jerry Lee Lewis had all the sweat and swagger of black R&B, but in his hands the style took on a parodic quality, part threatening, part caricature of threat. The rockabilly acts, though clearly copy-"cats," actually forged new comedic forms out of prevailing black traditions. When subsequently showcased for white mainstream audiences (often on primetime TV shows), their displays, images, and gestures became subversive challenges to uptight white norms by virtue of their somewhat "distant" relations to the black culture from which they had first been stolen.

Jerry Lee Lewis

The arrival of Jerry Lee Lewis in 1957—via records, TV, and cinema—signaled parents' worst nightmares realized. One can imagine their thought processes: here was a young, white, Southern Christian boy (before), and here was a young, white, Southern Christian boy on rock & roll (after). The wildest of the wild mid-fifties rock & roll rebels, Lewis performed with the possessed abandon of Little Richard, but he replaced camp theatrics with screw-loose danger; he courted raw black blues like Elvis, but neither softened nor slowed his own renditions for mass appeal; he tapped into the primal and sinister forces of roots music like Bo Diddley, but he added a bizarre spirit of gospel salvation to his profane sexual exorcisms. Jerry Lee Lewis did not so much push the envelope as rip it up and scatter the pieces to any who would listen. His subversive humor resided at the outskirts of his excess, where incongruity pitted sin against salvation, and where commitment to his craft lurched into (self)parody. His was the animalistic rock excess that we have since come to recognize in such fearless primitives as Iggy Pop, Darby Crash, and Henry Rollins.

Despite being tagged by parents as the poster child for juvenile delinquency and despite his unwillingness to tone down or compromise his style, Lewis was one of the more successful of the major mid-fifties rockers. Between 1957 and 1958 he racked up a string of successful hits, each characterized by Lewis's adept piano-pounding rhythms and on-the-edge vocal explosions. Residing within the R&B "leerics" realm, where words were thinly veiled metaphors for sexual conduct, Lewis played with puns, implied with innuendo, and vocalized sexual acts through flights of expressive swoons and surges, each complemented by a catalogue of less-than-subtle guttural noises. For Lewis, sex was neither the tender nor romantic world portrayed by so many of his peers; for him, it was pure physicality—sweaty and imposing. "Jerry's got the bull by the horn," he interjects during the manic three minutes that constituted his breakout single, "Whole Lotta Shakin' Goin' On" (1957). "We ain't fakin'" that "shakin'," he adds, loading fun to the orgasm pun. At one point Jerry Lee pauses the pounding to give directions to his lover: "All you gotta do, honey, is just kinda stand in one spot / Wiggle around just a little bit." Judging by the proceeding "Yeah-huh-huh-ha-ha," his instructions were carried out.[25] White middle-class parents stood aghast at this white boy, not only for singing such pornographic fare, but also for *acting out* these lyrics onstage and on prime-time TV. Conversely, young fans reveled in his sexual daring, his candid expression, and his testosterone-charged teen-titillations. For them, Lewis was conveying not only their own burgeoning sexuality but the pent-up frustrations of living within the siege mentality of a repressed, puritanical culture. Remember, this was a time when on TV and in most movies, married couples were still portrayed as sleeping in separate beds!

Jerry Lee earned the nickname "The Killer" for the way he slayed songs and audiences, and his predatory mission was apparent in tunes like "Great Balls of Fire" (1957), which took listeners on another sex-pun thrill ride into the dark excesses of our intrepid narrator. "Too much love drives a man insane," he drawls with telling self-disclosure, as the song drives through a series of onomatopoe(t)ic noises that transform the words on the page into a three-dimensional fantasy. Nerves, shakes, and shivers are fragmented into "dumb" utterances like "Mmmm" and "Mooooved."[26] The humor here is pre-lingual, pre-rational, pre-adult. It is pure id! "Breathless" (1958), likewise, continues to code sexual practice in sounds, this time "Ooooh" and "Brrrr," as The Killer pushes, pounds, and conquers until forced to come up gasping for air.[27]

Whether one regards it as incongruous or as a natural consequence, Jerry Lee Lewis's fiery (s)exorcisms had their foundations in a rigid conservative upbringing within an Evangelical community in Ferriday, Louisiana. Though born into a poor family, Jerry Lee had access to a piano and became an accomplished prodigy as a child. However, whereas his mother had hoped he would use his skills in the service of Christian faith, Jerry Lee was more drawn to the black boogie-woogie pianists who performed on the other side of the tracks. Encouraged to attend Bible college like his cousin, Jimmy Swaggart, Lewis still could not resist the draw of the profane R&B music scene, nor the decadence that world offered. At the age of twenty-one, he had already been married twice and served a spell in jail, but he still persisted with the musical ambition that would subsequently land him at the doorstep of Sun Records in 1956. Soon he was part of Sam Phillips's stable of white acts who sang the blues. Phillips regarded him as potentially the next Elvis and promoted him accordingly. Before long, Jerry Lee would be taking his split personality to rock & roll stages across America and beyond. With his left hand playing black boogie and the right displaying Liberace-like showmanship, Lewis fused gospel ecstasy with blues fatalism via the piano. The schizophrenic results speak to a resonant appeal—as well as the attendant danger—that constituted his artistic essence. With Lewis, the lusty humor so familiar within R&B was imbided with something as sinister as it was saucy, as provocative as it was playful.

Jerry Lee Lewis used his voice to trample down mainstream conventions, expectations, and rigidities. In his case, middle-class adult proprieties represented restraints on freedom of expression and they needed to be challenged, countered, and penetrated with all the arrows in his quiver. Middle-class parents wanted their kids to look decent and to act with decorum, so Jerry Lee unbuttoned his shirt and let his fiery red locks fly like whips, rolling his tongue with lascivious lust as he performed; middle-class parents wanted innocent lyrics and sweet songs, so Jerry Lee corrupted the speaking-in-tongues glossalalia of his family's Pentecostal sect into sacrilegious grunts of the primal and animalistic. Late in his career, he declared his staunch working-class pride with poignant reflection in the song "Redneck," co-opting and diffusing this conventionally middle-class insult tag by simply stating, "I'm just a redneck in a rock & roll bar."[28]

Much has been made of the wayward personal experiences that gave Lewis his legendarily checkered life. Indeed, his multiple marriages (the most famous being to his thirteen-year-old cousin, Myra Brown), his IRS problems, and his drug and alcohol dependencies certainly attest to the fact that Lewis did not subscribe to the typical middle-class life. However, in his life, as in his art, he has been unwilling to compromise or kowtow to social mores. This has made him a notorious figure over time, from one feared by parents but revered by their sons and daughters during the 1950s to one celebrated by the many successors who have inherited his edgy physical humor and spirited style for their own rock expressions.

BAWDY WOMEN

Despite the gender paradigm realignments of recent decades, popular music, like so many public art forms, is still a male-dominated phenomenon. Its boys-club, male-inscribed mythologies perpetuate a perennial machismo that has historically excluded or marginalized women to the outside of the performance realm, relegating them to the sidelines of audience participation. Thus, in the first half of the twentieth century, at a time when women's roles were circumscribed within clearly defined spaces and limited public opportunities, the fact that there were any subversive female practitioners at all within music is remarkable. But, though limited in number, certain women were key players in forming and fomenting the sounds and styles that constituted the forerunning aesthetics of rock & roll. Furthermore, many exercised a vibrant humor that served for survival purposes in the music industry shark pool; this humor was often trailblazing in nature, carving out spaces for empowerment that would provide hope for future generations of female rockers.

Though female rock humorists came of age in the 1950s, no discussion of such women is complete without acknowledgment of Bessie Smith and Ethel Waters, who spearheaded the heyday of the bawdy blues during the 1920s and 1930s. Resurrected and reformulated by female R&B shouters in the early 1950s, the genre enjoyed its second wave just prior to the rock & roll boom. Artists like Ruth Brown, LaVern Baker, and Etta James served as connectors from the female blues traditions of the past to the new upbeat R&B and rock & roll sounds. The edgier female performers of the 1950s used bawdy humor to fight back (symbolically) against postwar gender realignments that were forcing women from the workplace and back into the kitchen. In reaction to the frustration created by the pressures to conform to new patriarchal restraints, the celebratory roars and proto-feminist assertiveness of Big Mama Thornton and Wanda Jackson represented trailblazing voices of emancipation, symbolically suggesting a female identity thwarted by social and sexual containment but always liable to break free. Today, their thinly veiled innuendo lyrics and feisty blues voices can be heard in modern provocat-hers like Candye Kane and Beth Ditto. These women's contemporary updates of the form provide proto-feminist history lessons by reminding us of the enduring power and legacy of the bawdy blues tradition.

Big Mama Thornton

Willie Mae "Big Mama" Thornton left her mark on the history of subversive rock humor the moment she growled, "You ain't nothin' but a hound dog" in 1952.[29] Her only chart success over a thirty-one year career, Big Mama's single hit left a large impression. However, the decline of her career after 1957 and her frustrations with an industry that she felt never gave her her due left a decades-long mark on Thornton, too. The onetime 350-pound sassy comedienne was a mere 95 pounds when she died—a bitter alcoholic—in 1984. Some see her decline and fall as reflective of the fate of many women who had attempted to succeed in the early rock years, particularly those who were black and/or big. On the other hand, her larger-than-life frame and personality were ideally suited to the bawdy blues comedy-music tradition that predated and ran into rock & roll. A successor to Bessie Smith and Ma Rainey, Big Mama Thornton employed their same sassy humor, combative independence, and celebration of working-class black life.

"Hound Dog" embodies the Thornton persona she had crafted as a comedienne prior to entering the music industry. It parades the classic puns, extended metaphors, and sexual double entendres so popular within the bawdy genre. The song also has an intriguing history that mirrors the crossover developments of popular music during the early 1950s in America. Written by two Jewish men (Jerry Leiber and Mike Stoller), it was first recorded by a black woman (Thornton), then later rerecorded (in a very different fashion) by a white man (The King himself), and thereafter by many others (the Everly Brothers, Jerry Lee Lewis, and John Lennon, to cite but a few). Each artist has left his/her mark on the song in noteworthily different ways, though none have tattooed it with the ferocity that Big Mama did on the original.

The birth of "Hound Dog" as an idea came about when lyricist Jerry Leiber first met Thornton and took a gauge of her person and personality. He recalled, "She looked like the biggest, baddest, saltiest chick you would ever see. . . . I had to write a song for [her] that basically said, 'Go fuck yourself' but how do you do it without actually saying it?"[30] Once the song was written, Leiber and Stoller set to capturing Thornton's patented growl in the recording session. Stoller recalled offering suggestions, to which Big Mama would curtly respond, "Don't you tell me how to sing no song."[31] Whether riling her up helped craft the end product or whether Big Mama was sufficiently testy by nature, the vocal performance captured in "Hound Dog" is one of pure spit and vinegar. "You can wag your tail but I ain't gonna feed you no more" is the song's kicker line, extending the man-as-dog metaphor with a sexual pun on the "tail."

Big Mama's version of "Hound Dog" became a major crossover success for a "race" record (holding the number one slot on the R&B charts for seven straight weeks), though Presley's rendition became an international hit of huge proportions. History, though, increasingly favors Big Mama's version, which has become a cult classic to fans of pre-rock R&B and a touchstone song for many female artists and fans. Although she was never to repeat the success of "Hound Dog," Thornton continued to write and perform similar-styled bawdy R&B songs for her independent Peacock Records label. Many were popular, though by 1957 her old-school sound had been flanked by the emerging rock & roll trends; thereafter, her career went into decline, with Peacock ultimately releasing her from her contract. During her four-year heyday, though, the songs "I Smell a Rat," "Stop a-Hoppin' on Me," "I Ain't No Fool Either," and "Just Like a Dog" (the latter employing familiar imagery) continued to concretize her comedic mode within the feisty "take-no-shit" realm (as these titles suggest), where men are characterized as good-for-nothing exploiters and deceivers. One such song, "Ball & Chain," enjoyed considerable success when covered by Janis Joplin in 1967, yet despite Thornton being credited as its author, apparently she enjoyed few of its royalties.

Despite her final years of bitterness and cynicism against an industry she felt had systematically exploited her, Big Mama Thornton will best be remembered for carrying, then passing, the torch of the bawdy blues to the rock & roll era. Her proto-feminist resilience and comic resistance are stamped on her every ball-busting lyric, as well as in that one-of-a-kind, gravel-toned voice that delivers them.

Wanda Jackson

With its macho poses and locker room humor, rockabilly was largely a private boys' club. Females, of course, played an important role within the subculture, assigned either as the adoring screamers who bolstered the male performers' egos, or as the dreamy romantics who lay on their beds staring at their rebel-idols on the posters on their walls. Thus, when the teenage Oklahoma country singer Wanda Jackson, at the encouragement of her then-beau Elvis Presley, adopted the raging rockabilly style in 1956, she revolutionized not only the musical form, but also the role of women—particularly white women—within the rock & roll world. That she aimed to participate using the same renegade methods as her contemporary bad boys rather than compromising the form to the demure femininity of her gender-peers makes her contributions all the more shocking and radical.

Like her primary influences, Elvis and Gene Vincent, Jackson forged her sound out of her country roots and merged it to an R&B beat. Her voice, gravel-throated and assertive, had little connection to the Connie Francis–type femininity of her contemporaries; it had more in common with shouters like Jerry Lee Lewis and Little Richard. However, to describe Jackson as just a rockin' female singer is to understate her revolutionary role. Aside from her raw, feisty voice, Wanda also played guitar with swagger and aplomb, in addition to writing much of her own material—if only because there were so few songs from the rockabilly genre that posited a female narrative point of view.

Her songs from 1956 to the end of the decade provide a catalogue of some of the most subversive material of the era—and the funniest. Joanne R. Gilbert's female comedy designations of "the bawd" and "the bitch" are particularly applicable to this material.[32] Bawdy female blues singers like Bessie Smith and Ethel Waters had trailblazed this humor back in the 1920s and 1930s, but rarely had white women ventured into the *sordid* world of sexual innuendo. The establishment had deemed such humor to be understandable within the decadent black underclass, but it was not a style befitting an upright white lady, particularly one of Southern Christian stock. To flirt with such saucy stuff as Wanda Jackson did was to challenge norms, subvert the status quo, and turn hierarchies on their heads. Her first single, "I Gotta Know" (1956), was a case in point. Honing her Elvis-style hiccup vocal, Jackson satirized the prevailing male hits of the day, songs that posited either romantic illusions or "cool" boasting. Rather than passively wallowing in these conceits, or swallowing their deceits, Jackson set to debunking them with brutal "response" lyrics. "When you're on that floor, you're cool, man, cool / But when it comes to loving, you need to go to school," snarls the Queen to Elvis's King in a scornful put-down.[33] Such in-house humor had long existed in the combative jazz world, but it was rare within rock circles—at least, on records.

Besides debunking male self-aggrandizement and ego-driven myths, Jackson's humor also implicitly poured scorn on the prevailing female roles and attitudes of the time. Historian David Halberstam, in his documentary series *The Fifties*, spoke of the hypocrisy and repression that lay uncomfortably over gender and sexuality during this decade. Just as men were frustrated with the "gray flannel suit" world that had emasculated them after World War II, so women, too, felt stifled as they outwardly subscribed to the official line of contentment and normalcy and inwardly suffered an unspoken void.[34] Betty Friedan would soon give the condition a name with *The Feminine Mystique*. Likewise, the sexuality of women was a socially repressed topic, but the silence did not mean that sex had disappeared; it had merely been kept under wraps. Hence, just as Grace Metalious's 1956 barn burner *Peyton Place* had blown the lid off of this socially subscribed secret (in literature and later on TV), Wanda Jackson did likewise within rock & roll. Her outward demands for sexual fulfillment and outlandish demands for how she wanted it usurped traditional gender expectations and, as with *Peyton Place*, scandalized observers. In "Cool Love" (1957), Wanda insults then instructs: "You been playing it cool. / I been playing a fool. / Now don't you give me that cool love / Give me the kind I need."[35] Long before Madonna, there was Wanda!

"Fujiyama Mama" (1958) was Wanda Jackson's signature song. It was an international hit and enduring cult classic, and its lyrical references brought rockabilly to Japan, where it has remained since as a vital genre for both male and female musicians and fans. "I drink a quart of sake, smoke dynamite / I chase it with tobaccy and then shoot out the light," wails the Fujiyama Mama in her most bawdy of boast songs. Gravitating to "bitch" revenge humor, she then growls, "Well, you can talk about me, say that I'm mean / I'll blow your head off baby with nitroglycerine."[36] As displayed in her earlier single, "Hot Dog That Made Him Mad" (1956), Wanda was a woman not to be messed with, and should you step on her high-heeled shoes, she would respond by any means necessary. In "Hot Dog" the means is self-assured mockery: "He demanded to know just where I'd been / But I really put him in his place. / Instead of an answer, I laughed in his face."[37] Here, the sexual autonomy of Madonna meets the "bitch" assaults of Roseanne Barr, creating an intimidating identity the very antithesis of fifties female conventions.

As might be expected from her outsider status and audacity, Wanda Jackson never attained the mainstream rock prominence of the male contemporaries she so admired. But as with many of the finest and most radical artists, popularity does not define the art. History has proven to be more accommodating to Wanda's work than the shell-shocked audience who initially heard her. Critic Nick Tosches recognized her importance—as well as the fact that she was too hot to handle during the 1950s—including her in his *Unsung Heroes of Rock & Roll* book. The other Elvis, Costello, has also been a tireless advocate on her behalf, writing letters to the Rock & Roll Hall of Fame demanding her induction. Contemporary female alt-country figures like Neko Case, Tanya Tucker, and Rosie Flores have also recognized their debts to Wild Wanda, whether through tribute songs or in their own feisty independent styles. A born-again Christian today (the fate of many a rockabilly rebel, it seems), Wanda Jackson continues to perform on the nostalgia circuit, reminding new generations, through her strident songs, that subversive humor and rock rebellion in the 1950s were not the sole preserve of the more celebrated canon of male iconic performers.

NOVELTY HUMOR

Emanating from the same intellectual domain as Little Richard's "Tutti Frutti" and Gene Vincent's "Be-Bop-a-Lula," novelty humor became a dominant subgenre of late-1950s rock & roll. A celebration of "dumb" aesthetics, its essence and appeal were intimately tied to the teen demographic being targeted, though not exclusively. Even some "adult" humorists of the day, such as Stan Freberg and Tom Lehrer, got in on the novelty craze, though neither was particularly enamored of the new rock & roll sounds. Both acts used novelty means for satirical ends. Tom Lehrer could be particularly biting within the form, whether tackling trivial topics ("The Masochism Tango" [1959]) or more serious ones ("The Old Dope Peddler" [1953]). Mostly, though, novelty records were innocuous and inane, usually combining doo-wop vocal gibberish with childlike flights of fantasy. Sheb Wooley, for example, sang the faux-horror tale of the "Purple People Eater" (1958), while David Seville sang "Ting tong walla-walla bing-bong" in recounting his narrative of the "Witch Doctor" (1958).[38] Besides reinforcing the emerging generation gap, such songs lacked obvious incendiary purposes or effects.

Others within the field, though, were not so innocent and harbored goals merely coded in gibberish. "Transfusion" (1956), by Nervous Norvos, was a schlock ditty about car crashes, but subtly infused the danger, recklessness, and abandon of the alternative youth culture. It played to the "live fast, die young" charisma of James Dean and Jane Mansfield, both anti–role models from parental perspectives. Though novelty songs were usually presented within a pop context, often performed by quirky doo-wop vocal groups, occasionally the harder rock & roll acts also courted the genre. Carl Perkins's "Blue Suede Shoes" (1956) used a novelty concept to parlay a broader idea of subcultural identity, here around the beloved footwear of youth-rebels. Such songs added mystique to rockabilly as an in-club with its own codes of connection, rather than as just another music form. At once silly and superficial, such knowing humor essentially warned off squares and outsiders, symbolically saying "don't step on my" youth rebellion.

The most strategically subversive of the novelty humorists were songwriters Jerry Leiber and Mike Stoller, whose work with the Coasters adeptly walked the line between mainstream pop appeal and youth dissension. Brothers-in-arms with Chuck Berry in their sly lyrical purposes, Leiber and Stoller's novelty hits (performed by the Coasters), "Yakety Yak" (1958) and "Charlie Brown" (1959), were anthems of teen restlessness, accessible enough to penetrate the highest regions of the charts, but tricky enough to articulate a rebel-slacker, youth-versus-adult pose without undue censorship from above. Critic Steve Otfinoski had Coasters-type humor in mind when he asserted, "Like all good comedy, good novelty songs puncture the balloon of pomposity, expose the darker side of ourselves, and provide some life-affirming laughter in the face of civilization's pretensions."[39]

The Coasters

Next to the Platters, the most popular doo-wop R&B act of the 1950s was the Coasters, though many regarded them as a manufactured front for their dynamic songwriting team of Leiber and Stoller, who penned most of their hilarious hits. However, although the band did not write their own material, neither did Elvis Presley, and though they certainly were a vehicle for Leiber and Stoller's creativity, they were also much more. Like the Monkees a decade later, the Coasters complemented and carried out the visions of their so-called "puppeteers" with an action-packed performance style that showcased physical humor akin to the Marx Brothers; they also sang with a finely honed four-part harmony that boasted range, synthesis, and humor. Despite their skills and contributions, however, one cannot discuss the Coasters without focusing upon the sophisticated arrangements of Jerry Leiber and the socially aware humor of Mike Stoller's lyrics.

The Coasters took up the space created by bands like Hank Ballard & the Midnighters during the immediate pre–rock & roll years. The success of Ballard's trilogy of "Annie" songs in 1954 ("Work With Me Annie," "Sexy Ways," and "Annie Had a Baby") had shown the music industry that black R&B doo-wop bands had great potential to transcend racial ghettoization and to penetrate mainstream youth markets. The sound was accessible, melodic, and listener-friendly, and the doo-wop vocal concept worked well with lyrical humor and novelty topics. As crossover artists, the doo-wop humorists also trod sensitive territory as they navigated between the black and white worlds; this danger zone was ripe for the kind of subversive humor that Leiber and Stoller were intent to foist upon the unsuspecting public.

Leiber and Stoller themselves were not strangers to experiences of racial crossover. Two Jewish kids from East Coast working-class families, both grew up in bohemian, integrated environments where interracial dating was not uncommon and access to black popular culture was neither unavailable nor frowned upon. By the time they entered the music industry in the 1940s, Leiber and Stoller were wise to "hep" black culture: its music (mostly jazz), its street vernacular, its reference points. They would transfer this knowledge into future songwriting endeavors. Their early achievements within the R&B world included the 1953 success of "Hound Dog," a song they wrote for Big Mama Thornton. From this, Stoller learned an important lesson about the potential of using humor as a primary instrument in the musical mix, explaining, "There was something universal about the humor . . . that caught the teens."[40] By 1955, Leiber and Stoller were operating their own label, Spark Records, and had written and produced the hit "Riot in Cell Block No. 9" for the West Coast group the Robins. Atlantic Records took note and lured the rising songwriting duo on board, as well as half of the Robins, which they renamed the Coasters (as in the West Coast).

The Coasters would prove to be Leiber and Stoller's ticket to songwriting fame. During the latter years of the 1950s they produced one classic hit after another, each bearing the same hallmarks of slick production, engaging hooks, and lyrical comedy of the highest form. The team referred to their song-narratives as "playlets" and boasted (with their characteristic inverted snobbery) that they were in the business of writing records, not songs. What emerged were deceptively light numbers that had a novelty "dumb" surface quality and a subtly subversive underbelly. They brought intellectual insight to the common trivia of everyday teenage life. Like Chuck Berry (their only comparable lyrical peer), they inhabited the world of youth, playing with its habits and slang, not merely as a novelty exercise, but as a way into producing social commentary. As with Chuck Berry, their humor and simplicity were poses, disarming mechanisms that opened the doors for subversive cultural critiques.

Also like Chuck Berry, the Coasters discovered that "old" black guys singing about teenage (white) girls can ruffle the feathers of some. Such was the fate for "Young Blood" (1957), their song of desire that had certain suspicious critics waving the red flag of "teenophilia." The band reached safer ground with "Yakety Yak" a year later. Here, Stoller shifted the narrative point of view to the "everyparent" of imaginary Middle America. Simultaneously satirizing both ends of the generation gap, "Yakety Yak" mocked the smothering, restrictive practices of parents, as well as the carefree hedonism of their lazy kids. Capturing a slice of mainstream life, the song's staccato rhythm moved in parallel to the nagging of the narrator-parent, who warned, "If you don't scrub that kitchen floor / You ain't gonna rock & roll no more." For the song's central character and his "hoodlum friends," this was the ultimate threat.[41] Like similar satirical songs of the period, such as "Summertime Blues" (1958) and "Sweet Little Sixteen" (1958), the sympathies in "Yakety Yak" lay largely with the teenager, thus ensuring that the song be adopted by young listeners as a friend-in-arms, rather than as an authoritarian censure. The quantitative evidence to this end is that "Yakety Yak" was carried by youth consumers to number one on the national pop charts.

Capitalizing on their mainstream success, the Coasters took America by storm in 1959, releasing a series of Leiber-and-Stoller-penned hits, each packing a satirical punch pertinent to the times.

With "Charlie Brown," Stoller presented another generation gap struggle, but this time a third-person narrator told the tale of a stereotypical class clown-slacker-delinquent who, among his other rebel-sins, "calls the English teacher Daddy-O." In this instance, school substituted for the parent as the authority symbol, and bass singer Dub Jones was given Charlie's line of defense that would become the catchphrase heard from teens under siege across the land: "Why is everybody always picking on me?"[42] Implicit to the youth characters in "Yakety Yak" and "Charlie Brown" were the rock & roll influence and identity at the heart of generational tensions. These issues were tackled head-on in "That Is Rock & Roll," also released in 1959. The song was essentially a rebuttal—à la "Roll Over Beethoven"—to adult snobs and censors, personified with the accusatory "you" pronoun: "You say the music's for the birds / And you can't understand the words. / Well, honey, if you did / You'd really blow your lid. / Well, baby, that is rock & roll."[43]

Ever vigilant to the tastes and trends of mainstream culture, with "Along Came Jones" (1959) the band addressed the cult of the cowboy Westerns in 1950s popular culture. A staple of the movies, TV, and comic books, the Westerns had served to assuage the pervasive anxieties of the period—be it enemies within or beyond—with the comfort of hero stories with happy endings, rooted in a romanticized version of American frontier history. They provided sentimental relief by portraying a whitewashed America where men were real (white) men and women and blacks knew and accepted their ascribed submissive places. Ideological time capsules, they gave temporary escape from concerns about the bomb, communism, and rock & roll–inspired juvenile delinquents. For Mike Stoller, Westerns provided fodder for further cultural satire, an opportunity to operate his own six-shooter against a manipulative genre and the mediums that promoted it. Verse one establishes the narrator watching a typical TV Western. He describes how the evil gunslinger, "Salty Sam," is about to saw "Sweet Sue" in two, when "along came long, lean, lanky Jones" to the rescue. Our tired, cynical narrator, weary of the same old clichés, seeks alternative fare on the other channels, only to discover that "there was the same old shoot-'em-up and the same old rodeo."[44] Through caricature and satire, the song debunked a central mythological strain in the American consciousness, along with its attendant ideological assumptions and prescriptions.

When Leiber and Stoller left Atlantic Records in 1963, this presaged the decline of the Coasters' reign of dominance in popular music. Under changing lineups, they would continue to perform and record, even reclaiming some success with a version of "Love Potion No. 9" in 1971. However, their post–Leiber and Stoller career has largely been one of nostalgia, though they were recognized by the Rock & Roll Hall of Fame in 1987, inducted, appropriately, along with their original songwriting duo. Despite the fact that few would rank their work with the elite forces of fifties rock & roll, the Coasters/Leiber and Stoller, like Chuck Berry, established a method of high/low humor—bringing intellect and creativity to everyday culture—that would prove long-standing and influential to the more serious-minded novelty humorists of the future.

THE COMIC CRAZE AND OTHER VISUAL SPECTACLES

Prior to rock & roll, the establishment culture had felt challenged but not overwhelmed by the rebellious provocations of the youth-driven music styles. Isolated within specific racial and regional arenas, swing, jazz, and folk could be largely contained. However, with the technological and economic advances of the post-1945 period, new media outlets—many visually oriented—were increasingly available to access and receive the insurgent sights and sounds of the youth boom.

Many critics have pointed to "Rock Around the Clock" (1954), by Bill Haley and His Comets, as the song that shifted rock & roll from an underground seismic rumble to an international earthquake. Certainly, there is much truth to this assertion. However, on initial release the song was not an immediate hit. Not until the breakout movie *Blackboard Jungle* (1955) used it as its whip-crack theme introduction did the song ride up the charts. More than the song itself, the movie's visual images of delinquents in leather were instrumental in "cult"-ivating the emerging rebel-rocker persona of the time, the film ultimately serving as a proto-video for the marketing of the song as a teen anthem. Using the visual power of the movies, the humor in rock & roll's styles and attitudes could be illustratively paraded as subcultural markers.

With rock & roll's provocative wit working as much at the visual as the sonic level, film and TV were to prove important outlets for the movement's multiple expressions. Movies like *The Girl Can't Help It* (1956) brought the energized performances and outrageous stylistic flair of Little Richard and Gene Vincent to the uninitiated. *Jailhouse Rock* (1957) was the first of many movies that would help mold, manipulate, and maneuver the Elvis Presley image and style over the next decade. Even beyond rock movies, cult films like *Rebel without a Cause* (1955) and *The Wild One* (1954) helped foster the images of the rebel-rocker and sensitive outsider that Elvis and others would emulate so effectively. These movies, like rock & roll music, established narrative viewpoints opposing the adult mainstream, indicting it for its hypocrisy, crass materialism, and closed-mindedness.

Television, with its plethora of variety performance/talk shows, also proved a major outlet for the mid-fifties rock movement. The *Ed Sullivan, Steve Allen,* and *Milton Berle* shows were all instrumental in transforming key rock & rollers from regional successes into international superstars. Elvis Presley, Jerry Lee Lewis, and Little Richard all popularized their struts, wails, and multicolored styles through these televisual avenues. In turn, the physical humor that film and TV could showcase so effectively trickled down into the aesthetics of rock performance in general; as a result, even marginal acts like Screamin' Jay Hawkins and Esquerita—though they would rarely garner screen time—embraced the photogenic and the visual as essential components of their comedy and artistry.

The young TV industry itself, aware of the growing youth demographic, created specific music shows where rock & roll idols could promote their material and new dances could be invented, promoted, then sent out for further development in youth clubs and playgrounds across the land. The twist, the watusi, the mashed potato, and the stroll were just a few of the novelty dances that worked their way through the TV circuits on their way to the dance floor. Though these dances were permitted forms of (fore) play, their often-sexualized physicality (as with the jitterbug and the lindy hop of earlier decades) was not lost on either the perturbed parents or the practicing kids.

For the youngest fifties youth rebels, the comic book boom played a significant role in crafting subversive humor under the deceptive realms of fantasy and childish eccentricity. Comic books spoke the language of youth culture, appealing to readers' imaginative faculties through a voice and visual humor they could comprehend. Scare-comics like *The Crypt of Terror*, *Weird Science*, and *Frontline Combat* served edgy horror images and sci-fi fare to young children, their content often bringing frowns to the brows of concerned parents. One trailblazer, Harvey Kurtzman, had worked on these comics prior to launching the revolutionary *Mad* magazine in 1952 and *Panic* in 1953. Containing content that attacked social norms, parodied the competition, and brought ridicule to U.S. icons like GI Joe (who became GI Shmoe in *Mad* #10), Kurtzman used his magazines to further pry open, as well as politicize, the generation gap. Bravely broaching the sensitive parts of such taboo no-nos as racism, religion, and the bomb, he introduced youth culture to off-limits issues and to the weapon of satire. Kurtzman's comic books had a fifties rock & roll spirit that foreshadowed sixties polemics. For his troubles, he created a comic book scare that led to censorship and an investigative Senate committee in the United States. The British government, alarmed at the influx of these U.S. shock-comics, responded in 1955 by passing the Children & Young Persons (Harmful Publications) Act. Like the shock-rock of the mid-fifties, the comic book furor quieted by the end of the decade, but not before many of the most outrageous new rockers—Screamin' Jay Hawkins and Hasil Adkins among them—had drawn liberally from Kurtzman's grotesque spectacles, envelope-pushing innovations, and parodist techniques.

Screamin' Jay Hawkins

If the anti–rock & roll constituency within America needed a case study to illustrate its various fears and prejudices, Screamin' Jay Hawkins was their man. The image of the stereotypical primal savage, Hawkins brought his freakish persona—in all its outlandishness—to both stage and song. His style was literally "horror"-laden, and the screams, gurgles, and yelps that constituted his pseudo-operatic vocals uttered vague expressions that suggested themes ranging from voodoo to stalking. In other words, he was hardly the kind of entertainer Bible Belt parents wanted their kids to be within either eye- or earshot of. As usual, though, in the 1950s the music that elicited anxiety and consternation within mainstream adult circles fueled the fires of rebellion and celebration in youth reception. With Screamin' Jay, as parents saw evil horror, the kids saw a *Rocky Horror Picture Show*–style humor that we nowadays regard as innocent camp.

Though less effeminate than either Little Richard or Esquerita, the visual physical humor of Hawkins was cut from similar cloth. His flamboyant style and theatrical performances expressed the same excess and exaggeration as these peers, yet there was always something more sinister and unhinged about Hawkins. Tapping into the comic book craze of the post-1945 era, Hawkins crafted his image in the mode of cartoon horror, as a parody ghoul reveling in the dark side. He soon discovered that his choice of character was not always received with the good humor that he had envisaged. As with the reception of many comic books in the 1950s, Hawkins found that some people did not always get the jokes, or if they did, they still felt censorship was warranted on behalf of the poor young innocents who might witness such outrageousness. Though Hawkins's Dracula-like caricature provided his livelihood, it also limited his identity. Thus, from the first moment he added "Screamin'" to his stage name in the late 1940s to the time he finally lay down in his coffin for good in 2000, he was saddled with living within his alter ego as Screamin' Jay Hawkins rather than in reality as Jalacy J. Hawkins. Indeed, he once conveyed to writer Nick Tosches how this had taken its toll, saying, "I was forced to live life as a monster . . . I don't wanna be a black Vincent Price."[45]

Hawkins grew up in an orphanage in Cleveland during the 1930s Depression years. He studied piano and saxophone as a kid, but was also blessed with a Paul Robeson–like baritone voice. Putting his musical passions temporarily on hold, he pursued an early career path that took him from a term in the army to a stint as a boxer. Later, though, he returned to the music world, heading to Philadelphia in the late 1940s where and when the jump blues scene was hopping. Tiny Grimes hired him as a singer for his Rocking Highlander jazz-swing band, a curious novelty act with a sartorial taste for kilts. Jay quickly learned the possibilities of performance humor and the comedic potential of one's look. Going solo in the early fifties, he sought to carve out his own niche in the bustling R&B scene. In 1953, he recorded "Screamin' Blues" for Atlantic, but they deemed the track unsuitable for the label. Shifting to a small independent, Timely Records, Jay began to craft his "drunk" (and sacrilegious) aesthetic, recording and releasing "Baptize Me in Wine" and "I Found My Way to Wine" in 1954. The following year he put out "(She Put the) Wamee (on Me)," a title that foreshadowed things to come, as well as revealed the bizarre directions his imagination was taking. "Wamee" also marked a shift in Hawkins's vocal from a big blues delivery to the macabre growl that would become his signature style.

In 1956, Hawkins set about recording a ballad he had written called "I Put a Spell on You." To relax the band in the studio, a spread of food and alcohol had been provided for everyone. What happened next is the stuff of legend, the kind of mystery moment that also marked Elvis's "That's All Right" and Little Richard's "Tutti Frutti" sessions. To the shock of even Hawkins on the playback, it appeared that someone had put a spell on the recording session. Far from the blues ballad intended, the captured take of "Spell" was actually a sinister dirge, full of vocal screams, yells, and groans. The lyrics, on the surface suggesting a theme of pining and desire, had been magically transformed through the recording, reconstituted in meaning to a ritualistic mantra of possession and macho control. "I put a spell on you / Cause you're miiiiiinne," cried the pained Jay, emoting somewhere between pissed off and pissed drunk.[46] Clearly, there was humor in the excess, a parody venture into the tortured blues, but there was also something unsettling about this incantatory expression that evoked a stalkerlike psyche. Though as surprised as the band by the end product, the record label, Okeh, released the song, along with the following advertisement for radio stations that betrayed their concerns: "D.J.s—Be brave . . . Put a spell on your fans . . . Tie up your switchboard . . . If you get fired, we'll get you a job."[47] Beset with a backlash from parents and moral critics intent on protecting their sons and daughters from the "Spell," many radio stations protected the jobs of any would-be daring DJs by banning the song from the airwaves. Screamin' Jay, subsequently, suffered the same ostracized fate as his song, as he later recalled with characteristic hyperbole: "This record comes out and I've created a monster. Man, it was weird. I was forced to live that life of a monster."[48] Despite little airplay, and its status as the scapegoat of rock evil, the song became a cult classic during the late 1950s and has remained one to this day.

Capitalizing on the hype and furor that surrounded "Spell" in 1956, Screamin' Jay took his equally provocative stage act on the road. Employing props and duds complementary to the horror vibe of his music, he gathered up Henry (his skull on a pole), a coffin, and fuse boxes filled with colored smoke, then went forth to bring more comic shock to the kids and more anxiety to their parents. Adorned in bullfighter cloak, turban, red tuxedo, purple tie, and white shoes, Hawkins played on white fears of the black man, bringing his bogeyman menace to the youth of America. He parodied jungle stereotypes of the black man by celebrating cannibalism, as in his "Feast of the Mau Mau," in which he prescribed, "Pull the skin off a friend with a razor blade."[49] He lampooned fears of the predatory black man with the necro-humor of "I'm Your Man," in which he declared, "If I can't be your man while you're alive / I'll be your man when you're dead."[50] And in songs like "Constipation Blues" he showed himself to be plain bizarre—just for the fun of it.

The historical hangover of Hawkins's horror-humor—what critic John Dowell terms "slaughter"—has been of far more consequence than one could have imagined in the mid-1950s, when his songs barely reached the outskirts of the R&B charts. What was a deeply underground cult phenomenon then has since become a cottage industry. Its comedic strains have been regenerated through decades of the *Rocky Horror* subculture, while its more sinister wit has been played out on the national stage by shock-rockers like Marilyn Manson and the Misfits. Others who have been drawn to the inherent humor of the horror genre include metal tricksters like Ozzy Osbourne, White Zombie, and Slipknot, as well as punk ironists like the Damned and the Birthday Party. Each has theatrically adapted their own comic book comedy from cupboards and wardrobes of ghoulish ingredients; each has used the password of humor to tamper with the otherwise taboo topics of sexual perversion, nightmarish violence, and the subconscious realm of the irrational. Simultaneously silly and scary, the "act" that was Screamin' Jay Hawkins laid the foundations—and built the prototypical monuments—to one of the most appealing and long-standing traditions of subversive rock humor.

THE DAYS THE MUSIC DIED

Although technically the 1950s did not end in 1958, the rock & roll fifties largely did. Stripped of much of its danger by a sustained campaign of containment from the multiple arms of the national superstructure, rock & roll ventured into the sixties with a whimper more than a bang. During 1958, the year of the teen idol, the music industry offered idealized boyfriends in the form of Fabian, Frankie Avalon, and Paul Anka, when two years earlier it had put forward transformers and manic madmen like Chuck Berry and Little Richard. Instead of witnessing the gyrations of Elvis Presley or the piano exorcisms of Jerry Lee Lewis, kids were now being asked to read Pat Boone's new advice-to-teens book, *Twixt Twelve & Twenty—Pat Talks to Teenagers* (1958), which, among its pearls of wisdom, counseled that if a girl liked a boy to make sure that she talked to him about his interests.

The sustained adult backlash late in the decade pressured record companies to promote more wholesome acts (hence the rise of the teenage idol) and to desist from releasing provocative product. These moral arbiters even successfully censored such innocuous pop songs as the Everly Brothers' "Wake Up Little Susie" (1957) and Bobby Darin's "Splish Splash" (1958), illustrating the levels of hysteria being reached by the establishment in their containment campaign. When, in 1958, the sweet, angel-voiced Frankie Lymon sang "No, I'm not a juvenile delinquent," it was more than a little ironic that this innocent would be so defensive.[51]

Choices and personal circumstances also precipitated the changing of the guard at the close of the decade. By 1958, Elvis Presley had joined the army, Little Richard had retreated to the church, Jerry Lee Lewis had been ostracized for having married his thirteen-year-old cousin, and Chuck Berry had been convicted for transporting a teenage prostitute across state lines. A year later, in 1959, the death of rock & roll became literal as Buddy Holly, the Big Bopper, and Richie Valens all succumbed in a tragic plane crash. Adding self-destruction to accidental death, many of the independent record companies that had been so instrumental in bringing the key R&B and rock & roll acts into view a few years earlier were exposed and prosecuted as major players in the payola bribery scandal. Alan Freed, the man most responsible for the discovery and promotion of the decade's subversive rockers, became payola's most notorious guilty party.

As the decade drew to its close, observers could not be faulted for predicting that the rock & roll boom was exhaling its final gasps, and that sanitized industry-pop would soon be preeminent once again. Although fleeting signs of the old rock & roll spirit lingered in the surf music instrumentals of Link Wray and others, and a new record company called Motown was developing vocal group styles in new directions, little else appeared on the national horizon. As it turned out, the period from 1958 to 1962 proved to be but a calm before the storm, a brief naptime prior to America awakening to the next tumultuous rock revolution and its next wave of subversive rock humorists.

THE SIXTIES:

Humor Grows Up . . . and Away

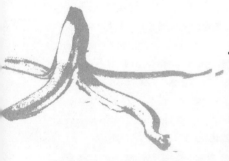

HE TRANSITION FROM 1950s to 1960s rock humor is primarily rooted in the demographic transformation of the baby boomers. Preteen and teen adolescents in the 1950s, rock & roll's first generation, had grown into their late teens and early twenties by the initial years of the following decade. The nature of their musical demands soon came to reflect this maturity as the often juvenile and novelty humor of the prior decade took on new seriousness and purpose; civil rights tensions and the emerging conflict in Vietnam engaged—and directly involved—the coming-of-age baby boomers in creating an environment where the sometimes-escapist fare of 1950s youth expression became increasingly irrelevant, if not inappropriate. The clever but silly wordplay that was featured so strongly in the output of fifties artists like Bo Diddley and Little

Richard was replaced with poetic high-mindedness and social satire; the physical humor that had made stars out of Elvis Presley and Jerry Lee Lewis began to take a backseat to political theater with intellectual insights; even looks and image—so central to the stage wit of posers like Gene Vincent and Screamin' Jay Hawkins—became regarded as superficial or were dismissed as trivial. Critic Nat Hentoff—perhaps with the San Francisco hippy bands on his mind—perceived a new type of anti-fashion humor in the au naturel style of sixties acts, saying, "Instead of hiding a so-called bad feature, they accentuate it, like a living caricature."[1] According to Hentoff, the swan was choosing to be the ugly duckling as a subversive gesture on behalf of candor and realism.

The underlying forces changing the face(s) and nature of subversive rock humor can be traced through two transforming artists of the period: Bob Dylan and the Beatles. The tentacles of their reach and influence can be felt, seen, and heard in all of the music of the decade and, as such, they not only serve as the primary precipitants of rock developments, but as significant symbols of surrounding and tangential movements as well. Dylan and the Beatles transformed rock & roll into rock music; they turned adolescent entertainment into serious art; they pulled humor up by the bootstraps, forcing it into new realms of the political, social, and psychological. With them, subversive rock humor grew up, up, and away into styles, intents, and territories that only five years earlier would have been unimaginable.

Revolutionary agents though they both were by the early sixties, both Dylan and the Beatles pointed to some of the primary roots of fifties rock & roll culture as the sources that had inspired them. And most of these influences were subversive humorists of one stripe or another. Dylan had grown up wanting to be the next Elvis Presley, and though he never mastered the pelvic gyrations of his hero, he clearly learned the power of image to effect influence and change. The Beatles, likewise, learned their trade studying the stagecraft and music of Elvis and other fifties rockers, taking tips from Little Richard on how a smile and a wink can open doors, or from Gene Vincent on how a studied pose or rebel lyric can endear you across class and gender lines. What Dylan and the Beatles added beyond their sources of inspiration was a new savvy sense of the sociopolitical. Sometimes explicit and sometimes veiled, topics transcended the purely personal, and humor was deployed as a weapon more than a shield. Inklings of such intents had been witnessed in the prior sly humor of Chuck Berry and the Coasters, but even their crafty lyrics were strategically coded and veiled. With the Beatles and Dylan, the proto-political humor of fifties subversive rebels emerged from the closet, was refitted in more stridently political clothing, and then was expressed with open confidence and passion. These trailblazers used humor as a primary weapon in their journeys of creativity. They transformed pre-political rebellion into a practicing political art.

At the start of the sixties decade, however, neither Dylan nor the Beatles registered on the rock radar, though the folk revival was underway with its sociopolitical figurehead, Pete Seeger, rallying the new troops. But even there, the movement was looking back rather than forward, pandering mostly to the "old school" authenticity of Woody Guthrie and the Weavers with conservative stoicism. Even the younger folk acts, like the Kingston Trio and Peter, Paul & Mary, filled their sets with clean-cut pop-folk rather than the edgier folk standards that might have ruffled establishment feathers. Though hardly a depoliticized movement, the folk scene in 1960 appeared to need a shot in the arm, a spark of inspiration from somewhere; within the next couple of years the necessary change-makers emerged from the ranks of a new youth vanguard.

SERIOUSLY FOLK

The folk music scene of 1962 America was splintered into three camps: the traditionalists (e.g., Pete Seeger); the pop folkies (e.g., the Kingston Trio); and the young radicals (e.g., Joan Baez). With the new additions of Bob Dylan, Phil Ochs, and Tom Paxton to the latter camp, a realignment—indeed, a coup d'etat—occurred that would alter not only the shape of folk music to come but also all of rock music. By 1963, college kids everywhere were propping up their acoustic guitars against their Dylan and Baez dorm room posters, dusting them off periodically for an occasional hootenanny where they could foist their new "poetic" songs on their roommates.

The rise to power of Dylan et al., however, owed much to the sustained struggles of Pete Seeger throughout the 1940s and 1950s (bridging the gap from folk's prior heyday in the 1930s Great Depression era). Seeger's involvement in the Campaign for Nuclear Disarmament (CND) protests in the U.K. during the 1950s had inspired him to start his own "topical" folk journal on his return to the United States. *Broadside* became the literary companion to the folk music culture, publishing original lyrics on the sociopolitical experiences of the time. Bob Dylan, Phil Ochs, and Tom Paxton not only contributed their work to the magazine, but they were cajoled by Seeger to politicize their content and to hone their rhetorical skills of argumentative satire. Mainstream TV "folk music" programs like *Hootenanny* (broadcast on ABC between 1963 and 1964) may have ignored the new politicos of folk, but journals like *Broadside*—as well as the numerous folk festivals springing up across the land—created ample spaces and outlets for the new radicals to disseminate their messages.

Rooted in but not tied to a folk tradition represented by Joe Hill, Woody Guthrie, and Pete Seeger, the new folk singers adopted these forerunners' penchant for the topical and sociopolitical while developing their own satirical methodologies into harder new forms. Pete Seeger's strain of populist humor grew more ironic, darker, and more forthright when it sprang forth from the pens of Dylan and Ochs. And while the issues of civil rights, freedom, and Vietnam were all confronted by the new radicals, personal idiosyncrasies were also integrated into their political humor. Indeed, by 1965, Bob Dylan's topical satires had all but disappeared, replaced with an esoteric, introspective self-scrutiny that upset many of the traditional folkies still craving the next "Blowin' in the Wind." By this time, though, Dylan had hypnotized his student following such that he could (and sometimes did) write anything and it would still be analyzed and decoded into multiple meanings with all the rigor that they brought to T. S. Eliot poems in the classroom. However, it was Dylan's "political" years of 1962 to 1965 that consolidated this collective youth adulation, and it was during these years that he and his primary peer, Phil Ochs, were at their most socially subversive and purposefully humorous.

Bob Dylan

When today's fans and critics reflect upon the content and character of Bob Dylan, the image that comes to mind is rarely that of the humorist. In fact, the long and dour expressions that have appeared fixed to his face for the past thirty-plus years have led people to associate him with a persona of maudlin seriousness and grumpy standoffishness. However, during the early years of his career—between 1961 and 1965—Dylan developed a performance style that fellow folkie Dave Van Ronk once described as "one of the funniest stage acts I think I've ever seen."[2] Moreover, in his incisive satirical lyricism of that period, Dylan established himself as an agent of change in the music industry and as the most influential subversive rock humorist of his generation. His was a style of "superiority" humor that harked back to the social satire of Greek theater, one that exposed hypocrisy and chastened the hubris of the establishment culture. Loved and idolized by millions within years of his debut performances, Dylan illustrated how humor can be used as a weapon for social change and as a means to inspire the forces that can bring about those transformations.

The origins of his trailblazing wit go back to his childhood roots in Minnesota, where, as music critic Janet Maslin observed, "Bob Dylan [became] the grand invention of Robert Allen Zimmerman."[3] Shedding his real name became his first escape from many skins, while his newly adopted name—in homage to the writer Dylan Thomas—represented the first of many masks he would adorn. Indeed, when playing a Halloween show in 1963, Dylan even tellingly quipped at one point, "I've got my Bob Dylan mask on." The implicit escapism of his *assumed* role/persona did not so much reflect the desire to hide a troubled childhood so much as to leave a dull one. A Jewish boy growing up in the predominantly Catholic town of Hibbing, Minnesota, the young Zimmerman was always something of an outsider in an outpost town where options for stardom and adventure were few to none. Thus, when Dylan found on his radio the daring blues of Howlin' Wolf and the lyrical exploits of country singer Hank Williams, he entered another world—one characterized by travel, discovery, and rebellion. By the time he reached the University of Minnesota for his freshman year, Dylan was attuned to the pioneers of roots music, as well as to the rebels of mid-1950s rock & roll. He had taken to wearing his hair in the elevated style of Little Richard, and he mimicked the ironic sneer of Elvis Presley. Most significantly, he was introduced to Woody Guthrie's picaresque autobiography, *Bound for Glory* (1943), a book that would inspire him to escape further into the adventure playground of fantasy and reinvention.

Drawn to the lighthearted anecdotes and travel sagas that never let the truth get in the way of a good story, Dylan adopted the tall-tale humor of Guthrie. Ready to try on the mask that had been years in the making, Dylan left the confines of the Midwest not only to find Woody Guthrie, but to become him. Discovering that Guthrie was dying in a New York hospital bed, Dylan, in the image of the mythical folk-poet troubadour, strapped his guitar to his back and hitched East to meet the man he called "the last hero."

Dylan's arrival in New York proved to be the inspiration for one of his first original songs, "Talkin' New York," later included in his 1962 debut album, the eponymous *Bob Dylan*. Taking on the talking blues style that had been popularized by Woody Guthrie and many other earlier folk and country artists, Dylan—like his predecessors—emphasized the intrinsic humor of the form, with its open scope for long-winded tall tales and wry narrative observations. "Talkin' New York" was a pivotal early song in his career as it established the myth of his persona, the (supposed) hardships that beset him, and the (supposed) institutional forces he had fought along the way. With self-deprecation, the song recounts his early attempts to adjust to the Greenwich Village bohemian coffeehouse set, where he was not immediately embraced as the poet of his generation.

The song informs, "Man there said, 'Come back some other day. / You sound like a hillbilly. / We want folk singers here.'"[4] As the narrative proceeds, Dylan reflects upon the trials and tribulations of his initial dealings with the cutthroat music industry, offering clear testimony as to why he would shortly thereafter hire the equally hardball Albert Goldman as his business manager.

Once established in New York, Dylan began to work on (ironically) *crafting* a more authentic folk persona to satisfy the demands of the city's "serious" folk set. Before long, he had created an extensive self-mythology, one flexible to circumstances.[5] A modern-day Cyrano de Bergerac, as his persona took on new fictions, he grew a reputation as an authentic truth-teller. Sometimes he was an orphan, other times part Native American; he told his peers that he had performed with old bluesmen (though they had died before Dylan was born); and sometimes—when lost in performance—he even demanded to be called Woody Guthrie! With a good humor that suggested a budding tall-tale trickster rather than the onset of psychosis, Dylan's early years saw him diligently practicing the art of reinvention and self-mythologizing. And it paid off. Even before his first recordings, he began to garner a reputation as a spellbinding performer, one who combined wry anecdotes with various stage antics. Dave Van Ronk recalled his "Chaplin-esque mannerisms" as "excruciatingly funny."[6]

Thanks to the support of longtime jazz impresario John Hammond, Dylan secured a major record deal with Columbia Records in 1962, though his self-titled debut was neither pushed by the label nor (maybe as a result) particularly successful. Furthermore, as was the folk convention of the day, the album was dominated by covers and included few of the many quality original songs that Dylan—even by that point—had written. Convention and Dylan, though, were incompatible, and by the next year the hardworking songwriter had loosened his ties to Woody Guthrie's songs and identity and had crafted an album's worth of original material. *The Freewheelin' Bob Dylan* (1963) proved to be his breakthrough album in so many ways—personally, artistically, socially, and politically; it also signaled the blossoming of a lyrical form of social satire that Dylan referred to as his "finger-pointin'" songs. Critics and fans were soon to realize that a new kind of subversive rock humorist was now in their midst, even if the musical form was still familiarly folk.

The *Freewheelin'* songs developed the long-established folk music tradition of the topical address, responses to the pressing sociopolitical concerns of the day. In Dylan's hands, the topical song took on new levels of contempt, vitriol, and sizzle, as a scornful mockery was employed to skewer various arms of the establishment. Delivered with sardonic spit(e), these were the songs that led critic John Orman to tag Dylan as "the expert in witty, passionate discontent."[7] "Masters of War" points the finger at political leaders who "build" the weapons, then "hide" when they are used. A thematic precursor to rebel-anthems like Creedence Clearwater Revival's "Fortunate Son" (1968)—and, more recently, the Beastie Boys' "In a World Gone Mad" (2003) and Eminem's "Mosh" (2004)—Dylan indicts with an accusatory "you" the leaders who make decisions they never have to face up to. Each verse is an outburst of distaste, a satirical portrait of war's cruel ironies. "You hide in your mansion as young people's blood / Flows out of their bodies and is buried in mud,"[8] Dylan charges scornfully, crusading, as Geoffrey Stokes once put it, as "a one-man generation gap."[9]

It was these *Freewheelin'* poem-songs that first established Dylan as the so-called "voice of his generation." Their impact was immense. "Audiences didn't just listen to Bob Dylan, they depended on him," observed Janet Maslin.[10] In the shadow of the Cuban missile crisis and growing atomic fears, Dylan succinctly voiced the dissenting sentiments of his nation's socially conscious youth with a humor that offered relief and that encouraged empowerment and resistance. His was a humor strictly for the serious-minded. "Talkin' World War Three Blues" saw Dylan using the intrinsically humorous talking blues genre for such ends. Here, he tells a cock-and-bull story with the underpinning sentiment that we live in a culture of fear and anxiety that is permeating our physical, mental, and psychological conditions. Dylan's treatment here is bizarre and lighthearted, ironically undercutting the obvious seriousness of the subject matter. "I dreamt I was walkin' into World War Three," he tells us before concluding, "It seems everybody's been having them dreams."[11]

Though war and the prospect of war are themes that hang heavy over many of the *Freewheelin'* songs, Dylan approaches them from various angles in order to implicate all guilty parties. In "With God on Our Side," he adopts a "we" rather than "you" pronoun to suggest our collective responsibility for political madness. Here, the blind faith and religion "we" selectively apply to justify genocide and war are addressed (and undressed) with mordant mockery and a dry delivery. "When the Second World War came to an end / We forgave the Germans and we were their friends," Dylan declares, before providing the ironic kicker: "Though they murdered six million, in the ovens they fried / The Germans now too have God on their side." If they are our friends now, they *must* have God on their side, runs the cultural logic that Dylan here wryly deconstructs. Later in the song, he shifts his scorn to the constituency that would be termed Nixon's "silent majority" by the end of the decade, cajoling sarcastically, "You never ask questions with God on your side."[12] Dylan's theological invocations (of which there were many throughout his career) showed not a distaste for faith, but a skepticism of its institutional and ideological misuse.

In his next two albums, *The Times They Are a-Changin'* (1964) and *Another Side of Bob Dylan* (1964), Dylan continued to produce finger-pointing anthems, though he also started to broaden his strategies and targets of humor. Cognizant of the enormous influence that the Beatles and other British Invasion bands were having on America's rock culture, Dylan showed a combination of respect and scorn for their contributions. Though he welcomed the musical innovations and energy that the Beatles were bringing, Dylan was not averse to offering a little mockery in response to their somewhat facile early love songs. Sending up the conventional love song bromides of the Beatles' hit "She Loves You" (1964), Dylan inverts the song's celebratory "yeah yeah yeahs" with his own "no no nos" in "It Ain't Me Babe" (1964). Bringing an incongruous opposite to the conventions of the love song genre, Dylan's first-person narrator speaks with cynicism and emotional distance to his lover, while echoing and inverting the language of the Beatles and their ilk: "I'm *not* the one you want, babe. / I'm *not* the one you need." Besides revoking the pervasive pop myth of the gallant romantic male, Dylan's inside humor reaches another layer as it captures the autobiographical truth of his own elusive and masked character. "Everything inside is made of stone," the trickster proclaims in an act of ironic self-disclosure, as if to repel the emotional scrutiny of his adoring fans while setting a critical distance by setting the record straight.[13]

Dylan's drift from external social satire to more internal personalized in-jokes reached its apotheosis in the fly-on-the-wall documentary film *Don't Look Back* (1967); here, director D. A. Pennebaker and his handheld camera followed closely in Dylan's footsteps during the course of his 1965 tour of Britain—his last acoustic tour. Bypassing the conventional rags-to-riches films still used by his peers, Dylan, in *Don't Look Back*, cultivates his anti-star myth in the midst of the heightened hysteria of Bob-mania. Rather than charming and entertaining the media in interviews and press conferences (as the Beatles had done in their *Hard Day's Night* [1964] promo-film), Dylan thwarts all efforts to quiz him, responding to questions with defiant sarcasm, combative insults, or merely questions back. Part petulant brat, part tortured artist, Dylan used this film as an opportunity to further craft an unconventional proto-punk belligerent persona. A raw humor is omnipresent throughout the movie, invariably employed as a means to ridicule the artistic and generational disconnect of a mainstream media of which Dylan was growing increasingly weary and wary.

The defensive shielding and anti-media strategies in *Don't Look Back* would serve him well as he proceeded post-1965 to upset his peers and fans by going electric (a sacrilegious act within the folk scene), and by eschewing his popular political-topical songwriting. Instead, he began to produce abstract, increasingly personal lyrics centered on the image rather than the narrative. Also thrown overboard in this mid-sixties makeover was Dylan's by-then established satirical method of humor. Increasingly, humor would become less pronounced (or obvious) in his work, as an avant-garde esoteric style took its place. This shift from serious humor to what appeared to be just seriousness was not an overnight operation, though, nor did humor wholly disappear from his repertoire. Transitional songs like "Subterranean Homesick Blues" (1965) marked the birth of his imagistic period, symbolically reflecting his withdrawal from channels of easy communication. His postulation at the time, "I don't want to write for people anymore,"[14] and the parallel song sentiment, "I don't want to work on Maggie's farm no more,"[15] were semi-joking declarations of this new assertive independence.

"Subterranean Homesick Blues," despite its obfuscating lyrical abstract expressionism, also casts out an array of rhyming dictates that offer suggestive, if quirky, nuggets of wit. "You don't need a weatherman to know which way the wind blows" became a go-to phrase for the youth counterculture, reminding fans in a concise fragment of the poetic pronouncements of "Blowin' in the Wind" (1963) and "The Times They Are a-Changin'" (1964). Another snippet, "Don't follow leaders / Watch the parkin' meters," despite its vague incongruity, seems to speak to a fan base that was willing to appreciate strident satire anywhere in Dylan's work they could find (or interpret) it.[16]

Other songs, like "Rainy Day Women #12 & 35" (1966)—with its counterculture-sensitive playful punning mantra "Everybody must get stoned"—showed Dylan willing at times to return to the types of humor that had once made him so endearing and inviting.[17] However, by the second half of the decade, Dylan had become an unrecognizable image of his former self. Outside demands and pressures made him jaded and often bitter, while his 1966 motorcycle accident brought him face-to-face with mortality, setting him on the path to his later Christian conversion. These artistic, professional, and spiritual retreats became literal, too, when Bob left the city for the protective enclaves of rural upstate New York.

Bob Dylan continues to write, record, and perform into these, his September years, to great acclaim, though humor has been a less-dominant feature of his work since the mid-1960s. While critics still occasionally note Dylan's enduring wit, they recognize it as parenthetical rather than pivotal to his craft of late. Eulogies are being woven implicitly into their analyses, too, as they ponder Dylan's influences, legacy, and place in history. There is no need or space to account for those here; suffice to say, one would have to list just about any thinking songwriter since 1963 if one were to start charting his impact. Within the field of subversive rock humor, though, one wonders whether Dylan will be given his due recognition as a pioneer and multifaceted wit. His brand of targeted social satire—so central to his early career—has lived on in all subsequent protest youth cultures, whether in the hippy and punk movements, or even segments of hip-hop culture. His attention to language and the revolution he brought to the song lyric—in what can be said and how it can be said—speak to the power and scope of his subversive humor, as well as its influence. Indeed, one wonders whether that other primary force of 1960s rock culture, the Beatles, would still have been writing variations on "Love Me Do" and "She Loves You" had Bob Dylan and his work not entered and transformed the songwriting world.

Phil Ochs

Because the early career path of Phil Ochs ran parallel to that of Dylan, it was largely in the latter's shadow and always a few steps behind. Each ventured East—Dylan from Minnesota, Ochs from Ohio—to land in the hubbub of the vibrant folk scene of New York's Greenwich Village at the dawn of the 1960s. Along with Joan Baez and Tom Paxton, Ochs and Dylan became centerpieces of the new folk guard, though Ochs would remain a cult mainstay as Dylan's journey elevated him to the cover of *Rolling Stone* and the front pages of rock history. Stylistically, both Ochs and Dylan were drawn to the topical songwriting oeuvre initially, though Ochs was always more inclined to this mode. Likewise, both often employed the whimsical talking blues form as a means of conveying their topics and humor, though Ochs brought more of an overtly political edge to his writing. By the mid-sixties, each had outgrown the limitations of the acoustic folk sound, as well as the time-and-place constraints of topical writing. However, though they both went electric and spread their lyrical wings into more personal areas, it was only Dylan who enjoyed success in the process.

Dylan, though, was not so inclined to compare himself to Ochs, regarding his peer as a singing journalist more than a folk singer. This intended insult was actually a quite accurate designation of Ochs's style, and it also highlighted the fundamental difference between Ochs's writing and Dylan's own. Though both wielded an incisive satirical sword in their treatment of the pressing topics of the day, Ochs's song-stories were always limited by the specificity of the incidents on which they were based. Conversely, Dylan gave his "finger-pointin'" songs an edge and imagistic reach that enabled them to speak beyond their subjects and to transcend their real-life situations. Dylan's topical writing always had one eye on the future, while Ochs was invariably stuck in the present. As such, Ochs actually had more in common with his hero and folk antecedent, Joe Hill, who at the beginning of the twentieth century had dedicated himself to capturing the struggles of the disenfranchised and downtrodden through a combination of journalistic detail and biting satire. Like Hill, Ochs was an avowed socialist and a member of the Industrial Workers of the World (popularly known as the Wobblies). Neither was bashful in their political candor, and both saw their missions as spreading the word and unifying the forces of opposition to oppressors. Humor, for them, was not an adornment, but a strategic weapon that could appeal to—and thus attract—followers. Ochs was to pay tribute to Hill, not only in continuing the tradition of topical folk protest, but in his reverential biographical song "Joe Hill" (1968), which charted his hero's courageous exploits and final execution at the behest of the American "justice" system.

Whereas Dylan was intent, early on, to sever his ties to a folk scene that he found increasingly conformist and conventional, Ochs was very much part of its proud continuum, though his edgy satires certainly suggested that he was willing to sharpen the political bite of the genre. *All the News That's Fit to Sing* (1964) established Ochs as a major player on the new folk stage, though the title did little to dispel his reputation as a singing journalist. His on-the-spot early skepticism of U.S. involvement in Southeast Asia was reflected in "Talking Vietnam Blues," in which he mocked the deceitful official "speak" that referred to the bomb-dropping, gun-toting American troops as "trainees" and advisors.[18] Ochs's sophomore effort, *I Ain't Marching Any More* (1965), boasted two songs that were to be embraced as sing-along anthems within the antiwar movement: "Here's to the State of Mississippi" and "Draft Dodger Rag." In the latter he offered a tongue-in-cheek self-help list of reasons one might invoke to avoid the draft, among them: "I always carry a purse," "I'm addicted to a thousand drugs," and "I ain't no fool, I'm a goin' to school."[19]

A lesson that Ochs learned from Hill was to use titles and chorus lines as the attention-getters, for protest songs that did not reach out and excite protestors were wasted exercises. Always audience-conscious, Ochs's titles were often striking and ironic. "The Cannons of Christianity," "I Kill Therefore I Am," "I Like Hitler," and "You Can't Get Stoned Enough" were titles-as-slogans, meant to catch the eye, then the ear; they used humor as the magnet for audiences to reflect upon the songs' serious concerns and their (implicit) calls to action. This strategy of humor, inspired by Joe Hill, would be passed on to subsequent satirical humorists, such as the Dead Kennedys' Jello Biafra, whose own song titles—among them "California Über Alles," "Holiday in Cambodia," and "Kill the Poor"—are cut from the same caustic cloth.

Another Ochs song with a striking punch line, "Love Me, I'm a Liberal," was the popular standout from his 1966 *In Concert* album. This song—like some of Dylan's during this period—saw the satire swing inward at the sympathetic in-crowds. A put-down of the ideological compromises of liberalism, Ochs assumed the voice of his targets, letting hypocrisy emerge from their own mouths. "I love Puerto Ricans and Negroes / As long as they don't move next door," asserts the "unreliable" narrator. And then in a further in-joke, this time into the inner sanctum of the folk "institution," the singer boasts, "I go to all the Pete Seeger concerts."[20]

This caricature humor, using stereotypical figures to voice their own contradictions and inconsistencies (and thus dig their own graves), became a familiar strategy of Ochs's protest style. In "Outside a Small Circle of Friends," from *Pleasures of the Harbor* (1967), he applies this technique to a real-life incident that occurred in New York in 1964, when a woman died after being assaulted three separate times over a thirty-minute period while in clear view of thirty-eight citizen onlookers, all of whom responded by doing nothing. Ochs used this well-publicized news story as a springboard to comment upon the erosion of humanity and personal responsibility in the modern age. With acerbic satire he assumes the role of one of the bystanders, who comments, "Maybe we should call the cops and try and stop the pain / But Monopoly is so much fun, I'd hate to blow the game." Though the song was known more for its controversial line "Smoking marijuana is more fun than drinking beer" (which got it banned from the airwaves), "Outside a Small Circle of Friends" has proven to be one of Ochs's more resonant statements, its central news story allegorically making the timeless point that indifference is the enemy of empowerment, protest, and change.[21]

Although Ochs continued to write into the latter years of the 1960s, his documentary style began to lose favor as the more esoteric abstractions and personal introspections of the counterculture grew more in vogue. Ochs attempted to ride with the trends to varying degrees—going electric and writing love songs—but his transitions never took hold with the public. He continued his commitments to social activism, though, performing outside the 1968 Democratic Convention in Chicago when many other acts were too fearful to put themselves in that conflict zone. However, the mass popularity he sought continued to elude him, and his move to Los Angeles to ride the folk rock bandwagon alongside the Byrds and the Mamas & the Papas failed to elevate him above his preexisting cult status. Seemingly resigned to his fate, he masked his miseries in self-effacing humor (and prophesy, as it turned out) by titling his last two studio albums *Rehearsals for Retirement* (1969), which included "No More Songs" as its closer, and *Greatest Hits* (1970), of which he had had none, and which included all new material.

Creatively running near empty as his career entered the 1970s, Ochs started to exhibit increasingly erratic behavior. Besides his embarrassing and poorly received stint as an Elvis "impersonator," complete with gold lamé (or lame) suits and 1950s repertoire, Ochs also started to bomb in more personal ways. Frustrated by his artistic decline, he turned more and more to alcohol as solace, and this, in turn, exacerbated a worsening bipolar disorder. Furthermore, a mugging incident in Africa left his vocal cords permanently damaged. Little was heard from Ochs thereafter until the news came down in 1976 that he had hanged himself at his sister's house in New York; he was only thirty-five years of age.

Rock history has always placed Phil Ochs within its shadows, and though his artistry never showed the scope or development of his rival/peer Bob Dylan, his no-holds-barred satirical treatment of the sociopolitical concerns and incidents of his day have left a mark on subsequent artists. In recent years, Ochs has enjoyed something of a reappraisal, his aggressive wit striking a chord with the more literate constituency of post-punk rock. Both the Weakerthans and They Might Be Giants have paid tribute to Ochs's political activism and humorous methods by covering his songs, and Jello Biafra and Mojo Nixon revived "Love Me, I'm a Liberal" during the Clinton era, thus suggesting that not all of Ochs's singing-journalist numbers were stuck in time. Phil Ochs's principal disciple may well be Britain's Billy Bragg, an artist who has helped carry the torch of social activism and satirical lyricism into the current century. His tribute song, "I Dreamed I Saw Phil Ochs Last Night," on *The Internationale* (1990), was a fitting cross-reference ode that alluded to Joe Hill, Phil Ochs (not Dylan), and himself as connected links in the chain of purposeful (and serious) folk humor.

GIRL POWER

The conventional critical line from many serious rock critics concerning the "girl groups" of the early 1960s is similar to their reactions to the bubblegum pop acts of the latter part of that decade: They are generally regarded as temporary groups with interchangeable parts, faceless female puppet singers with every string pulled by some Svengali manager-producer-songwriter; their songs are seen as formulaic, cookie-cutter, and indistinguishable from one another, all addressing the same inane adolescent theme ad nauseam. Subversive? No way! Humorists? Maybe if you are laughing *at* them! Though there is certainly some validity to such dismissive generalizations (vis-à-vis bubblegum as well as the girl groups), this portrait offers only part of the story on only a portion of the many groups who ruled the charts in the early sixties under such names as the Chiffons, the Marvelettes, the Exciters, and the Crystals.

The vitriol that some rock critics have leveled at the girl groups has been motivated largely by the fact that these *acts* tamper with the great myths of rock culture: creative autonomy, the artist as author, instrumental musicianship. Such enduring myths, however—built by rock purists largely on romantic delusion rather than reality—speak primarily to rock's patriarchy, with its predilection for rugged individualists and independent artist-adventurers. The girl groups, though, were neither trivial nor "un-rock" in their lack of these macho ideologies. Indeed, they were subversive by virtue of their avoidance of them. In fact, they were further subversive by seeking the *extremes* of the feminine, in opposition to the codified conventions that had been established by the male-dominated industry. You would find few phallic guitars or saxophones when a girl group performed; but neither would you see the sexless, sanitized *objects* that populated most female pop groups throughout the 1950s. The girl groups, interestingly, were both assertively female and just plain assertive.

In a chapter entitled "Why the Shirelles Mattered" in her book *Where the Girls Are* (1994), Susan J. Douglas explains that the girl groups represented the first musical effort to capture the real experiences and dreams of teenage girls. Their songs consisted of girl talk about girls by girls for girls; they were diary entries made public; advice songs parlayed by (as opposed to just about) young females. In content, they addressed the often contradictory and mixed emotions that most adolescent girls felt about their lives. As a result, some songs spoke to passivity and conformity—because girls experienced those feelings—and some expressed boasting and rebellion—because they had those inclinations, too. Unlike much male rock, in which the party line of parties and lines (i.e., sex, drugs, and rock & roll) is expected to be unquestioningly accepted, girl group lyrics were subversive in their embrace of inner-self contradictions, with their recognitions of shame, guilt, and uncertainty—all no-no's in rock-swagger myths. Not surprisingly, therefore, Douglas and others have pointed to the Shirelles' 1960 girl-anthem, "Will You Love Me Tomorrow," as a central song in female pop history. A should-I-or-shouldn't-I song about sex, the female narrative point of view addresses the real concerns of sexual intimacy and commitment for teenage girls. Not only had sex been a taboo topic for female performers to this point, but the fact that the song charted torn, conflicted feelings rather than presenting a pat "adult" moral line spoke to an emotional complexity rarely seen in any areas of rock culture. These were new messages and new voices that starved female adolescents could cling to, talk about, and learn from as they made their difficult journeys into womanhood. As such, they were both empowering and radically innovative.

To suggest, however, that all girl groups were transgressive and rebellious in nature would be to overstate the argument. For every Shirelles-type song shaking up gender conventions, there were many others toeing the traditional line, playing passive roles and imparting adult-friendly moral messages or no message at all: novelty dance songs like Little Eva's "Loco-motion" (1962) and "Old Smokey Locomotion" (1963), or the Chiffons' conveyor-belt "Fine" songs ("He's So Fine" [1963], "One Fine Day" [1963]) come to mind. But even these had their own elements of female empowerment: the Little Eva songs giving "space" for girls to dance alone or together, and the Chiffons positioning the boys as passive objects and the girls as the active voyeurs "eyeing them up." Such implicit role reversals were subversive within the conventions of the rock narrative framework.

Little Eva was no Madonna and the Chiffons were far from riot grrrls. However, with New York's Shangri-Las such comparisons may indeed be made. These feisty Queens kids not only subverted the expectations of patriarchal society and the myths of male rock culture, but they also tore up the girl group rule book at the same time. Their fatalistic tales embodied all the excess melodrama one witnessed in their peers, but they were ratcheted up to hilariously parodic proportions. Turning on the soap opera excesses, the Shangri-Las transformed tragedy into tragicomedy and drama into (self-)parody. Their songs of courting the forbidden, flouting authority, and boasting of conquests, when combined with their image as semiandrogynous street rebels, awoke baby boomer girls from the slumber of post-fifties conformity, guiding them toward their subsequent feminist awakenings. Douglas, a boomer herself, paid tribute to the trailblazing influence of the Shangri-Las on her and her female peers when she commented in reference to the group's famous anthem, "There's a good reason why, even on our deathbeds, we'll still know the words to 'Leader of the Pack.'"[22]

The Shangri-Las

At the essential core of the Shangri-Las was relief humor—for girls. This worked contextually by virtue of ironic juxtaposition. Perhaps more than any other artistic field, rock music was (and still is, to a lesser degree) male-dominated, its productions, projections, and receptions all constructed around the presumption of the male gaze and consciousness. The emergence of the girl groups in the early 1960s and their immediate rise to the higher echelons of the charts challenged the male hegemony as well as its tenets and myths. By speaking directly to the silent girl demographic—about them, through their voices—an alternative aesthetic was produced that set itself in ironic inverse to conventions. With the Shangri-Las, the irony penetrated a secondary plane, for besides being one of the leading lights of girl group music, they also set themselves in comic contrast to the conventions of their own subgenre. Deconstructing their own formula became a means of subverting the more conventionally feminine principles of the girl groups, a way of empowering and celebrating girls who were alienated outsiders within their own gender. With their anthems to teenage runaways, defiant "bad" girls, and their "bad" (sometimes soon-to-be-dead) boyfriends, the Shangs sent shock waves through a populace of mainstream parents that was forced to reconsider whether their own daughters were really who they appeared to be.

The methods of the Shangri-Las' subcultural subversions were rooted in literary conventions of "type" humor, tragicomedy, and melodrama. Within their sonic theater, they breathlessly recounted vivid and timeless tragic teen tales by inhabiting—via first-person narration—the pained internal and external existences of their songs' misfit characters. Skillfully using their "everygirl" voices to represent these rebel-types, they crafted what Greil Marcus called "blazing, hokey teen morality plays," or what their principal songwriter, Jeff Barry, regarded as soap operas with sound effects.[23] The end products were three-minute packaged farces that voiced the frustrations and yearnings of girls, while projecting the possibilities of female subjectivity.

Like many of rock music's female subversives (Patti Smith, Debbie Harry, Karen O, to name a few), the Shangri-Las hailed from New York City. Consisting of two twins (Mary Ann and Margie Ganser) and two siblings (Mary and Betty Weiss), the girls grew up in respectable middle-class environments but caught the teenage bug for pop music early. By the time the band were hitting stages in 1963, the age range of the Shangri-Las was between fifteen and seventeen.

Being teenagers, they were vulnerable to the preying managers and producers that populated the music industry. It turned out that the Shangs crossed paths with some of the more notorious of these characters. Jeff Barry and Ellie Greenwich were one of several married-couple songwriting teams at New York's Brill Building, affectionately known as "teen pan alley." Barry and Greenwich had written hits for many of the girl groups—among them the Crystals and the Ronettes—and they also penned most of the major hits the Shangri-Las were to record. Along with the legendary manager-producer-songwriter George "Shadow" Morton, Barry and Greenwich wrote and produced the band's classic hit, "Leader of the Pack." For Jeff Barry, writing girl group melodramas would prove a training stage for his subsequent dominance in the world of bubblegum pop a few years later, where his tongue-in-cheek excesses would be given comparable free rein. Signed to Red Bird Records, the Shangri-Las also worked with the label's heads, Jerry Leiber and Mike Stoller, two stalwarts of novelty pop production and the writers responsible for some of the great humor songs of early rock & roll with the Coasters.

Surrounded by such managerial and creative forces, it is not surprising that the Shangri-Las broke fast and big. Their debut single, "Remember (Walkin' in the Sand)" (1964), was successful but failed to distinguish the band from the hordes of other girl groups then on the scene. With "Leader of the Pack" a few months later, team Shangri-La struck gold while simultaneously carving out a radical niche within the form. A theatrical blockbuster, "Leader of the Pack" was an example of melodrama in the extreme. Bypassing the themes of idealized and innocent romance that had dominated "white girl" music for decades, here frustration, rebellion, and tragedy took center stage in an explosion of farcical excess. A modern-day *Romeo and Juliet* vignette, the song showcases the band members as characters engrossed in "girl talk." Their interplay, complete with slang-speak interjections of "Uh-uh" and "Mm-hmm," shows the teens in united idolatry of the song's mythical rebel "boy."[24] Unfolding like a scene from *West Side Story*, the song dramatizes the world of the generation gap, where the parents just don't understand and the rebel without a cause is just misunderstood; only "the girl" can save him. Alas, at the climax, the sound effects of a screeching motorbike skid and smashing glass inform listeners of the fateful demise of the leader of the pack.

Despite its send-up excesses and obvious parody of types and myths, the song made the adult authorities who controlled the airwaves fearful of the romance of rebellion that lay within. Many radio stations on both sides of the Atlantic refused to play the song, and the popular British TV pop show *Ready Steady Go* demanded a different song be performed when the Shangri-Las arrived to promote it. Despite the stir caused (and perhaps partially because of it), "Leader of the Pack" dominated the charts in the United States and U.K. over the next year.

Quick to capitalize on the mega-success of this single, team Shangri-La set to crafting a band image less conventionally girl group and more geared to the iconography of the rebel "bad" girls portrayed in their new songs. Out went the skirts, blouses, and high heels, and in came spike-heeled leather boots, skintight slacks, and catsuits. Soon, the band was being promoted as the anti–girl group. Ironically, as their African American girl group peers were pressured to accommodate themselves to the mainstream white-dominated industry and audience, the Shangs replaced their publicity smiles with sneers, while striking poses in attire that suggested that these were girls not to be messed with. Such images were more in tune with the bawdy black blues women of generations past than with those (white and black) of the early 1960s. Such images were also significant in awakening girls everywhere to the limitations that had been put on their identities and the imaginative possibilities for reconstruction that lay out there. Douglas reflected upon the proto-feminist iconography of the Shangri-Las, saying they "mattered because they helped cultivate inside us a desire to rebel."[25] And for Douglas, the real-life subversions of songs like "Leader of the Pack" were tangible. As she notes: "By allying herself romantically and morally with the rebel hero, the girl singer and listener proclaimed her independence from society's predictable expectations about her inevitable domestication."[26]

Understandably, the Shangri-Las will always be remembered and recognized for the achievement and long-standing influence of "Leader of the Pack," but it was by no means their only major hit. Between 1964 and 1966 the band produced over a dozen hit singles, most developing the darker side of girl group topics. "Give Us Your Blessings" and "I Can Never Go Home Anymore," both released in 1965, tapped into many of the same comedic techniques that had brought "Pack" such mass adulation. Both were runaway melodramas told as narrative tales from the perspective of a headstrong rebel girl; both characterized parents as the deniers of romance and consummation; both resolved in tragedy and/or disappointment. "Blessings" mirrored "Pack" but shifted vehicles with a car crash ending in which *both* lovers die.

Perhaps exhausting the specificity of their rebel girl subgenre, the Shangri-Las faded after 1966 and eventually called it quits in 1968. Various medical issues thwarted subsequent attempted comebacks, though the band enjoyed something of a rebirth during the height of the punk rock era when they scored a hit for the second time with "Leader of the Pack" in Britain and enjoyed a successful reunion show at the New York punk mecca, CBGBs, in 1977. That show was attended by members of Blondie and the Ramones, two bands that had been greatly influenced by the Shangs' brand of mock-drama; critic Lester Bangs, a long-time supporter of subversive rock humorists, was also in attendance.

Although recognized for their contributions to the girl group era, the Shangri-Las have not been given the kind of critical acclaim that they perhaps deserve; this is maybe because they were deemed minor players by virtue of their association with this "minor" female form. Within the world of rock bands, though, the Shangri-Las' influence has been long-standing and far-reaching. The "bad girl" imagery that brought camp comedy to 1970s acts like Joan Jett (and the Runaways), Suzy Quatro, and Girlschool would have been unthinkable without the precedent of the Shangs. Subsequent purveyors of this subgenre—Sahara Hotnights, Damone, even the Spice Girls—have employed the band's potent combination of parodic girl-zone melodrama to potent and amusing ends. Perhaps the most curious illustration of how memorable and insinuating the vivid musical theater of the Shangri-Las has been was reflected in the reusage of their opening catch question from "Leader of the Pack"—"Is she really going out with him?"—subsequently referenced by the Damned in their punk debut single, "New Rose," and later in the title of Joe Jackson's biggest hit single.

MID-SIXTIES TURNING POINTS

By the mid-1960s, the new folkies, girl groups, and British invaders had jump-started excitement into an American rock engine that had been stuttering since the end of the 1950s. Though none of these movements—besides folk—operated in explicitly political ways, each symbolically or tangentially spoke to the pervasive social trends of youth dissent and liberation struggles. Nowhere was this more apparent than in the African American civil rights struggles within the United States, which had been accelerating in intensity and support since the 1950s. Folk protestors like Dylan, Ochs, and Baez had been vocal on social issues in much of their work, but one can also see that implicitly many of the British bands and girl groups were contributing to the momentum that was aligning the massive baby boom youth power bloc to the civil rights fight. In their open embrace of old black blues and more recent R&B, the British acts paid tribute to the accomplishments of black America, and by virtue of the fact that most of the girl groups were African American in makeup, they symbolically sent out signals of empowerment and attainment, not only for females, or for black females, but for black America in general. America may have been refusing to integrate and accommodate, but the rock culture was showing the way.

The serious concerns at the heart of society at this time account, somewhat, for the dea(r)th of humor within black music culture. There was a sense within Motown and beyond that serious times necessitated serious culture, or at least a culture that would be taken seriously. Thus, the "street" flamboyance that had characterized the visual humor of black acts like Little Richard and Screamin' Jay Hawkins in the 1950s was increasingly replaced with the upwardly mobile, high-couture culture of the Motown acts and girl groups. Frantic antics and mayhem moves were substituted with formal dance steps and middle-class decorum. It was not that humor had disappeared from black music, only that it had been temporarily put on hold at a time when the public image of black people was deemed paramount in the struggle to be accepted and to reap gains within the white, male, adult establishment.

By the mid-sixties, though, there were signs that the physical swagger was returning to black music, that black pride was trumping assimilation as a strategy, and that humor was being heralded again as an important strategy of cultural self-defense and counterattack. Soon, James Brown began to dominate the black soul (music) landscape with his carnival showmanship, and Sly & the Family Stone embarked upon a series of crossover maneuvers that included a multiethnic and cross-gendered band playing a melting pot music that drew from white psychedelia as well as black blues, soul, and funk. Both of these acts had the confidence to use humor (both physical and lyrical) to raise the spirits of black (and white) youths, as the civil rights era extended into the "black power" movement. By the end of the decade, radical satirists like Gil Scott-Heron and the Last Poets were bringing their *black* humor to the scene, replacing the light, bright gestures that characterized early-sixties "integration" ambitions.

Within white rock culture other turning points were also noticeable in the mid-sixties. The topical and sociopolitical lyricism of the folk trailblazers was beginning to seep into the broader rock culture at the same time as the rock aesthetic was starting to alter the folk paradigm. Sex and drugs became central topics of rock songs, less veiled in innuendo than before, and represented in myriad forms of sometimes eccentric expressions. The so-called "sexual revolution" was gaining steam and gathering in adventurous youths who were fed up with living by the proprieties and stale orders of the establishment adult culture. These youths—growing into their late teens and early twenties—wanted to break free, to experiment, and to create their own culture to reflect their imaginations and realities.

A more esoteric, abstract humor began to shade the rebel postures and subversive intents of the new waves of rockers, bringing eccentricity, whimsy, and sometimes sick humor into the mix as ingredients of the new art. Absurdism, the bizarre, and a flaunting of the forbidden signified a seeking of new forms over old, utopian dreams over conventional compromise. Sometimes the resulting rock was subversive, sometimes it was too abstract and too obtuse for one to know, but it always came with an aura that evoked the spirit of experimentation and a subconscious sense that whatever these kids were doing, they appeared to be laughing *with* each other and laughing *at* their generational opposition.

This mid-sixties rock trajectory toward a collective youth voice, alongside the simultaneous trend that celebrated one's unique expression, created a craving for communal as well as individual sustenance and representation. Nowhere were these parallel strains more apparent than in the hippy movement forming around the San Francisco Bay Area. Sparked by the merging of the idiosyncratic folk poetry of Dylan with the group rock adventures of the Beatles, the resulting genre of folk rock became the basis for the San Francisco sound. The most representative band in this transition was the Byrds, who soared to success in 1965 by sounding like Dylan and the Beatles simultaneously—this particularly illustrated by their biggest hit, the Dylan-penned "Mr. Tambourine Man" (1965). The Byrds, moreover, not only drew from these prior forces but also developed them into a new hippy humor that was to dominate late-sixties rock culture. In songs like "Eight Miles High" (1966) they complemented drug-punning lyrics with the new psychedelic drones of San Francisco guitar rock (though the band actually hailed from Los Angeles).

A contemporary of the Byrds, Country Joe McDonald similarly drew from early-sixties folk roots in developing his own folk rock style. A central figure in the San Francisco/Berkeley rock scene, McDonald expressed his sociopolitical concerns through a warped, bizarre, and idiosyncratic lyrical humor that revealed that something had been going on in the mid-1960s to alter the language, tone, and demeanor of subversive rock humor at both individual and communal levels.

Country Joe & the Fish

The forty-year (and counting) career of Country Joe McDonald started and continues at the counterculture frontier outpost of San Francisco, California. After thirty-three albums, he still uses the city as his stage to rage from the left on behalf of his primary sociopolitical concerns: civil rights, the environment, and peace. When talk show "shouter" Bill O'Reilly recently compared McDonald to Fidel Castro, Joe no doubt received the charge as the utmost compliment.

Joe McDonald was that rarest of late-1960s counterculture protestors: one who had actually served in the armed forces. After serving in the navy as a young man, McDonald headed to San Francisco with the intention of attaining a college education. However, he soon became distracted by the political activism that was flourishing around Berkeley, and he became drawn to the so-called "underground," where activists, hippies, dropouts, and artists were carving out new lives, philosophies, and artistic endeavors. Joe joined the in-crowd, bringing his guitar and singing skills to the Berkeley String Quartet and the Instant Action Jug Band in the early 1960s. These acts drew inspiration from folk and other roots music, and exuded an upbeat energy of irreverent humor and carnival-like celebration.

By the mid-sixties, San Francisco was getting a reputation as a transitional site where alternative culture and radical politics were given space to flourish. A longtime outpost for beatnik dissent and artistic adventure, the city was a magnet for alienated young people of many stripes. As the sounds of Dylan and the Beatles seeped into the atmosphere of San Francisco, they mixed with the bohemian consciousness that had taken hold. Soon, the city was producing its own musical acts, with their own stylistic distinctions, morphing folk and rock into a drug-fueled psychedelic style that was free-form in both musical structure and lyrical expression. The Grateful Dead, Jefferson Airplane, and Big Brother & the Holding Co. would soon become the central bands of this psychedelic vanguard, but it was Country Joe McDonald who laid the foundations for this musical explosion, he who established the sociopolitical consciousness upon which these philosophies would coalesce.

Country Joe & the Fish came together in 1965; the Fish was guitarist Barry Melton. Other musicians would come and go over the following years, but the constant mainstays of McDonald and Melton remained. The founding of the band was for political as much as entertainment reasons. In order to provide support for the upcoming Vietnam Day Teach-In at Berkeley, in October 1965, Joe decided to provide a live show as well as a promotional recording. The resulting self-recorded, self-produced, and self-promoted EP included two songs from local act Peter King and two from the newly formed Country Joe & the Fish entitled "Superbird" and "I-Feel-Like-I'm-Fixin'-to-Die Rag." These would prove to be signature tunes in Joe's repertoire.

"Superbird" embodied the stylized political humor that had been brewing in San Francisco in recent years. Its mockery of the U.S. president captured the dissenting spirit in an eccentric, childlike style that was becoming the pervasive attitude of the city's youth movement. "Look up yonder in the sky now. / What is that, I pray? / It's a bird, it's a plane, it's a man insane. / It's my President L.B.J.," Joe gleefully sings. Later in the song the demarcations of the generation gap are made apparent, as Joe rallies the hippy troops to fight back with their own weaponry: "Gonna make him eat flowers. / Yeah, make him drop some acid."[27] Such neo-agitprop humor became the hallmark of Country Joe's oeuvre, establishing a style that disseminated throughout the harder edges of the protest movement later in the decade. His alternative humor also tapped into the more apolitical factions of the counterculture, those busier crafting a new personal consciousness than confronting the political establishment.

The second song on the legendary debut EP, "I-Feel-Like-I'm-Fixin'-to-Die Rag," was a call-and-response anthem that became the model for San Francisco rock humor, as well as a standard go-to sing-along song for antiwar protest gatherings and marches across the country. To this day it remains the (only) song that (most) people (can) cite when the name Country Joe McDonald comes up. An anthem for a generation it may have been, but Joe remembers writing the song in thirty minutes. Recollecting on his official website, he wittily refers to the song as an example of "GI humor," meaning that it incorporates various complaints but frames them in a fashion whereby you would not get in trouble for voicing them.

The song articulates its anti–Vietnam War grievances by addressing the various parties involved in and/or affected by the war: the draftees ("Put down your books and pick up a gun / We're gonna have a whole lotta fun"); the generals ("You know that peace can only be won / When we've blown 'em all to kingdom come"); Wall Street financiers ("There's plenty good money to be made / Supplying the army with the tools of the trade"); parents ("Be the first one on your block / To have your boy come home in a box").[28] That the song is set within the context of a happy sing-along "rag" melody only serves to further elevate the pointed ironic incongruity of the forthright content. The mountain of angry letters sent in after the band performed the song on the *David Frost Show* in 1969 indicates the disturbing effects of such black humor; it also underlines how, though the song was empowering to youth protestors, it was equally provocative (though in a decidedly different way) to the "silent majority" adult culture.

"Fixin'" proved to have an interesting life subsequent to being first set to wax in 1965. The record label, Vanguard, insisted it be left off the band's debut album, *Electric Music for the Mind and Body* (1967), squeamish that the song's inflammatory content might meet with a backlash from the censoring forces of the music industry and beyond. It was, however, rereleased on the next album, as a psychedelic rag, complete with carnival organ and trippy sound effects. It also incorporated the song's infamous "FISH" cheer introduction, which consisted of an audience shouting back the four letters of the word in collective unison. By the time Country Joe unleashed the song to the attendees at the Woodstock Music Festival in 1969, the FISH cheer had undergone changes more befitting to the increasingly dark and militant moods of the times. Having revamped it there as the "FUCK" cheer, Country Joe had—as he then put it—"300,000 . . . fuckers" chanting this symbolic "middle finger," concretizing Woodstock as its own symbol of an alternative youth nation. An emblematic song of its time, "Fixin'" (and this performance of it in particular) has since become a much-referenced historic signifier of the divided nation as well as an indication of how such black humor had become the last-resort gasp of the exasperated, frustrated, and angry youth peace movement by the end of the decade.

A great many of the bands in the Bay Area in 1967 drew from the slapstick, satire, and political consciousness that Country Joe

& the Fish had been feeding into the city's regions. The band's trailblazing efforts not only spawned a regional rock renaissance that changed the music culture but they also established San Francisco as a home for the new alternative FM radio and progressive media. It was San Francisco, for example, where *Rolling Stone* magazine, in 1967, initially set up shop, Jann Wenner and his gang of young upstarts dispensing a brand of "gonzo" rock journalism wholly attuned to the spirit of their adopted city.

Country Joe & the Fish—like *Rolling Stone* in its early years—were representative of their place and time. They signify a turning point in rock history during the 1960s when whimsy began to merge with satire, and when anti-establishment irreverence became an integral and integrated attitude of the youth subcultural expression.

BUBBLEGUM POPS UP

The imaginative reach and high art aspirations of mid- to late-1960s rock propelled the form across new frontiers of music and humor. Rock developed into a boundless art form limited only by the creative visions of its purveyors—and few recognized any limits. It had certainly been a long, strange journey in a short time from the innocent simplicity of much 1950s and early 1960s rock to ambitious albums like *Pet Sounds* in 1966, *Sgt. Pepper's Lonely Hearts Club Band* in 1967, and *In-A-Gadda-Da-Vida* in 1968. However, in rock history—as in all histories—reactions are invariably met with counter-reactions, forces met with counter-forces. Such was the case during the final years of the decade, a period, many believe, when rock had reached its artistic zenith. The bubblegum genre that popped up in 1968 was—in many respects—a counter-reaction to a rock culture that had been following the lead of the Beatles in seeking sounds of increasing complexity and that of Bob Dylan in constructing lyrics of philosophical and/or abstract purposes. Such developments saw rock songs increasingly resembling classical suites and lyrics morphing into poetic compositions. These serious endeavors reached their apotheosis in the exploratory music of "art rock," a subgenre characterized by multitextured songs with extended instrumental dynamics and complex lyrical imagery. Where art rock bands like Iron Butterfly, Pink Floyd, and Yes constructed lengthy and densely layered symphonic workouts, bubblegum pop songs were short and simple, elemental and elementary; where art rock recognized the album as its medium, bubblegum was represented by the single; and as art rock pitched its ambitious projects to selective and serious-minded audiences, bubblegum shamelessly marketed its three-minute products for mass consumption. In response to the rising intellectual objectives of art rock and the counterculture, bubblegum popsters offered what one might call an over-the-counterculture.

One of the principle reasons rock proper had become more sophisticated in its humor and expression was that the baby boom kids were coming of age. That left the next wave of pre-pubescents without a music they could relate to or call their own. Mixing comic book ideas with nursery rhymes and baby-speak lyrics with fast, catchy dance beats, bubblegum "bands" like Ohio Express, 1910 Fruitgum Company, and the Archies took the U.S. and the U.K. charts by storm between 1967 and 1972. The fact that these acts did not actually exist as such, but were mere fronts for the songwriting-producer team of Jerry Kasenatz and Jeff Katz was of little concern to the adoring masses of preteens. For them, the rock their elder siblings listened to was too weird and uninviting; they wanted primal, simple(-minded) pleasures to which they could sing along and dance. As such, bubblegum was not only a tacit reaction to rock snobbery, but it was also the second coming of the novelty pop that had dominated the U.S. charts in the late 1950s.

Unsurprisingly, not all listeners received bubblegum with open arms and hearts. For serious rock fans and critics, it was an abomination, a worrying sign of a step backward after the many great leaps forward. They saw bubblegum as contrived and formulaic, fabricated fronts for business-minded controllers who plugged in whatever studio musicians were needed to create a top-ten hit. The Archies, a TV cartoon band, did not even pretend to be real! As with the reaction to the girl group phenomenon a few years prior, the reason for the backlash against bubblegum was largely that it broke the sacred code of rock credibility: authenticity. Both fake and faceless, bubblegum offended the prevailing rock myths of artistic creativity and rebellious opposition to the powers that be. Behind the cartoons or actors in silly costumes were those powers, manipulating every detail with Wizard of Oz–like deceit.

Despite its dismissal as the very worst pap of pop, bubblegum has its roots and bore its fruits in some of the most respected rock quarters. One can see early Beatles songs (the original boy band) as the template upon which bubblegum crafted its material ambitions. Just ask the Monkees! Even within the counterculture's inner sanctum, one could interpret the Tiny Tim phenomenon—along with his hit "Tip-Toe Thru' the Tulips" (1968)—as more bubblegum fare than hippy absurdism. And within critical ranks, where the urge to burst the bubble was strongest, rock writer-rebel Lester Bangs was as tireless an advocate on behalf of the form as he had been in defense of the girl groups. In both cases, he admired how the pomposity and phony myths of rock bands were being penetrated and exposed, their own fakery unveiled, and their own product revealed as just that—product. For Bangs, the beautiful irony was that despite its commercial trappings, bubblegum was actually less phony and more authentic than rock proper. In their genre study, *Bubblegum Music Is the Naked Truth* (2001), editors Kim Cooper and David Smay actually make their dedication out to Lester Bangs, recognizing his longtime support of this much-maligned genre. Over time, Bangs's position has gathered support, just as the genre itself has become more accepted and recognized on its own terms.

There is clearly ironic humor in bubblegum existing in juxtaposition to high-art rock in the late 1960s; it provided a knowing wink and a constant reminder of bottom-line realities in much the same way that dada and pop art had provided a challenge within the fine arts. Furthermore, there are other aspects of gum humor that reveal (perhaps) subversive angles. Bangs has pointed to the in-house double entendres in some of the lyrics, to wordplay that shows the songwriters subverting their own "innocent" fronts. He sees sexual innuendo in both Tommy Roe's "Jam Up and Jelly Tight" (1970) and the Ohio Express 1968 hit, "Yummy Yummy Yummy" (with its rhyme-line "I've got love in my tummy").[29] Some have also read drug references into such lines as "Pour your sweetness over me" from the Archies' "Sugar Sugar," a number one hit on both sides of the Atlantic in 1969.[30]

Though the U.S. bubblegum boom burst around 1972—perhaps an eventual victim of its own corporate facelessness—the trend adapted and expanded in the U.K. and beyond. On the more glittery edges of the U.K. glam rock movement in the early seventies, the influence of bubblegum aesthetics was pronounced. Early Sweet songs like "Wig-Wam Bam" (1972) and "Little Willy" (1972), both written by bubblegum writer-producers Nicky Chinn and Mike Chapman, paved the way for the band's future pop career; Marc Bolan, as he drifted from hippy indulgence into (the) glitter camp, was not averse to adding some gum to his glam; Gary Glitter (a.k.a. Paul Gadd) likewise adopted the elemental features of bubblegum as he crafted his space age Liberace image. (Glitter's efforts to reach the gum's pre-pubescent constituency would later go too far when he was jailed for downloading child pornography in 1999 and more recently convicted for having sex with minors in Vietnam. One might perceive a somewhat parallel scenario in the recent legal troubles of Michael Jackson, who, lest one forgets, once led the premier soul-bubblegum group of the late sixties alongside his brothers.)

Beyond glam rock, other major pop acts of the 1970s, like Abba and the Bay City Rollers, also operated by the bubblegum playbook, though where the genre reached its most subversive and humorous adaptations was within the late-seventies punk rock movement. The Sex Pistols' how-to-be-stars satire (on album and film), *The Great Rock 'n' Roll Swindle* (1979), could just as easily have been addressing any bubblegum band, while the Ramones' embrace of childlike simplicity in lyrics and hooks showed the band to be studious fans of the form. As with bubblegum, the humor of punk's back-to-basics model was an implicit (and often explicit) satirical counter-reaction to the self-importance of many of the rock idols/idles of the day.

Nowadays, bubblegum continues to pop up periodically, bringing rock's higher ambitions back to pop's down-to-earth realities. One might note, for example, how modern gummers like Hanson, the Spice Girls, and Britney Spears emerged in the wake of the early-nineties grunge seriousness. The bubblegum genre itself is also increasingly being praised for its primary charms and unpretentious dumb humor. As a result, alternative acts have more frequently entered the fray, embracing the form and pushing its extremities up more ironic avenues. Sweden's Sahara Hotnights and the Hives, as well as Japan's Shonen Knife and Guitar Wolf, suggest that the geographical reach of bubblegum rock is also expanding; these and other bands are currently providing some of the cutting edges and wit of what has been termed "bubblecore," a subgenre exploring the possibilities inherent in sonic simplicity and humble (though tongue-in-cheek) humor.

THE ROCK COUNTER-COUNTERCULTURE

If escapism and self-indulgence were primary characteristics of much of the psychedelic humor coming from both sides of the Atlantic during the mid- to late 1960s, there were other contemporaries less enamored with these journeys into withdrawal and (inevitable) apathy. Oppositional forces—led by Frank Zappa and Lou Reed from the West and East coasts of the United States, respectively—set about creating a counter-counterculture. With their feet firmly grounded (rather than with their heads airily in the clouds), these artists brought a cold, hard stare to the realities of 1960s America. Down-to-earth pragmatists, they had little time for the abstract indulgences coming from the hippy enclaves of San Francisco; indeed, Lou Reed once dismissively referred to that city's bands as "untalented bores."[31] Whether exposing political hypocrisy with their mordant wit or stripping rock of its bloated excesses through parody, the new cynics of the counter-counterculture harnessed humor as a weapon rather than a whim, and they had their sights set to "bullshit detector."

Their style of attack-humor was refreshing, though not original. Indeed, the "sick" and/or "black" humor that Zappa and the like-minded practiced had been firmly established and developed within other art forms during the late 1950s and early 1960s. Lenny Bruce, the original "sick" comic, had been crafting his brand of stand-up satire during the early sixties until its and his excesses led to his untimely death in 1964. Bruce's urban-ethnic style was streetwise and raw, using language and an attack mode hitherto unseen in comedic circles. Besides the influential legacy Bruce left to the likes of Richard Pryor and George Carlin (among many others), his incisive stabs were embraced by rockers like the Fugs and Zappa. The Fugs tested the limits of mainstream tolerance, much as Bruce had done, with word-centered neological assaults that touched the raw nerves behind American hypocrisy and superficiality. Songs like "Coca-Cola Douche" (1966) had censors hounding the band much as they had the beleaguered Bruce ten years earlier. Zappa was, likewise, blessed (or cursed) with Bruce's twenty-four-hour antennae for all things phony and wrong with his nation. His razor-sharp inquisitions into both the rock counterculture and the broader national culture made him both beloved and despised—depending on whether or not you were a target of his short-fuse satirical assaults. Prodding and challenging on behalf of "freaks" rather than hippies, Zappa progressed the outsider-looking-in black humor tradition that had been gaining credence in sixties literature (through Ken Kesey and Joseph Heller), stand-up comedy (through Lenny Bruce and Dick Gregory), fine arts (through Andy Warhol and Peter Blake), and film (through Stanley Kubrick and Lindsay Anderson). On all artistic fronts, humor was hardening into cathartic outbursts aimed at a world that seemed increasingly irrational, out of control, and hell-bent on self-destruction.

The Mothers of Invention

When young music prodigy Frank Vincent Zappa joined the small-time Los Angeles R&B combo the Soul Giants in 1964, humor was about to be taken in bold new directions. Immediately assuming leadership of the group, Zappa changed the band's name to the Mothers and led them to the heart of the city's underground music culture. By 1966, they were signed by jazz specialists Verve Records, who promptly pressured the band to change their name again to something less "suggestive." Soon they were the Mothers of Invention, and their debut release, *Freak Out!* (1966), was a declaration of intent as well as an album that revolutionized rock humor.

Musically, *Freak Out!* did not signal a grand departure from the R&B styles that the band had been performing over the prior two years, but Zappa added some of the new experimental sounds that he had been working with in his studio. *Freak Out!* arrived on Verve's doorstep as a double album (rare for a new artist) and contained the services of a seventeen-piece orchestra (stretching the purse strings of the fledgling label). Never one for less-than-dramatic gestures, Zappa further broke the mold (and the rules) by crafting *Freak Out!* as a concept album (making it a forerunner of its kind).

At a time when countercultural rock bands were aligning themselves with the sensibilities and philosophies of the Haight-Ashbury hippy subculture, Zappa used this album as a platform, not only to critique the oppressive conformity of the establishment culture (as his peers were doing) but also to take aim at the apathetic complacency of the counterculture itself. Dissing and dismissing "flower power," Zappa proposed "freak power," a movement for creative nonconformists who were not dulled or disabled by drugs or alcohol. *Freak Out!* was a satirical assault on hypocrisy and escapism everywhere, and if the sandal fit. . . . As such, the album has proven to be a trailblazer of its kind, outlining an attitude and methodology less in tune with abstract hippy escapism and more associated with future "straight edge" punk practitioners like Henry Rollins and Ian MacKaye.

The Mothers of Invention's follow-up album, *Absolutely Free* (1967), consolidated the shock methods and satirical styles of their debut. Here, Zappa ratcheted up the sarcastic provocations further, juxtaposing songs about phonies from all social classes, generations, and geographical locales. In a relentless parody of pretensions, Zappa could barely contain his distastes. "Plastic People" aims high, sneering at the Middle American dimwits that ran the country in the interests of their own self-serving conservative "principles." A similar satire on squares and "fascists" follows in "Brown Shoes Don't Make It." Continuing on the theme of conformity, Zappa, in "Status Back Baby," zaps the blinkered preoccupations of young high schoolers unable to think beyond the scope of their own peer groups (a topic he would return to in his eighties hit "Valley Girl"). He described the song as being about "acne America."

Whereas the hippy counterculture romanticized youth and scorned adulthood into disconnected worlds of good and evil, Zappa made no such discriminations or distinctions. Apathy, conformity, and small-mindedness are not the traits of any particular age group or social class in Zappa's world; they are all-pervasive "opiates" that serve to keep the entire populace in a perpetual state of idiocy and impotence. Never afraid to bite the hand that feeds, Zappa felt a particular responsibility to provoke the slumbering state of a youth culture that was wasting its energies on escapist indulgences and stylized rebellion (as he saw it). He directed his scathing humor with sustained satire on the Mothers' third album release, *We're Only in It for the Money* (1968). The album arrived a year after the summer of love, and Zappa used the visual art of the album cover to send out a preemptive flare. Created by Cal Schenkel, the sleeve neatly parodied the by-then-infamous collage cover of the Beatles' *Sgt. Pepper* album, at that point the musical rallying point for the hippy subculture.

And if the ironic appropriation of this renowned iconic shot, set against the scornful title, was not enough to suggest Zappa's sardonic theme, the songs within surely did. "Are You Hung Up?" the album's opener, is a surrealistic skit played out through the voices of drug-addled hippies conversing in an incomprehensible slang-speak that makes little to no sense. "Who Needs the Peace Corps?" continues the "question authority" parody approach, with another "unreliable" hippy narrator telling us tales from his Kerouac dream-book. "I'll stay a week and get the crabs and take a bus back home. / I'm really just a phony but forgive me 'cause I'm stoned," rambles the speaker, an emblem of more "plastic people" lost in self-indulgence.[32] Zappa used the title, "Who Needs the Peace Corps?" to comment wryly upon the credibility (or lack thereof) of the youth culture's professed idealism. Started as a program of international public service by the Kennedy administration at the start of the 1960s, the Peace Corps' purpose was—to paraphrase JFK—to show what young people could do for their country, not what their country could do for them. The wasted hippies begging for change on Haight and Ashbury Streets or the escapist fantasists of Manson-like cults were not quite what Kennedy had had in mind. While Zappa by no means references the Peace Corps in order to endorse it (indeed, he regarded the program as exploitative of cheap labor and as self-serving, on the part of the government), he used it in this song as a point on a symbolic measuring stick marking the distance between counterculture idealism and practice.

The focus for Zappa's humor is usually his lyrics, but this was not his only avenue of comedic expression. In fact, on the written page Zappa's words do not reflect the full effectiveness of their humor. Unlike Dylan's "poetry," Zappa's lyrics demand their musical accompaniment and vocal articulation in order to reach full effect. In this regard, he and his band used the humor of form and formula in ways similar to those used by the Bonzo Dog Doo-Dah Band. Like the Bonzos, the Mothers were highly skilled musicians with eclectic styles and tastes. Over Frank Zappa's thirty-three-year career, he and his bands ventured into just about every genre that has been heard in twentieth-century popular music. Big band, blues, classical, doo-wop, electronica, funk, rock, hard rock, progressive rock, jazz (fusion), pop, proto-rap, and reggae are but a few of the styles Zappa tinkered with, bringing pitch-perfect parodic exaggeration to each.

Another outlet for the Mothers' all-purpose satire was the live stage. As their consistently striking album covers suggested, the band regarded visual humor as a significant weapon in their arsenal. Likewise, Mothers performances in the late 1960s have become the stuff of legend. Indulging Zappa's "shock" aesthetics, which he learned from theater and art movements (as well as rock), gigs were often anarchic and prop-propelled, though always well-rehearsed and note-perfect. During one legendary show in 1967 (as the Vietnam War and its protests were escalating to new levels), Zappa invited two soldiers from the audience onstage to dismember some baby dolls that he introduced as "gook" children. Such raw black humor somewhat trumped the comparable gesture that the Beatles had made with their "butchered" dolls image on the cover of *Yesterday and Today* (1966), tapping into the kind of "sick" humor that even Lenny Bruce would have been reticent to touch.

Zappa disbanded the Mothers of Invention then reformed it with new members at the end of the 1960s, and from then on his band lineups were flexible and ever changing. What remained consistent were the caustic satire, absurdist high jinx, and shock (sometimes scatology) of his lyrical content. Topics would change with the times, though, and Zappa appeared to have his resistance impulses rejuvenated with the election of Ronald Reagan to the U.S. presidency in 1980. Horrified by the behind-the-back deals Reagan's administration struck with the religious right, Zappa purged his frustrations on the 1981 album *You Are What You Is*, which described the new televangelists in "Dumb All Over" and their shameless embezzling in "Heavenly Bank Account." His growing political engagement reached a peak when he led the counter-charge against the Parents Music Resource Center, a group of senators' wives who were pushing for censorship and/or "advisory stickers" for albums *they* deemed offensive.

Rumors swirled that Zappa was gearing up to enter the political fray as a presidential candidate himself by the end of the eighties, but a 1991 medical diagnosis revealed that he had prostate cancer, bringing that goal (or rumor) to an end. He died in 1993, leaving the Zappa legacy to his four children: Dweezil,

Moon Unit, Ahmet, and Diva Muffin (yes, the humor ran deep!). Two years later he was posthumously inducted into the Rock & Roll Hall of Fame.

Subsequent artists have attempted to keep Zappa-style subversive humor alive by either adopting his methods, attempting to cover his complex songs, or just referencing their hero. Zappa is name-checked in the Dead Milkmen's "Let's Go Smoke Some Pot," the Ramones' "Censorshit," and "Weird Al" Yankovic's "Genius in France," while Deep Purple's famous "Smoke on the Water" was apparently written about a Mothers of Invention concert in Germany that was brought to a premature close when a fan burned the venue to the ground. Perhaps the most curious fan of Zappa is the author turned revolutionary turned president of Czechoslovakia, Václav Havel, who recognized the artist's subversive spirit by making him a culture attaché to his nation in 1990. Zappa was the perennial outsider looking in, and this would be as close as he would come to being recognized by the political establishment he had spent the prior thirty-three years lampooning.

The Fugs

A combustible combination of the trivial and the serious, the Fugs were both wildly ahead of their time and poignantly part of it. Their humor, which ranged from locker room lewdness to provocative political satire, was too outrageous ever to be embraced by the general public and too edgy to be ignored by the eagle eyes of the authorities. During their initial reign of terror—between 1965 and 1969—they pushed envelopes, ruffled feathers, trampled on taboos, and attracted the attention of the FBI along the way. And they did this by using a humor that was as subversive as Greek theater and as infantile as Andrew Dice Clay.

The band was formed in and around the radical New York City Peace Eye Bookstore in 1964 by literary mavens Ed Sanders and Tuli Kupferberg, who initially perceived the idea of the rock band as a joke. They were partially right. Joined by drummer Ken Weaver and later by Holy Modal Rounders' folk pranksters Peter Sampfel and Steve Weber, the band took their name from a euphemism that Norman Mailer had been bullied into using as a substitute for "fuck" in his 1948 novel, *The Naked and the Dead*. Mailer would later return the hat-tipping reference by writing about the Fugs' performance at the 1967 Washington anti–Vietnam War rally in his *Armies of the Night* (1967). (Apparently, Sanders and Kupferberg were not the only artists amused by Mailer's adoption of the term "fug," as legend has it that Dorothy Parker's first words to Mailer when she met him were "So you're the man who can't spell 'fuck.'" But I fuggin' digress.)

Starting from their manifesto premise of "personal freedom, no more war or poverty, and lots of fun," the Fugs set out to capture the idealistic developments of the growing youth counterculture, but they aimed to do so by drawing on the styles and attitudes of their gritty New York home base. As writers, they took a literary approach to lyricism, but working within the rock format, they recognized the importance of using a language that could speak directly and with immediacy to a youth demographic. Sanders and Kupferberg also drew from inspirations other than literature: they admired the subversive gestures of Greek theater; they studied the art-politico theories of the dadaists; they listened to folk musicians from Joe Hill to Bob Dylan for pointers on techniques of communication. From each source they learned how humor can be a tool and a weapon, how it can open avenues of free speech, and how it can attract and appeal, empower and impact. For avowed political radicals like the Fugs, a humorous approach was deemed the most strategically effective, though few could have suspected how far they would push its limits of acceptability and decorum.

The Fugs started out working from a Phil Ochs–type folk template, writing topical songs with a harsh satirical style. They drew from the imagery around them as well as from popular conventions. They incorporated jingles, rhymes, chants, and clichés that audiences could latch onto and recite in unison at protest rallies and concerts. Musically, they constructed simple folk forms, then mixed them with the rhythms and sound effects emerging from the burgeoning psychedelic and folk rock scenes. They toured the city, then the country, picking up tips and passing on their own to like-minded acts—like Country Joe & the Fish and the Mothers of Invention—with whom they crossed paths.

This introduction to the world of rock & roll led to their debut album release, in 1965, *The Village Fugs: Ballads & Songs of Contemporary Protest, Points of View & General Dissatisfaction.* Its raw lo-fi sound was as much garbage as garage, while its ragtag combination of loose jams and off-kilter Everly Brothers–style harmonies betrayed the reality that the album had been recorded in just two afternoon sessions. Too raw and amateur for broad appeal in 1965, *The Village Fugs* is now (of course) a cult classic of underground lo-fi deconstruction to be filed next to one's Guided by Voices, Pavement, and Piss Artists albums.

With a larger budget and more time in the studio, the Fugs' eponymous follow-up album in 1966 and bootleg *Virgin Fugs* in 1967 revealed the band finding their "voices"—both musically and lyrically. With a muckraking drive and a mocking attitude in spades, the band sang of the "C.I.A. Man" (1967): "Who can squash republics like bananas? / . . . Fuckin' A, man / C.I.A. man."[33] They sampled gunfire sound effects into the outrageous and absurd "Kill for Peace" (1967), a song with a war-mongering narrator who makes the speakers of Randy Newman's "Political Science" and the Dead Kennedys' "Kill the Poor" seem like doves: "Kill 'em, kill 'em, strafe those gook creeps!" demands Kupferberg, channeling his "redneck" speaker. "The only gook an American can trust / Is a gook that's got his yellow head bust."[34] These lyrics are harsh by any standards, but that they were written and sung during the height of the Vietnam War years is both remarkable and daring. The Fugs were rarely subtle and often juvenile, but their raw parodies cut to the heart and frayed the nerves of their times as forthrightly as any other artist of the decade.

Beyond the war, the Fugs also spoke to issues closer to home and to their own cultural in-crowd. Longtime advocates of the indulgences of sex and drugs (and rock & roll), the band often brought a self-effacing humor to their own excesses. "My Bed Is Getting Crowded" (1966) and "Dirty Old Man" (1965) were wry admissions that these aging beatniks were enjoying the fruits of their labors, while "New Amphetamine Shriek" (1966) proclaimed, "If you don't like sleeping, and don't want to screw / Then you should take lots of amphetamines too."[35] Elsewhere, Sanders and Kupferberg laugh at their own literary roots, mixing highbrow pastoral writing with crude pornography. In the transcendentalist parody, "Elm Fuck Poem" (1966), Sanders recites, "How I love to rim your bark slits / Kiss the leaves above your dripping elm crotch."[36] This must have been what Kupferberg meant when he told critic Bruce Pollock, "Let's say we were a little bit sarcastic about the love thing."[37]

Although the Fugs were never welcomed into the bosoms and hearts of the broader rock culture—or even the general counterculture— they had attained a modicum of cult success by the late 1960s and had become a staple performer on the antiwar and civil rights protest circuits. However, at the peak of their popularity, in 1968, the pressures from the attention they were receiving reached unbearable proportions. Never just another band, the Fugs used shock tactics and political candor that drew a lot of backlash attention. Besides the FBI, Postal Service, and police constantly scrutinizing band operations, looking for evidence of "obscenity," the Fugs received numerous death threats and a fake bomb scare during 1968. Under the pressures of the controversy they were creating, Ed Sanders decided to withdraw from the madness and retreat back to the world of books. Tuli Kupferberg continued his Fugs-style interests in subversive politics and performance with a new troupe, Revolting Theater, but that was an even more underground operation than the Fugs had been. Little was heard from either Sanders or Kupferberg until the mid-1980s, when they decided to reunite the Fugs for the Reagan era. The band has intermittently played together since, even recording a couple of new studio albums for die-hard fans and newcomers to the Fugs-fold.

Listening to the Fugs today, one is struck by how "1960s" they sound, yet also how outside of their era their lyrical exploits seem. Sick "toilet" shockers like "Coca Cola Douche" and "River of Shit" are taboo-transgressing even by the standards of the most outrageous sixties acts. Indeed, their harsh lyrics (whether political or just profanity-laced), alongside their anyone-can-do-it attitude to songwriting, have as much in common with punk rock successors as with their hippy contemporaries. When I listen to "Dirty Old Man" I am reminded of the test-your-limits provocations of the Macc Lads and GG Allin, and when I hear "Kill for Peace" I connect it to the political bile and subversive parodies penned by the Dead Kennedys and the Sex Pistols. And when I consider the Fugs historically and geographically, I think of the traditions of New York City: its combative humor, its bohemian pride, and its rough-mannered attitudes and articulation. A counter to the dominant whimsy and childlike escapism of the California-based counterculture bands, the Fugs offered a New York state of mind—and a rebuttal—in the form of some of the blackest and sickest confrontational humor of the decade.

The Velvet Underground

Formed in the midst of the British Invasion then recording and performing during the ascendence of the West Coast hippy movement, the Velvet Underground, from New York City, embodied the essence of incongruity to both scenes. Antithetical to everyone and everything around them at the time, the Velvets sought to counter both the mainstream and the counterculture with the attitude, whatever you are, we are your opposite. Their incongruous humor did not always register as humor at the time, though the years since their demise in 1970 have seen their comedic cachet rise with the realization that within the dark corners of their bleak musical constructions lies a cynical and sarcastic humor aimed at undermining the institutional conventions of rock culture. Rebelling against the so-called rebels of West Coast rock, the Velvets crafted an antagonistic, subversive humor that would later be picked up by the glam, heavy metal, proto-punk, punk, post-punk, industrial, goth, alt, and indie genres—to name but a few—that followed.

The band's oppositional incongruity to the counterculture operated on many fronts, macro and micro, during the late sixties. Whereas the West Coast artists celebrated nature, bright colors, and visionary drugs like acid, the Velvets were urbanites, dressed in black leather, and wrote about downer drugs and downer experiences; whereas the West Coast bands wrote utopian songs about freedom and celebrated the ideals of peace, love, and understanding, the Velvets were dystopians who casually described the subterranean worlds of deviant sex, sadomasochism, and violence; and whereas whimsy and communal laughter fueled the spirit of counterculture humor, the Velvets sneered with sarcasm and presented wry observations in deadpan tones. Ostracized or largely ignored by the bands, fans, and critics of their day, the Velvets stood alone, gleefully wallowing in their own isolation and differences.

Incongruity appeared to come naturally to lead singer and songwriter Lou Reed. While pursuing his day job as a staff pop songwriter at Pickwick Records in 1965, Reed was writing songs about drug addiction ("Heroin") and S&M sex ("Venus in Furs") in his spare time. This, remember, was just a year after the Beatles had shaken and stirred the nation with songs about holding hands and how much she loves you. Reed's lyrical (mis)adventures, by contrast, seemed like they were from another planet, yet they were actually candid and realistic in their portraits of decadent NYC lifestyles. Nevertheless, set against the pop hedonism and escapism then invading U.S. shores, Reed's words were incongruous to the dominant rock narratives of the time.

Also working on the outskirts of mainstream music at the time was John Cale, an avant-garde electric viola player who was developing his drone techniques with composer La Monte Young. Desirous to bring experimentation to the rock world and impressed with Lou Reed's alternative guitar tunings, he joined forces with Reed, the two mixing their talents and interests into an alchemy that was bound to result in explosive musical potions. With the subsequent addition of Sterling Morrison on guitar and, later, Mo Tucker on drums, the "classic" Velvet Underground lineup was established.

The instrumentation provided by these four unconventional players immediately disturbed listener sensibilities and expectations. While Cale dislocated songs by washing them in a drone of viola, Tucker eschewed the standard practices of rock drumming, injecting primitive tom-tom beats while avoiding the usual stressed accentuations of snare cracks and cymbal crashes. Guitars, likewise, rode waves of feedback or jangled passively, creating atmospheric effects rather than precise notation or solos. The resulting cacophony of abrasive noise and minimalist arrangements ushered in a rock sound unprecedented at the time, but one that has become omnipresent in modern alternative rock. For most listeners at the time, the Velvets' sonic constructions were headache-inducing assaults on the ears (think "Sister Ray" [1967]), but for a few fellow outsiders they were the sounds of inspiration and outlets to the future. Iggy Pop recalls being turned on to the band in the late sixties, saying, "I heard other people [i.e., the Velvets] who could make good music—without being any good at music. It gave me hope."[38]

Although few recognized or regarded the Velvets' raw, jagged sounds as comedic, their humor operated by context, in its outrageous incongruity to the standardized sounds of the time. As Jefferson Airplane and the Grateful Dead were receiving plaudits from *Rolling Stone* and others for their innovations within the rock form, next to the Velvet Underground's music, these bands sounded tame and accessible, even conservative. Listening to the Velvets with this perspective in mind, we are amused by their blanket separation from the rock trends and expectations of the time, even from those deemed radical and revolutionary.

Besides their sound, image was another area of the band's contextual subversion, and with Andy Warhol on board as manager and executive producer between 1966 and 1967, this became a particularly pronounced element of the band's artistry. Pre-Warhol, the band already offered a striking visual identity, Lou Reed looking sinister in black leather and shades, Mo Tucker looking androgynous with her *boy*-next-door style, and John Cale looking plain weird with his Elizabethan fringe haircut. Through Warhol, though, they acquired the striking blonde model Nico as an alternative lead vocalist, and the band became integrated into Warhol's multimedia traveling "circus" roadshow, The Exploding Plastic Inevitable. Accompanied by leather-clad "whip" dancers and playing against a backdrop of Warhol's imagistic film projections, the Velvets stood statically onstage, expressionless, often with their backs to the audience. At a time when Mick Jagger was strutting around stages and Jimi Hendrix, Pete Townsend, and Keith Moon were ceremoniously destroying their instruments nightly in the name of rock authenticity, the Velvets offered an incongruous—if no less affecting—stage (anti-)presence.

Warhol made image an integral aspect of the band's packaging and marketing, too. His design for the band's debut album, *The Velvet Underground & Nico* (1967), featured a large yellow banana with the instruction alongside to "peel slowly and see." What one saw upon peeling was a bright pink banana. The humor of this gimmick worked on many levels, though principally, the contextual one was the most significantly subversive: Just as Warhol's "object" pop art silk screens comedically deconstructed the expertise and high-mindedness of prior "romantic" art, so the banana cover provided a minimalist antithesis to the dense, rainbow-colored, psychedelic hippy art of the period. Sexual innuendo is obviously at play in the visual "pun" of the banana, while others have noted that this image also alludes to the ongoing myth of the time that smoking banana peels can get you high, a put-on that Donovan further perpetuated in his single "Mellow Yellow," which was also released in 1967.

Perhaps the most striking element of the Velvets' rock incongruity was vocal. In the late sixties, vocal delivery was a key marker of legitimacy within the rock counterculture, and the kind of expression exuded by Janis Joplin and Jim Morrison was associated with the "truth" of the blues. Conversely, the Velvets brought a different kind of truth through a deadpan delivery that never lapsed into sentimentality or melodrama. If cynicism and sarcasm are detectable in Lou Reed's flat reportage vocal style, Nico betrayed no emotions at all. Her icy delivery was made even more clinical by virtue of her stark German accent. These styles were disconcerting, as though the conventional intimate subjectivity of vocal emoting had been displaced by a remote objectivity bordering on disconnection. Furthermore, the vocal style within Velvets songs underscored the lyrical contents, which were equally matter-of-fact and ambivalent. "Waiting for the Man" (1967), sung by Lou Reed, is a case in point. In a monotone drawl, Reed casually captures a day in the life of a typical heroin addict. The numbed existence of the addict is exemplified by Reed's dry narration. "He's never early, he's always late / First thing you learn is that you've always got to wait," Reed states, succinctly capturing the power position of the dealer in relation to the helpless dependence of the junkie. A slight tonal shift enters the song near the end when Reed deadpans, "I'm feeling good, I feel oh so fine" after his fix, but this is followed by the knowing realization, "Until tomorrow but that's just another time."[39] The subtle shift in vocal inflection captures the junkie's "oh so fine" momentary release from his perpetual prison, while the juxtaposition of the two lines/lives creates a paradoxical black humor both pathetic and sadly amusing.

"Heroin" (1967) is an equally bleak narrative about drug addiction, but again, a wry humor infiltrates the nihilism of the song's portrait. Our expectations are inverted from the opening line, "I don't know where I'm going," which identifies life, not heroin, as the crisis at hand. "I have made a big decision," he tells us, luring listeners into expectations of his dreams and ambitions. Instead, he informs, "I'm gonna try to nullify my life," ironically blackening the hopes of the first line. The humor here is so dark it is barely visible, but incongruity is again the key that unlocks the paradoxical phrases and underscores the irony of the junkie's assertions. "It's my wife and it's my life," the speaker says of his addiction, the positive imagery of this line deflated by the context of entrapment it is associated with. Throughout, the music drones, then charges, then settles, echoing the highs, lows, rush, relief, and pain of the narrator until, exhausted, he offers his final conclusions, prefacing each desperate line with the ambiguous prefix "Thank God": "Thank God that I'm as good as dead / Thank God that I'm not aware / Thank God that I just don't care."[40]

Perhaps needing relief from such biting sarcasm as much as his listeners, Reed sometimes incorporated lighter strains of humor into Velvets songs. If the pessimistic portraits on the debut release reflected a contextual incongruity to West Coast whimsy, by their third album, *Velvet Underground* (1969), the band were forthrightly addressing their adversarial peers. While "Jesus" appeared to suggest an ironic take on the "Jesus freak" spirituality seekers within the counterculture, "Beginning to See the Light" was a direct satire of this phenomenon. With a skipping rhythm and excitable vocal style that both register as mock-happy when set next to the (ab)normally dour tones of the band, Reed parodies the caricature happy-go-lucky hippy escapist who celebrates, "There are problems in these times / But wooo, none of them are mine."[41] How does one know this is a parody? Answer: Reed really does let out a "wooo" here! "I'm Set Free" is equally sarcastic at the expense of the hippy "seekers" with its chorus line, "I'm set free . . . to find a new illusion."[42] Reed would return to this satirical style of writing early in his solo career with the song "Vicious" from *Transformer* (1972). Reed loads proto-punk scorn into its opening anti-hippy put-down, "Vicious / You hit me with a flower."[43] Ouch, indeed!

Although the Velvet Underground would continue in name into the seventies, most consider the band finished when Lou Reed left in 1970 (and some others when John Cale was fired in 1968). Reed would continue to exhibit the kind of cynical black humor that had characterized his prior work into the next decade, songs like "Vicious" and "Walk on the Wild Side" (1972) indicating that he had lost little of his street smarts and smart-ass humor. By mid-decade, though, as punk was breaking through from the underground on both sides of the Atlantic—each side drawing sustenance from Velvet Underground aesthetics—Reed, as he had with the counterculture of the sixties, chose to run counter to the new trends. With gestures of self-parody verging on self-loathing, Reed spurned the newcomers by mocking his own past with the mellow pop collections of *Coney Island Baby* and *Rock and Roll Heart* in 1976. "I Believe in Love," from the latter album, has Reed babbling about his "belief" in "the Iron Cross" and "good-time music."[44] Even Lester Bangs, a longtime supporter of the Velvets, could only bemoan this descent/dissent into self-parody, speaking of Reed's "punch lines that kept losing their punch."[45]

Since his mid-seventies lull, Reed has returned to form intermittently, reviving the narrative bite and cynical spit(e) that once defined him. Still performing today and still hailed as the original punk provocateur, Reed watches as generations of alternative rockers from myriad musical genres draw inspiration and attitude from his past work. Critics, too, have come around to the Velvets, giving them their proper due, if belatedly. *Rolling Stone* (in 2003) listed *The Velvet Underground & Nico* at number thirteen in their "500 Greatest Albums of All Time," while both *Spin* (in 2003) and *The Observer* (in 2006) credited it as *the* most influential rock album of all time. The bands impacted by the Velvets since 1966 are far too numerous to cite here, but Brian Eno perhaps captured their legacy best when he noted that not many people bought *The Velvet Underground & Nico* when it was first released, but all of those who did went on to form their own bands.

RETREATS INTO THE FUTURE

If black humor and bubblegum represented—consciously or not—alternatives to the far-out creations emanating from the psychedelic and art rock counterculture, they were by no means the only reactions going on. The year of 1967 had been a hectic one, replete with major artists the Beatles, Stones, Doors, Cream, Jimi Hendrix Experience, and Jefferson Airplane all releasing significant albums; the rock scene appeared to be riding a great wave of innovation and creativity. Change was everywhere, each band upping the ante of artistic ambition and consciousness-raising on their (and others') recent releases. Surely the momentum could not last; surely the transformational impetus could not prevail. It didn't.

The immediate post-1967 years saw catastrophe strike the counterculture on many fronts: Martin Luther King Jr. and Robert Kennedy, both youth-inspirational leaders in the struggles for civil rights and to end the war in Vietnam, were assassinated in 1968; the 1969 Woodstock Music Festival, a city-on-the-hill (at least, in a field) symbol of communal cooperation and the counterculture's value system of peace, love, and understanding, was followed a few months later with the violent bloodbath of Altamont; in 1970 and 1971 rock culture lost three of its leading innovators—Jimi Hendrix, Janis Joplin, and Jim Morrison—to premature (and needless) deaths; the Beatles, once the symbolic embodiment of the rock *group*, fell apart, acrimoniously fighting among themselves in the media or in the courts.

The expansive world of possibility felt during the 1967 summer of love had, within a year or two, transformed; the scene soon turned to siege, as withdrawal and jaded defeat became the new sentiments replacing enlightenment and confrontation. The retreats at the end of the decade signaled the end of an era, as rockers looked back to folk and country cultures for escapist solace and a place to hide. Simon & Garfunkel's resigned and plaintive *Bridge Over Troubled Water* (1970) album symbolized the counterculture's flight from electric rock's combative styles and eccentric whimsy into a new introspection that would dominate rock over the forthcoming years. The back-to-the-land romanticism of the hippy subculture became a literal withdrawal at the turn of the decade. The new consensus seemed to be that the only way to escape from Nixon's American culture of violence, oppression, and commercialism was to escape into nature and yourself. Rock in the early 1970s would represent this calm after the storm, the emergence of the singer-songwriter—alone with an acoustic guitar or piano—signaling the breakup of the communal (band) concept and the birth of inward-looking individuals with only bleak strains of humor in their hearts.

THE SEVENTIES:

Radical Cynicism

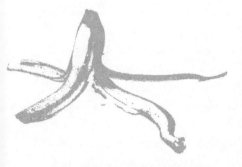

I N ONE OF the more pensive moments of his fin de siècle "gonzo" novel, *Fear and Loathing in Las Vegas*, Hunter S. Thompson reflects upon the collective feelings of the counterculture around 1966 and 1967. He writes of "that sense of inevitable victory over the forces of Old and Evil," of the belief that "our energy would simply *prevail*. We had all the momentum . . . We were riding the crest of a high and beautiful wave . . . " However, fast-forwarding to the then-present 1971, Thompson bemoans the evaporation of those optimistic sentiments, saying, "So now, less than five years later . . . you can almost *see* the high-water mark—that place where the wave finally broke and rolled back."[1]

As Thompson's character/alter ego continues to reflect upon the "passing" of the 1960s, he finds an apt metaphor in the changes in drug consumption with the dawn of the new decade, musing that "'Consciousness Expansion' went out with LBJ . . . and it is worth noting, historically, that downers came in with Nixon."[2] Lou Reed similarly perceived drugs as indicators of cultural identity and expression. He was being only partially glib when he said that the difference between the Velvet Underground's cynical street poetry and the West Coast's escapist hedonism was that the Velvets did heroin and their counterparts did acid.[3] Just as drugs played an integral part in characterizing the rock—and the rock humor—of the 1960s, so too would they be a factor in the succeeding decade.

A historical argument exists in some quarters that drugs—as much as anything else—were responsible for the death of the sixties, that the revolutionary dream of a collective utopia ultimately turned into a nightmare of drug-induced, self-indulgent excesses. The long, strange trip of the counterculture may have started with "we," but it ended with "me." Drugs cannot change the world, the argument went, they can only change the self. And though drugs would continue to play a significant role in seventies rock culture—breathing new smoke, as it were, into new strains of rock humor—drug-inspired rock would be increasingly oriented to the individual rather than the collective, to personal freedom rather than mass consciousness, and toward sardonic cynicism rather than celebratory idealism. No more would the childlike whimsy of Country Joe McDonald and the San Francisco set permeate rock humor; instead, the harsh sarcastic sneers of post-Velvets gutter-punks and the embittered satire of post-sixties souls in retreat would provide the wit that would simultaneously reflect and comment upon the "Me" decade.

Sixties unity was further undermined by the reality that rock had grown up and fled the nest in myriad directions. The burst of creative ambition that had made the late sixties such a musically exciting time opened up new options and possible directions. Furthermore, the rock-listening demographic was ageing, its older advocates drawn to more adult-oriented fare and its new disciples demanding quite the opposite. The result was expansion and fragmentation, an opening up of the rock field to the point where it splintered into multiple genres. By the early 1970s, the catch-all genre of "rock" had been replaced with singer-songwriters and folk rock at one end of the spectrum and everything from funk to heavy metal on the other, the former kinds of music played on "adult-oriented rock" (or AOR) radio, the latter types secluded on the outskirts of the dial.

As the industry splintered, so it also grew. What had been termed the counterculture was becoming the culture. No longer manning the barricades on the margins, the big rock acts of the seventies embraced the mainstream. Artists like Elton John, Fleetwood Mac, and Peter Frampton became big-business acts, playing stadium tours and living in luxurious mansions. Their records were slick and inoffensive, but they lacked the sharp humor, imagination, and energy of their predecessors. By the mid-seventies, such mainstream rock dominated the airwaves and stadiums of America and beyond.

But as the profitable conveyor belt continued, an air of complacent staidness took hold. Young people, particularly, began to crave a shot of energy, an element of surprise, some excitement. And if the industry (and its bloated rock star stooges) would not provide an alternative, then the kids would provide it themselves. The glam, metal, funk, and punk genres that came into being in the seventies were youths' answers to the anemic state of rock culture. These genres used raging humor in defense and attack against the corporate forces that had sanitized the rock form. Entrenched in the margins, these new youth genres lobbed satirical missiles and missives, not only at the forces of the present, but also at the failed myths and promises of the past. As the decade unfolded, these new primal movements provided the energy that would invigorate rock culture then and for decades to come. Their counteractive humor provided the principal front against corporate blandness, drawing sustenance from their participants' status as youths marginalized by their social class and/or race and/or education and/or gender and/or sexuality and/or age.

Beyond the new youth factions of glam, funk, metal, and punk, subversive rock humor could also be detected within the mainstream body. As enemies within, these upstarts provided a second front against the "sellouts" and profiteers of rock's ruling hegemony. From within Los Angeles, home to so many of the super-groups and AOR singer-songwriters of the 1970s, cynics like Warren Zevon and Randy Newman provided humorous counter-thrusts to the earnest introspections of their peers.

LOST IN L.A.

Long the locus of the American Dream mythos, the letters "L.A." have always conjured up more than just the physical city of Los Angeles. Sunshine, wealth, sea, blue skies, freedom, eternal youth, beauty, and fantasy are but a few images and ideas that come to mind when the city's name is evoked. During the 1960s, the idealism and escapism of such acts as the Mamas & the Papas, the Beach Boys, and the Byrds defined perceptions of the city. California itself, as Mama Cass sang, truly was a kind of "dreamin'." As the seventies dawned, L.A. remained center stage on the rock landscape, though its emerging artists began to express quite different emotions. Gone were the communal hippy vibe and fantasy hedonism; in their place emerged a new introspection and serious lyric poetry. Post-hippy Angelian residents like Joni Mitchell and Jackson Browne, exhausted and confused by the failures of the counterculture's idealism as well as by the violence, commercialism, and fragmentation that had taken hold of the "peace" movement, withdrew into self-examination and solipsism. Although not totally humorless, these "singer-songwriters" dispensed with the whimsy, playfulness, and good cheer of the hippy high tide, bringing forth a new undercurrent of personal anguish, alienation, and bitterness. Sometimes a self-deprecating humor lingered uncomfortably over their confessionals, but invariably their lyric-poems were sad and serious in tone and content. Indeed, there's little room for anything but tears and misery as one follows Joni Mitchell undergoing personal therapy throughout the harrowing "diary" songs on her cathartic *Blue* (1971) and *Court and Spark* (1974) albums.

Indeed, speaking to a twenty- and thirtysomething demographic of mostly middle-class white (ex-)students, the new L.A. songwriters channeled the poetic spirits of Sylvia Plath and Anne Sexton as they gazed within, as if to say, "We failed to change the outside world; perhaps we can transform ourselves." Or, as Janet Maslin observed: "Even the most euphoric of flower children were beginning both to need and feel their solitude, and to feel the strain of artificially imposed selflessness."[4] Sometimes narcissistic, sometimes penetrating, the likes of James Taylor and Carole King performed—like Joni Mitchell—psychological self-analysis in search of a new personal authenticity. This pursuit often resulted in heady stuff, with intimate outpourings of distress, depression, and frustration delivered first-person to the listener. Not surprisingly, these autobiographical confessions lacked the kind of eccentric humor that had become such a dominant force in late-sixties rock music.

To some, such songwriting was pure self-indulgence, therapy not art. Such critics found the humorless ramblings of these spoiled middle-class would-be poets to be the recognizable tags of the emerging "Me" generation. That these detractors were growing weary or were just not interested in the sensitive self-revelations of the singer-songwriter brigade is not surprising; that some of these critics were peers and artists working within the same fold was. Tom Waits, for example, though a fellow L.A.-based singer-songwriter, represented a very different literary approach to lyricism, one that looked outward rather than inward. His tales of winos, bums, and hard-luck loners evoked the California of Charles Bukowski or the Beats. Also eschewing the autobiographical "I" and casting their imaginative scope beyond the internal rumblings of the self, L.A.-insider singer-songwriters like Warren Zevon and Randy Newman challenged the parameters of the form's style and content. Their satirical injunctions skewered the internal conventions of rock norms, but they also looked beyond, offering detailed tall tales and pun-fueled observations on their immediate and broader cultural surroundings. Zevon and Newman showed that there was a new type of singer-songwriter in town, armed with attitude and humor and not afraid to use them.

Warren Zevon

As bizarre and outlandish as many of Warren Zevon's 1970s story-songs seemed, in many respects they were also oblique but pointed documentaries of time and place. Zevon's muse was the Los Angeles in which he networked and operated, and which he ultimately satirized. A player at the heart of the L.A. singer-songwriter scene, he served as an enemy within—both to its other practitioners and to himself. As his peers and friends (the Eagles, Fleetwood Mac, and Jackson Browne among them) offered laid-back reflections on the alienated self in the burnout period of the post-sixties, Zevon offered insurgent urgency and a wild-man imagination. His songs ranged from faux-jaunty rockers about criminal misfits to tortured ballads on longing and lost love. In all instances, he infused his writing with a deadpan humor—sometimes targeted externally, sometimes self-deprecating—that was influenced by California's hard-boiled literary and film tradition. A wordsmith to the core, Zevon was one of rock's most literary and literate lyricists and humorists.

Though he afforded himself generous poetic license, the woefully comic misadventures in songs like "Roland the Headless Thompson Gunner" (1978) and "Mama Couldn't Be Persuaded" (1976) also reflected upon Zevon's own family upbringing. According to Zevon, his father was an itinerant gambler and gun-wielding gangster who never let the family get in the way of a get-rich-quick scheme. That thrill-seeking spirit was inherited by Zevon himself and manifested during his own legendary "cowboy" drinking years (the seventies and eighties), and in the characters featured periodically in his tall-tale songs. Like Woody Guthrie, Zevon had a fascination with rogues and populist heroes. His "Frank and Jesse James" (1976) echoes Guthrie's own outlaw odes and shares the same populist point of view. In his song, Zevon narrates how the James gang rode against the railroads, banks, and governor, "And never did they ask for a word of thanks."[5]

Zevon's music reflected a general interest in Western myths that was pronounced among the L.A. rock set. Frontier themes and cowboy characters provided parallels for counterculture romanticism, and by the end of the sixties various artists drew analogies between the death of the counterculture and the closing of the frontier. Indeed, the exhausted cowboy became a fitting metaphor for the lost idealists of the post-sixties rock culture. Neil Young's *After the Gold Rush* (1970) and the Eagles' *Desperado* (1973) albums captured and spoke to this pervasive mood. More cynic than sentimentalist, though, Zevon transferred his desperados to less romantic settings, such as Russia, Cuba, and Honduras in "Lawyers, Guns, and Money" (1978), or the Hollywood Hawaiian Hotel in "Desperados under the Eaves" (1976). The latter satirized L.A. rock's self-indulgent coke and booze set (of which he was an active participant). Set the morning after the night before, Zevon's "I" narrator reflects upon his dead-end life as he stares into his "empty coffee cup." The hotel has become his last-stop enclave, a protective womb of money-no-object self-annihilation. "Heaven help the one who leaves," he warns. Like the Eagles with "Hotel California," Zevon here looks into the abyss of seventies rock life in the fast lane. And as the like-minded Jackson Browne concluded a couple of years later, it was "running on empty." However, whereas the Eagles and Browne presented their funereal forecasts with pain and earnest desperation, Zevon's treatment embodied the sardonic tone of the satirist. The conclusion of the song has his character "listening to the air conditioner hum."[6] Then, with soaring irony, the string section carries the song into a two-minute mantra of epic melody, with Zevon plaintively humming the sound of the air conditioner into the tunnel of nothingness. Never has the void sounded so glorious.

Taken from the Jackson Browne–produced *Warren Zevon* (1976), "Desperados Under the Eaves" serves as a personal reflection of his own alcoholic demise, as well as a pointed metaphor of L.A. rock's narcissistic Roman Empire–like debauchery, the dirt behind the California daydream duly revealed. Elsewhere on this album, Zevon punctures the romanticism of California dreaming. In "Join Me in L.A." he quips, "They say this place is evil / That ain't why I stay," and in "The French Inhaler" he digs beneath the glitz, glamour, and phoniness of the Hollywood starlet (of rock and film).[7] Describing a scarves-clad woman who sounds suspiciously like Stevie Nicks,

Zevon unveils the sad emptiness behind the vain Hollywood party brigade. "Drugs and wine and flattering light / You must try it again until you get it right," he observes, succinctly capturing a Hollywood hedonism as alive and kicking today as then and before.[8]

Zevon's (self-)parodies of L.A. rock star indulgences and the increasing separation of rockers from both the real world and their fans reflected similar perceptions emanating from the burgeoning punk rock genre. It was tough for street kids to relate to the existential crises of having too much money and too many groupies at one's beck and call. Zevon, ever the poet of the misfit and loser, sympathized with punk's embittered rage, welcoming their revolt in "Johnny Strikes Up the Band" (1978), a tribute to Johnny Rotten. "They'll be rocking in the projects," Zevon predicts of the new insurgence.[9] Zevon's grotesque song characters, furthermore, shared punk's danger, unpredictability, and wildness. "Excitable Boy" (1978) comically juxtaposes a jaunty melody with its lyrical tale of a high school rapist/murderer who later digs up the grave of his victim "and [builds] a cage with her bones."[10] Such disturbed and bizarre imagery reflected the macabre humor of Zevon, as well as his wild imagination and sense of detail. "Werewolves of London" (1978), his biggest hit, likewise charts the journey of a debauched character on the rampage. The song's "hairy-handed gent who ran amok in Kent" was like a rebel rocker, a dandy whose "hair was perfect."[11] Within the rock mainstream, where corporate conservatism kept lyrical f(l)are within tight and formulaic confines, the arrival of "Werewolves of London" in the U.S. top thirty was a breath of fresh air equivalent to the Sex Pistols ripping up the U.K. charts with "God Save the Queen" a year prior.

Although his occasional commercial success and general critical acclaim have largely revolved around upbeat, madcap character songs, Zevon also wrote many personal relationship songs over the course of his career. Invariably driven by pain, loss, and longing, his love songs rarely celebrate the happiness of love, and the humor therein is of the self-effacing kind. These songs—"Hasten Down the Wind" (1976), "Reconsider Me" (1987), "Nobody's in Love This Year" (1989) among them—are heartbreaking ballads that certainly do not evoke the belly laughs of his comic adventure story-songs. However, the humorist, when serious, is one to take seriously. Because the comic often hides his/her emotions behind the mask of humor, when private emotions are expressed they often feel both weightier and more authentic. Such is the case with the sad poignancy, though never sentimentality, that Zevon brings to these reflective songs. There is resilient courage to songs like "Accidentally Like a Martyr" (1976) and "Empty-Handed Heart" (1980) that resonates because we expect Zevon to retreat behind his more comfortable wall of humor. But he does not. The quality humorist can thus generate additional emotive power by foregoing as well as using the art of wit.

A similar comedic courage is in evidence in Zevon's later songs, which both predict his future ill health and demise and comment upon them. Ironically, the *Life'll Kill Ya* (2000) and *My Ride's Here* (2002) albums were both written and released before he was diagnosed with terminal cancer. These titles would thus appear quite prophetic, except for the fact that Zevon had long stared into the face of death. Early songs like "I'll Sleep When I'm Dead" (1976) were mischievous ruminations on his dancing-with-death decadence and alcoholism. However, by *Life'll Kill Ya*, his "F. Scott Fitzevon" days were well behind him, and his conversations with the grim reaper contained a wry rather than raucous humor. The album's title track—as well as such other cuts as "My Shit's Fucked Up" and "Don't Let Us Get Sick"—showcases a gallows humor of unblinking bravery, and on the title track he wittily observes an eternal verity: "From the President of the United States / To the lowliest rock and roll star / The doctor is in / And he'll see you now."[12] The cover sleeve of *My Ride's Here* has Zevon blankly staring out from the window of a hearse. Along with his final album of goodbyes, *The Wind* (2003), Zevon's last three releases offer the ultimate challenge to the humorist: how to act in the face of imminent death. That he responded with humor in dignity and dignity in humor is a tribute to his strength and courage.

Other tributes poured in once Zevon's fate became publicly known. For decades, fellow comedian David Letterman had admired and supported Zevon's work, and on October 30, 2002, he dedicated the whole hour of his show to saying his farewells to his friend. "Enjoy every sandwich," Zevon responded when Letterman asked him how to face impending death. Other comedian-friends, Hunter S. Thompson and Dave Barry, also rallied to his side, as well as longtime musician-fans like Bob Dylan, Neil Young, and members of REM.

Subverting the inner sanctum of his own L.A. songwriting circle, the formulaic clichés of the conventional love song, and even death itself, Warren Zevon cast a broad comedic net over his thirty-year career. His grotesque characters and (a)cute observations of human foibles and frailties have made him the leading comic noir rock writer of his generation. And despite his storied association with other L.A. singer-songwriters, his work actually has as much in common with the subsequent punk cynics who arrived as antagonists to that school of rock. Zevon's current cult popularity among the more literary-minded of indie rockers suggests that his style of word-centered songwriting may be rare, but it has not been forgotten.

Randy Newman

Randy Newman cannot be trusted; therein lies the essence of his humor. A master of the unreliable-narrator literary device, Newman has often been burdened with the inevitable consequences of being wrongly associated with the "I" of his speakers. "Short People" (1978), for example, his biggest hit, is narrated by a bigoted "height-ist" who states—among other put-downs—that "short people have got no reason to live."[13] A diminutive fellow himself, Newman no doubt presumed that listeners would perceive the purpose of the song to be a satirical criticism of mindless prejudice. However, for some, the joke went right over their heads (so to speak). They thought the narrator *was* Newman and that the song's extreme and absurd statements (e.g., "You've got to pick them up just to say hello") were reflections of the songwriter's prejudices. Such misreading (or maybe satire-denial) even reached the Maryland legislature, where a certain 5'5" member sought to ban the song from the state's airwaves. Newman, perplexed by the vitriolic feedback he was receiving, also reveled in the moment, never missing an opportunity at his live shows to reiterate how much he *really* hated short people.

This experience—not the only one of this kind in Newman's career—begs the bigger question of the satirist's responsibility for the reception of his/her work. The answer lies in what constitutes effective satire. For the humor to work through the outlet of the unreliable narrator, that speaker must be sufficiently exaggerated for listeners to be able to discern that character as caricature; the speaker must also be extreme and disturbed enough for us to question his/her veracity and credibility. Thusly mocked (by his/her own words), the narrator is strategically distanced by the controlling artistry of the author. That author, in turn, must have moral purpose behind his/her mockery, using superiority humor in the tradition of Greek theater, where the targets are worthy of chastening, and the victims rhetorically rewarded. For the most part, Randy Newman has attained this balancing act with the concomitant restraint and provocation necessary for such a subversive strategy to be successful. In some instances, though, such as in "Old Man" (1972), with its mocking denunciation of the central character's blind faith and worthlessness, even Newman has doubted whether his "ageist" narrator was effectively unreliable. Conversely, the artist, surely, should not be held responsible for lazy misreadings such as those proffered on "Short People" by the Maryland legislator and others.

Like that of fellow Los Angelian Warren Zevon, Randy Newman's humor has strong literary influences. But whereas Zevon drew from the comic noir of his city's hard-boiled novelists, Newman's style of satire dates back to the less-than-reliable narrators of Geoffrey Chaucer and such practitioners of the form as Jonathan Swift, Mark Twain, and J.D. Salinger. Their narrator-centered satire pursued the common purpose of social comment through ridicule, attained by letting exploiters, hypocrites, racists, and liars expose their own deplorable flaws. Randy Newman works within this tradition.

Where Zevon satirized the in-crowd characters and decadent spaces of Los Angeles in the mid-seventies, Newman tended to skewer his hometown through more general indictments against the greed inherent within the American Dream during the "Me" and "Mean" decades of the seventies and eighties. "It's Money That I Love" (1979) and "It's the Money That Matters" (1988) offer Zappa-like stabs at vapid materialism; L.A. lingers in the subtext, the "elephant" in the lyric. Where he does directly take on the city, as in "I Love L.A.," Newman is actually at his most satirically half-hearted. Here, the writer's attempt to be both affectionate and mocking is largely unsuccessful, as the mocking element lacks sufficient punch to trump the affection. It is not surprising, and hardly a product of misinterpretation, that "I Love L.A." has become a sports stadium rallying cry—a good-hearted tribute to the city—since the song's release. Such a reception, one suspects, was only partially Newman's intent, though it was almost entirely his fault.

This ambivalent employment of satire runs the risk of the intended message getting lost in translation, even when the authorial juggling act is inspired by good intentions. Tackling such raw-nerve topics as slave-trading ("Sail Away" [1972]) and imperialism ("Political Science" [1972]), Newman often applied his bag of tricks to individual characters who, while dislikeable, also deserved sympathy. By writing multifaceted characters rather than the more conventional (within humor) one-dimensional "types," Newman established difficult challenges for himself, for it is a lot easier to laugh *at* stock characters than to laugh *with* and feel *for* realistic ones—while still laughing *at* them. It speaks to his sophistication as a humorist that he rarely settled for the easier constructions and receptions of the former type.

The concept album *Good Old Boys* (1974) involved Newman crafting historical themes of Southern economic hardship during the Great Depression years of the 1930s. Set in the Deep South, the songs work through the narrative voice of Johnny Cutler, a fictional character. Cutler is a hard-drinking, working-class mill employee, ignorant, a failure, but a man proud of his home, hearth, and family. Although intent on exposing the Southern racism of the likes of Johnny Cutler, Newman also refuses merely to mock a character who is afflicted in other respects (poverty, lack of education). The comedic result is an ambivalent form of satire, with layers of subversion, but also with uneasy and uncertain authorial positions on its issues. "Rednecks," the album's most controversial cut, is an example of satire with daring balance and sophistication. The song starts with Cutler describing a TV talk show he has watched the night before. The show is hosted by a "smart-ass New York Jew" (apparently Dick Cavett), and the main guest, racist Georgia governor Lester Maddox, is "set up" for a dose of ridicule next to an opposing all-liberal panel, audience, and host. Cutler, offended, poignantly says of Maddox, "Well, he may be a fool but he's our fool / And if they think they're better than him they're wrong." By this point (the end of the first verse), Newman has managed to turn audience sympathies against the "redneck" racist narrator; however, he has also drawn them back by highlighting the self-righteousness of the liberals who have manufactured this unfair fight. But just when we are connecting to the dignity and humanity of the narrator, Newman returns to his primary purpose of mocking his racist speaker, who boasts, "We're rednecks . . . and we're keeping the niggers down." Nevertheless, Newman returns to his second-tier target at the end of the song as he lists the various "cages" of racism that exist throughout the North ("Harlem in New York City," "the South-Side of Chicago," "Hough in Cleveland," "East St. Louis," "Fillmore in San Francisco," and "Roxbury in Boston"), thereby underscoring the blinkered hypocrisy of his cast of liberal characters.[14] "Rednecks" is a tour de force of satirical bite, an equal-opportunity assault on all offenders. That it can still create critical space for empathy with Cutler reflects the considerate humanity of Newman's humorist project.

The *Good Old Boys* album, though time-capsuled within its 1930s setting, addresses a geopolitical subtext that still resonates today: the national neglect of the South. "Louisiana 1927" (1974) recalls the massive flood of that year, the devastating destruction it brought to the city of New Orleans, and the desperate feelings of the largely poor populace who helplessly witnessed the federal government's uncaring inaction. "They're trying to wash us away," bemoans the maudlin singer/narrator.[15] Not surprisingly, this song has been much cited and covered in the wake of the recent flooding of New Orleans and other Southern coastal regions when governmental authorities stood idly by, just as they had in 1927.

"Political Science" (1972), a song originally intended as a mockery of America's global ambitions in the wake of the spreading Vietnam War, also has much prescience in relation to America's international role at the start of the twenty-first century. Narrated by another American "redneck" type, the opening lines are "No one likes us / I don't know why." Mirroring Merle Haggard–style national braggadocio, the speaker suggests the appropriate course of action: "Let's drop the big one and see what happens." Throughout, the narrator bemoans international ingratitude for all the aid the United States passes out, resolving that the only way to teach the rest of the world how to be "peaceful" and "free" like America is to bomb them into submission. Loaded with irony and bristling with absurdly comic statements of justification, such as "Asia's crowded," "Africa is far too hot," and "South America stole our name," Newman rails against the ignorance and insularity of Americans' global perspective, as well as the economic motivations at the root of its foreign policy impositions. Reviewed in the wake of the recent invasion and occupation of Iraq, "Political Science" is a testament to the curious fact that reality can sometimes catch up with satire. One can almost hear Donald Rumsfeld's dismissal of "Old Europe" when the song's narrator justifies "dropping the big one" because "Europe's too old."[16] Whether these songs reveal the timelessness of good humor or merely that history is destined to repeat itself, Newman's songs of decades past are proving of late to be quite uncanny in their prophetic reach and resonance.

Randy Newman's most caustic social satire songs were released on his three great seventies albums, *12 Songs* (1970), *Sail Away* (1972), and the aforementioned *Good Old Boys* (1974). Although he has intermittently continued to record studio albums since, he has mostly turned his talents to writing film scores, following in a family tradition that includes various uncle and cousin composers.

These works have developed a lighter humor, and their critical and popular acclaim have brought Newman fifteen Oscar nominations (and one win). This renown has made him the broadly successful artist that his rock career never did. For his sins, he has even enjoyed the backlash of counter-parodists, and he has been caricatured on the TV shows *Mad T.V.*, *Family Guy*, and *Queer Duck*.

Within rock traditions, despite often being lumped in with the other singer-songwriters of the early seventies L.A., Newman has operated quite differently. While James Taylor, Joni Mitchell, and Jackson Browne used introspection as a way to reveal common feelings, Newman—like Warren Zevon—took the L.A. road less traveled, looking outward in order to look inward, imagining characters and voices that would reflect not only their own selves but also the culture and communities within which they lived. By employing humor as the means to their spectacles, Newman and Zevon were able to re-see their worlds for others, broadening perceptions by expanding imaginations.

FIGHT THE POWERS

The roots of the radical strains of 1970s black music were most immediately located in the "black power" movement that had developed during the second half of the 1960s. The most visible and magnetizing symbol of black power to young African Americans was the Black Panther Party for Self-Defense. The Black Panthers not only hardened the youth civil rights struggle but they also brought a separatist strain to the movement. By the late 1960s, the integrationist Martin Luther King–led NAACP was seen (by many) as floundering, as too accommodating as it attained insufficient gains. In reaction, the Malcolm X–inspired black power movement attracted many young African Americans to a more extreme expression of black politics, one not reliant on handouts or concessions from the white political establishment. Taking their lives and culture (and sometimes the law) into their own hands, black power advocates sought self-sufficiency and self-affirming pride.

This development had its correlative in rock culture, too. Moving away from the conciliatory "please whitey" sounds and images of Motown and the girl groups, artists like James Brown and Sly & the Family Stone began to strike out and to speak out. Brown's "Say It Loud, I'm Black & I'm Proud" (1968) became the signature song of black power, and Sly's *There's a Riot Goin' On* (1971) brought candor to black realities of social degradation and urban militancy. These paved the way for the arrival of some key black acts at the turn of the decade. Both Gil Scott-Heron and the Last Poets brought a new street style and grit to black music; moreover, they introduced an incisive satirical approach that had been markedly absent from much black music of the previous decade. It was as if the serious survival instinct of black reality in the 1960s was finding a new self-confidence in its expression, a new pride that enabled black culture to reinvigorate its indigenous humor for the seventies. *Rolling Stone* critic Geoffrey Stokes concurs, saying, "[T]he subversive sentiment underlying the joke would remain buried until the twin notions of black pride and black power caught fire among the younger generation of blacks."[17] Unmasking hypocrisy and exposing injustice with vernacular wit and sarcastic stabs, the proto-rap militancy of Scott-Heron and the Last Poets captured the new mood—one famously articulated in the stand-up comedy of another young innovative upstart making waves at the time, Richard Pryor.

Eclecticism and diversity were the positive trends of black music going into the seventies, with separation and disunity being their negative underpinnings. Motown, a staple of stability and black music visibility during the prior decade, was splintering as the company headed into the 1970s. It was no longer able to contain its key artists within its strict formulas: Stevie Wonder and Marvin Gaye began to write with the social realism and self-reliance that the black power movement had fostered. Their unwillingness to play by Berry Gordy's rules suggested that the company's strategy of accommodating white expectations was no longer acceptable to the new consciousness of young black America. As Motown underwent its identity crisis, Philadelphia International Records moved into the vacuum with a roster of sweet soul acts like the O'Jays, the Three Degrees, and Harold Melvin & the Blue Notes. Although hardly subversive, the so-called "Philly" sound produced grooves more attuned to the laid-back "cool" of early 1970s black music. Other emerging artists, like Curtis Mayfield, also represented the new style, exuding self-confidence with a dash of street arrogance. His soundtrack music for "Blaxploitation" ghetto movies like *Super Fly* (1972) connected his style to hip street credibility and black self-assertion. The genre's exaggerated pastiche of crime film conventions also gave such music a sly tongue-in-cheek edge. Despite black power's influence on the products of early-seventies black culture, the overall state of affairs was somewhat uninspiring and staid—much as it was in the white rock culture of the period. The slow crawl of reggae music from Jamaica to the United States gave indications that radical black music was afoot, but young urban blacks were craving some home-grown sounds that would reinject the same kind of energy, wit, and wisdom that James Brown and Sly & the Family Stone had offered in the preceding years. They found it in an unconventional eccentric called George Clinton, a funk pioneer who promised to "rescue dance music from the blahs."[18]

Clinton's celebratory but hard-edged humor—in his bands Parliament and Funkadelic—gave a subversive strain to black music in the seventies that would contribute to the birth of rap music and hip-hop culture at the close of the decade. Alongside Clinton, black power satirical rabble-rousers like Gil Scott-Heron provided a radical wit that set itself against the formulaic disco and "buttered" soul spread across African American (and white) culture throughout the decade.

Gil Scott-Heron

Although the increased militancy of the black underground in the late 1960s had drawn artists like Marvin Gaye, Stevie Wonder, and the Temptations into more sociopolitical territory—both in terms of their lyrics and their more Afrocentric musical styles—the trajectory of most black music was, as noted, toward the kind of gentle string-laden soul that would later morph into disco music. One new soulful artist of the period who refused to take this mainstream route was Gil Scott-Heron. Quite the contrary, his jazz-soul-funk "poems" moved with the rhythms of the hard urban streets and the militant cynical consciousness of the black power movement. Like that of his peers the Black Poets, Scott-Heron's literary songwriting made him only tangentially connected to rock culture, but his fused-forms style also gave him a distinction and a voice unique to the times.

Scott-Heron's poetic sensibility was inspired and molded during his childhood. Gil's parents divorced when he was young; his Jamaican-born father was an ex-professional soccer player for Scotland's famous Celtic club, and his mother was a college-graduate librarian. Born in Chicago, Gil experienced the tense years of (de-) segregation when the family moved to Tennessee. As a teen he moved to the Bronx in New York City, where he witnessed the burgeoning black power movement firsthand. After a year at Lincoln University in Pennsylvania, he published his first novel, *The Vulture*, and dropped out to become a professional writer.

By 1970 he was combining his writing skills with a growing passion for jazz, soul, and African music. His debut album release of that year, *Small Talk at 125th and Lenox*, was greeted by the radical in-crowd as a revelation for the revolution. With his sardonic all-out assaults on white hegemony (represented by the government, corporations, media, and police), Scott-Heron proposed strategies for self-defense based on those of the Black Panther Party. Like that organization, Scott-Heron called for self-consciousness and self-determination, taking individual responsibility for community survival. Moreover, he articulated such serious messages with an urgent and pointed humor. Combining the vernacular satire of Dick Gregory and Richard Pryor with the articulate aggression of Amiri Baraka, Scott-Heron provided a powerful relief humor by airing the feelings and frustrations that urban black communities sublimated and dared not voice. For many, he became the voice of the collectively repressed.

The striking centerpiece of his debut album was "The Revolution Will Not Be Televised" (1970), a cut many cite as the prototype of the rap form. In the fire-and-brimstone voice of an apocalyptic street preacher, Gil warns of the impending black revolution. Originally inspired by a Last Poets' piece that envisioned the TV coverage of a black street uprising, Gil's sequel proclaimed that "the revolution will be live." With its "you" pronoun pointed directly at young black urban youth, the song develops into a sociopolitical action manifesto, a wake-up call with a how-to and how-not-to program. Throughout, Gil points to the myriad enemies of the revolutionary consciousness, skewering each with vernacular wit and pertinent allusions of the time:

- **Mediation:** Warning would-be revolutionaries that television—in all its forms—is the opiate of the masses keeping black people inert and inactive, Scott-Heron wittily twists Timothy Leary's hippy mantra, saying, "You will not be able to 'plug in, turn on, and cop out.'" With its transmissions of false reality, a whitewashed world, and the ideal of passive reception, television is shown to be a systemic tool to keep black people in a condition of mindless escapism when they should be "in the street looking for a brighter day."

- **Drugs and alcohol:** "You will not be able to lose yourself on skag / . . . Or skip out for beer during commercials," admonishes the narrator. As he similarly expressed in subsequent songs like "The Bottle" (1973), "Angel Dust" (1978), and "The Needle's Eye" (1971), Gil regarded drugs and alcohol as more "opiates" that disable, disarm, and dispirit black people, destroying the broader community's survival. Ironically and sadly, he has fallen foul himself to cocaine addiction in recent years.

- **Political establishment:** "The revolution will not show you pictures of Nixon blowing a bugle and leading a charge by John Mitchell, General Abrams, and Spiro Agnew to eat hog maws confiscated from a Harlem sanctuary." Besides mocking these primary symbols of national power and black exploitation (the Abrams reference alluding to the disproportionate drafting of black youth onto the front lines of the Vietnam War), Gil also ridicules establishment black leaders who have turned their backs on the struggles in the streets, instead becoming cozy with the broader white political establishment: "There will be no slow motion or still life of Roy Wilkens strolling through Watts in a red, black, and green liberation jumpsuit that he had been saving for just the proper occasion." Wilkens, then executive director of the NAACP, was seen, like his organization, as out-of-touch with young black America. Tired of the negotiated accommodations of the NAACP and other "old guard" black rights organizations, Scott-Heron was increasingly drawn to the activist philosophies espoused by Malcolm X and the Black Panthers.

- **Police:** "There will be no pictures of pigs shooting down brothers in the instant replay. / There will be no pictures of pigs shooting down brothers in the instant replay," Gil instantly replays. The slang term for the police—the most visible "arm" of the white establishment presence—"pigs," had by the seventies become ubiquitous in black communities and beyond, reflecting the broadly held feeling that the police were the state's most immediate oppressor.

- **Women:** Within the macho, quasi-militaristic world of Black Panther politics—not to mention the male-dominated and male-defined world of rock music—women were either romanticized objects (at best) or (more commonly) second-class citizens. Feminists, who by the early seventies were felt by the black power movement to be co-opting their struggle and stealing their public thunder, were often the recipients of backlash scorn and reactionary sarcasm; Gil's media envy is articulated in "Revolution" when he bitterly opines, "There will be . . . no pictures of hairy-armed women liberationists and Jackie Onassis blowing her nose."[19]

Although hardly the model of political correctness, "The Revolution Will Not Be Televised" signaled a rare shout-out from the streets at the start of the seventies, a newsflash from an angle you would never see on TV. It was also a precedent recording that young upstarts like Chuck D and KRS-One heard from within their own respective urban pockets, inspiring them to their own future songwriting provocations.

Many of Scott-Heron's early songs modeled the oratory methods preferred by the Last Poets, a barren backdrop of an African bongo beat employed rather than a full band. The result was that his lyrical substance and deadpan delivery could be showcased. Two such song-poems, "Brother" (1970) and "Whitey on the Moon" (1970), adopt this kind of bare, voice-activated arrangement. In the former, Scott-Heron conducts an examination of his own youth culture, censuring "brothers" for their laziness, irresponsibility, and anti-educational inverted snobbery: "Jumping down on some black man with both feet 'cause they're after their B.A. / But always missin' when your B.A. is in danger. / I mean your black ass!"[20] (He would later level a similar missive at the "gangsta" rappers of the early 1990s with "Message to the Messengers" [1993], a rebuke to their gunslinger romanticism and dumb-slang posturing.) "Whitey on the Moon" targets outward, exposing America's convoluted priorities through ironic juxtapositions and the use of incongruous humor. Employing the repetitious parallelism oft used by black preachers, the speaker elevates the irony of the title-refrain as it sits against the escalating social crises he describes: "A rat done bit my sister Nell (with whitey on the moon) / Her face and arms began to swell (and whitey's on the moon). / I can't pay no doctor bill (but whitey's on the moon) / Ten years from now I'll be paying still (while whitey's on the moon)."[21] As each line/problem triggers the next, the vernacular disdain of the key line interjects like an irritating reminder of "whitey's" ignorance and negligence of the perennial inner-city ailments that remain untreated.

Such comparison-mode "black" humor is also at the heart of "Pardon Our Analysis (We Beg Your Pardon)" (1975), an address to President Ford in the wake of the Watergate pardon of Nixon: "We beg your pardon," puns the narrator. "Because the pardon you gave was not yours to give."[22] Meanwhile, the petty crimes of black youths that lead to their disproportionate incarceration in the nation's prisons are not so readily pardoned, observes the speaker. "H2O Gate Blues" (1973) further airs Scott-Heron's observations of Nixon affairs, while as the decade closed a new target for his trenchant satire arrived courtesy of the incipient president Ronald Reagan. With the decay of city infrastructures, increased violent crime, and clampdowns on youth protest, the seventies had not been a progressive decade for urban black America, but Reagan's promised welfare cuts and general conservative agenda presaged a new political threat to the poor. Caricaturing Reagan in "Re-Ron" (1984) as a deluded nostalgic, Scott-Heron forthrightly declared, "We don't need no re-Ron," suggesting that his second-term administration signaled more politics as usual (or worse).

Outflanked by a new school of political rappers in the late 1980s (Public Enemy, KRS-One), Scott-Heron's recordings became increasingly sporadic. Worse, his personal life began to spiral downward as he fell victim to the very drug addictions he once so passionately warned against. Seen by many as the "god-pop to hip-hop" today, Scott-Heron's legacy continues to inspire the more militant and literate of rappers, like the Coup and Mos Def. One can see his "cool" brand of social satire elsewhere, too, in the amateur "slam" poetry of city coffee shops and in the caustic stand-up comedy of Dave Chapelle and Chris Rock. Like the funk pioneer George Clinton, Gil Scott-Heron broadened the horizons of what black music could do, should do, and by the end of the seventies, would be doing.

WHAM GLAM!

Just as bubblegum in the late 1960s had implicitly served to chasten the excesses of a self-important rock culture, so the contemporaneous emergence of heavy metal, likewise, symbolized a back-to-basics trajectory. Minimalist and stark rather than elevated and ambitious, heavy metal put primal aesthetics back into rock. Ozzy Osbourne's Black Sabbath, Iggy Pop's Stooges, and the MC5 were proto-metal humorists, in essence; their excessive parodies of rock primitivism were the sonic equivalent of giving the finger (or two for U.K. practitioners) to the new dominants of corporate rock and art rock, as well as the beatless, fey poets of the singer-songwriter scene. Heavy metal bands were as combative and aggressive lyrically as they were musically. Some channeled their aggression into infantile assaults and abuse (Ozzy, Iggy), while others articulated with a political purpose (MC5). Either way, the results were always full of extremist humor.

One strain of the U.S. metal scene that developed in the early years of the 1970s was glam-metal, a subgenre that has intermittently resurfaced since in various guises. The figurehead of glam-metal in its infant years was Alice Cooper. His tongue-in-cheek theatrical "act" proved to be an immediate influence on other emerging homegrown performers, as well as on developments across the Atlantic. Kiss, who followed in Cooper's fake-blood-spattered trail, used similar comedic exaggeration in their stage and sonic creations. Their infantile antics became so beloved among America's preteens that by the mid-seventies Marvel Comics created a Kiss comic book. For "Kiss Army" kids—too young to appreciate the poetic sensibilities of singer-songwriters or the AOR mid-tempo ballads of stadium rockers—their heroes gave them symbols of the outsider, the visceral pleasures of rock noise, and a good old-fashioned taste of rebellion. Kiss live shows were carnivals for the kids, complete with fire-breathing, face-painting, costume-wearing, blood-spitting, tongue-wagging, and smoke-bombing. The dramatic glam humor that lay cheerfully over it all provided camp contrast to the serious sincerity of the sixties "authentics." And along the way, ironically, international pop stars were made of its dark breed of leading cast members.

The international success of Alice Cooper and Kiss highlighted another development that distinguished glam acts from the more doggedly "purist" 1960s counterculture bands: the alternative rocker could simultaneously be a mainstream pop star. Glam's ability to magnetize the media, "elect" appealing pop candidates, and mix melody and style with a gritty sound enabled the genre to operate across demographics and to occupy each side of the mainstream-marginal fence. Apparitions of authenticity and artifice coexisted without question, a knowing wink and wry smile providing the only indicators of their wily methods.

Alice Cooper

Sociologist Philip Ennis refers to the year 1970 as "the pause" in rock history, a time when creative momentum waned and death and violence came to replace the hippy mantra of peace and love.[23] However, as disunity and confusion pervaded the official counterculture, a new underground was emerging. And as hippies bemoaned the death of the authentic going into the new decade, glam rockers fashioned themselves for a future of the fake. Alice Cooper (both the individual and the band) were propelled by an ego and ambition that would have been dismissed as crass phoniness during the 1960s. For Cooper, though, such a charge was worn as a badge of honor. Star-struck, the former Vincent Damon Furnier sought to be "elected" by transforming allusions into illusions, and gory horror into camp humor.

Young Vincent started his rock career in a number of British Invasion–type beat bands in the mid-1960s. By the time he had crafted the outlandish stage shows and faux-horror imagery of Alice Cooper a few year later, he had fallen out of step with the musical tenor of the times. On the West Coast, where they were initially based, the band's musical theater seemed like a throwback to the shock humor of Screamin' Jay Hawkins and Little Richard, and their visual spectacle was not the kind then sought by the L.A. hippies, as Cooper recently noted: "L.A. just didn't get it. They were all on the wrong drug for us. They were on acid and we were basically drinking beer."[24] Apparently taking the right drugs were the Detroit audiences who had been opening their arms to the harsh proto-metal assaults and aggressive stage antics of bands like the MC5 and the Stooges. The band thus relocated east, returning Alice to the Motor City, the place of his birth. There they discovered young and receptive crowds willing to participate in the band's gore-filled drama.

Alice Cooper had already released two albums—*Pretties for You* (1969) and *Easy Action* (1970)—on Frank Zappa's label while in L.A., but their style gained more focus on arriving in Detroit. Cooper took pains to synchronize sardonic lyrics of teenage rebellion with a raw attack of guitar riff rock; these were then illustrated onstage by a complex choreography of props and gestures that highlighted the danger and humor of the musical quotient. By the early seventies, Alice Cooper shows were garnering popular support, critical intrigue, and media sensationalism. Like Malcolm McLaren with the Sex Pistols a few years later, the band never let the truth get in the way of bad (i.e., good) publicity. When an article was published claiming that Cooper had ripped the head off of a chicken and drank the blood, the band (at the encouragement of Zappa) did little to dispel the sensation (which was wholly false, though it did put some ideas into the mind of Ozzy Osbourne). Zappa and Cooper further realized that such stories provided amusing means by which to hammer more nails into the coffins of the sixties "love" generation.

Capitalizing on the growing hysteria, Alice Cooper took their spectacle to cities across America. Like a Las Vegas show witnessed through the eyes of Hunter S. Thompson, the band's bastardized Broadway shtick centered around the "trashy transvestite" Alice. Dressed in tight leather, gold lamé, satin, and lingerie, he painted his face with garish and sinister black makeup. Stalking the stage with his pet boa constrictor and a (Marilyn) Manson-like stare, Cooper played with his props like a kid in a torture playground. Serving up fake beheadings and hangings with onstage guillotines and trick nooses, he welcomed the adoring masses to his nightmare. It was part circus, part magic show, and teenage misfits reveled in this *Rocky Horror* stage show, but they were not the only ones. By the mid-seventies many celebrities had gotten wise to the best show in town, as Cooper welcomed such unlikely attendees as Groucho Marx, Mae West, and Salvador Dalí to the proceedings. Marx and

West both perceived that this "shock rock" display was but an interesting update of vaudeville traditions, while Dalí saw the same surrealistic humor he had engaged in his own artwork. Following the era of intellectual posturing and art rock introspection, Cooper's contrived visual farce offered an audacious alternative artifice, with a wicked bite in its tail worthy of his pet snake.

If grotesque visuals were Alice Cooper's calling card, they were also complemented by the carefully crafted lyrics that consolidated the Alice mythology; these invoked further unrest between and within generations. "I'm Eighteen" (1971) and "School's Out" (1972) provided stark generation-gap anthems in the tradition of Chuck Berry, Eddie Cochran, and the Coasters. They drew a line in the sand, demarking Alice's youth in antagonistic opposition to the parent generation. Appropriating the shocking ideas and imagery of Stanley Kubrick's controversial film version of *A Clockwork Orange*, Alice wrote "Department of Youth" (1975), a spoof fantasy of a youth political takeover, and "Generation Landslide" (1973), a social satire and cautionary tale of youth uprisings in the face of their sellout, washed-up parents. More cartoon fantasies than dystopian science fiction, such songs still touched the raw nerves of the newly emerging "next" generation gap. Hot from banning the *Clockwork Orange* movie, British lawmakers sought to protect vulnerable youth from Alice Cooper, too, voicing objections and calling for concert cancellations in the Houses of Parliament. Presaging the later situationist antics of the Sex Pistols, Alice Cooper responded to the adult institutional backlash by embracing the hysteria and ratcheting it up with sarcastic disdain. In "Go to Hell" (1976), they offer their own self-effacing response to the growing critical unease, aping the voice of a concerned adult citizen: "For criminal acts and violence on the stage . . . for all the decent citizens you've enraged / You can go to hell."[25] And if hell was where Alice was heading, he always made sure he was appropriately dressed for his descent.

Such self-deprecation and ironic asides appear in many of Cooper's lyrics. "Elected" (1973), for example, despite its apparent simplicity, has him simultaneously mocking phony politicians, sixties authentic affectations, and himself, all in another rallying cry on behalf of the new youth. "Kids want a savior, don't need a fake," deadpans Alice. "I wanna be elected."[26] Other times, as in "Teenage Lament '74" (1974), the youths themselves bear the brunt of Cooper's satire. Speaking through a Coasters-style woe-is-me kid, the narrator whines about the adult world and the torturous peer pressure of keeping up with the latest glam fashions. "What a drag it is, these gold lamé jeans," he complains.[27]

Proclaiming himself the voice and image of the new decade, Cooper aimed much of his subversive wit at the past, mocking the self-righteousness and social consciousness of the sixties generation. However, he was also quite happy to turn to the present for satirical sustenance. "Billion Dollar Babies" (1973) was a succinct slogan for the "Me" generation, a testament to the self-indulgences of mainstream rock culture. In "Wish I Were Born in Beverly Hills" (1978) he pursues the same theme by observing a caricature-type of the period. "I swear I couldn't drink half as much as she spills," the narrator jokes at the expense of a typical Hollywood decadent.[28]

Alice, it turned out, could and did drink that much and more. Indeed, alcoholism became his coping mechanism as the Alice Cooper star rose throughout the seventies. By the eighties he had become the "billion dollar baby" he had once ridiculed, and he found it increasingly difficult to keep the stage persona "Alice Cooper" at arm's length from the real thing. After returning from an extended session of rehabilitation in the early eighties, Cooper saw that his star had been eclipsed by the new barrage of punk and "hair" metal bands, each inspired to varying degrees by his trailblazing innovations.

Like that of the Velvet Underground, the influence of Alice Cooper on subsequent rock music is too broad to fully account for. The hallmarks of his theatrical style, raw sound, and lyrical provocations can be seen in the glam-punk of the New York Dolls, the British punk of the Sex Pistols and the Damned, the eighties metal of Guns 'n' Roses and Danzig, and the nineties shock rock of Marilyn Manson and Norwegian black metal. With his updates on burlesque entertainment, Alice Cooper brought new (fake) blood to old forms, while conveying a new identity to the seventies decade by gleefully severing the c(h)ords to the past generation.

PROTO-PUNK PROTOTYPES

The Velvet Underground are one of the most influential bands in the history of rock music. In their minimalist style, decadent image, and cynical attitude, they—more than anyone—have provided the three-pronged template for subsequent punk and post-punk insurgences. Before the Ramones and Sex Pistols would transform the Velvets' vision into punk proper, though, certain other proto-punk acts fanned the flame and carried the torch. These bands might be divided into two camps, each projecting a distinctive side of the Velvets' essence: the Big Apple hard-glam street-rock side was represented by the New York Dolls, while the alienated art geek side was played out by Boston's Jonathan Richman & the Modern Lovers. Both sides shared the central Velvets traits of minimalism, decadence, and cynicism, and each projected an ironic humor that set them in stark contrast to most of the mainstream rock and pop developments of their times.

As seventies rock grew more complex, its productions more slick and bombastic, the proto-punk bands were not the only detractors who took to the road less traveled. Although they found few compatriots within the rock industry epicenter, the proto-punks had loud and enthusiastic support from the underground (and sometimes mainstream) music press. U.S. rock journalists like Lester Bangs, Dave Marsh, and Greg Shaw, as well as U.K. counterparts like Charles Shaar Murray and Nick Kent, had trumpeted the call for back-to-basics rock music throughout the barren years of the early seventies. Their celebrations of mid-sixties garage bands and of the raw power of the Stooges and the MC5 were as enthusiastic as their denigrations of the singer-songwriters and stadium rockers. The arrival of dirty decadents like the New York Dolls and amateur ironists like Jonathan Richman brought glimmers of hope, if only flickering and isolated ones. Young aspiring punks were also taking note of the winds of change that these acts were ushering in. Soon-to-be Sex Pistol Paul Cook recalled how the New York Dolls provided comic relief from the standard fare and dull trappings of the British live rock TV show *The Old Grey Whistle Test*, hosted by the less-than-amused "hippy" Bob Harris. "They were really funny," Cook remembers. "And they just didn't give a shit, you know."[29] The godfather, Lou Reed, was also cognizant of the proto-punk rumblings of the early seventies, which he analyzed with characteristic ironic candor: "There were those who were trying to become much better musicians . . . and those who were trying to forget what they already knew."[30]

Proto-punk humor was the wit of provocation, of offering the incongruous in the face of the rational, of playing the contrarian on the outskirts of a rock culture that had become entrenched within the repetitious routines of overplayed clichés, gestures, and rituals. By busting taboos and breaking through to new topics (or new perspectives on old topics), acts like the New York Dolls mocked the boredom of their trappings by acting out an exaggerated version of that boredom. Their humorous parade of "trash" anti-aesthetics provided the initial rumblings of what would soon be an earthquake within the industry and beyond.

New York Dolls

Few were aware of it at the time, but the New York Dolls—perhaps more than any other early-seventies band—signified a musical line in the sand, a point of irreversible separation from 1960s rock aesthetics and its lingering ideals. Indeed, they represented not just a break but the very antithesis to that prior era. Musically and lyrically, and in attitude, gesture, and image, the New York Dolls were the anti-sixties, flaunting their contrarian arsenal with a scornful laugh and a childish pout.

Despite often being associated with the glam rock genre of the times, the New York Dolls were as much apart from as a part of that movement. Whereas David Bowie, Marc Bolan, and Brian Ferry headed for the high road to pop stardom and indulged their bohemian fantasies with new post-sixties escapist withdrawals, the Dolls took the low road back to the New York dives and back alleys from whence they had come. Lead singer David Johansen saw his band's mission as "bringing it back to the street."[31] There were no space oddities or lounge lizards to be found in the world of the New York Dolls, just "kick-ass" rock & roll and a live-fast-die-young attitude.

The glam tag was applied to the New York Dolls largely because of their taste for outlandish attire. Even here, though, the Dolls differed somewhat from their British counterparts. When Bolan or Bowie played dress-up, they sought to create new fantasy characters and worlds, to take their fans on exciting adventures. Dolls' glam, though, was rooted in the real transvestite world of New York City. It denoted a world of hookers and drug addicts, rather than aliens and male models. More thrift shop combos than high couture, the Dolls' style brought "gross" exaggeration to cross-dressing; essentially, they were a comment upon glam as much as a manifestation of it. Their high-heeled boots, rubber outfits, and sinister makeup had been purchased from the Malcolm McLaren SEX boutique end of London's King's Road, rather than the high-fashion Antony Price end. As such, the Dolls' more macho cross-dressing pointed the way toward punk's sartorial harshness and away from glam's elitist adventure playgrounds.

Future Heartbreakers' manager Leee Childers remembers 1970 and 1971 New York Dolls gigs as "very, very funny."[32] He recalls how, though the male attendees were discomfited by the band's aggressive "fag" look, the women knew immediately that they were straight. Like Alice Cooper, the Dolls offered a harder, more heterosexual take on glam than their U.K. counterparts; they were intent on scaring and sensationalizing as much as on entertaining. Each drew from theater, the Dolls inspired by the "Ridiculous Theater" popular in the New York underground at the time. Unlike Alice Cooper, the Dolls' shows were not prop-driven, but their slovenly gestures and combative attitudes toward their audiences (some claim David Johansen started the punk tradition of spitting at the front rows) created a bare-bones urban theater that reflected the decadent underworld outside.

Johansen regarded the band's drama as a subversive counterpoint to the self-indulgent stadium rockers that had come to dominate and dilute rock culture, saying, "Rock and roll stars were like 'Wow, I got my satin jacket and I'm really cool and I live in this gilded cage and I drive a pink Cadillac.' Or crap like that. The Dolls debunked that whole myth and that whole sexuality."[33] Although their rough gestures and raucous guitar rock sentenced them to perennial cult band status, their snub of rock elitism and return to rock basics endeared them to critics like Lester Bangs (in the United States) and Nick Kent (in the U.K.) who had been campaigning for a roots rock revolution. Locked for the most part within a New York club circuit of Max's Kansas City, the Mercer Arts Center, and the Diplomat Hotel (with an occasional excursion to England), the Dolls did not usher in a revolution, but they certainly laid the foundations and rallied the forces that would later transfer to the CBGBs scene and the subsequent punk uprising.

Bucking the trend toward technical virtuosity, the Dolls symbolically proclaimed an anyone-can-do-it attitude in their music. Without breaking new turf, they managed to deliver their distorted Stones riffs into something quite original. There was an amateurish swagger to Johnny Thunders's guitar style that alluded to R&B and mid-fifties rock, yet it was somehow outside of those sources, too. Future Sex Pistol Steve Jones studied this unconventional yet rooted sound as he prepared to start his own band. There was something ironically "dumb" in the simplicity of the Dolls' style, a natural limitation one hears in Bo Diddley and the Velvet Underground. Despite itself, it just works.

Lyrically, too, the Dolls wrote against the grain of their times. The cynical simplicity of their lyrics was a significant feature of their "dumb" humor, contrasting with the intellectual "poetry" of the singer-songwriters and the wry sensibilities of art rockers like Roxy Music. Dolls lyrics were minimalist and vacant, coursing around a circular flow of boy/girl/New York/sex images. In songs devoid of sociopolitical relevance (or relevance to much else), the Dolls offered striking titles in place of delving lyrical content. "Personality Crisis," "Frankenstein," "Bad Girl," "Pills," "Trash," and "Vietnamese

Baby" are all provocative titles from the band's eponymous 1973 debut album. What is startling about these songs is how little one learns from listening to the lyrics, yet how much one is drawn into the Dolls' world merely by the titles and chorus lines alone. They evoke crisis, alienation, rejection, self-destruction, and outsider status, yet such provocative ideas are barely developed in-song. Such attention-grabbing minimalism was classically proto-punk, conveying a short-attention-span ironic dumbness that the likes of the Ramones would soon craft into a more discernible aesthetic.

This childlike simplicity was particularly appealing to manager-in-waiting Malcolm McLaren, who saw in the band the kind of primitive rebellion and subversive humor that he had enjoyed as a kid listening to Chuck Berry and Gene Vincent. However, in trying to craft an image to complement the band's lyrical primitivism, McLaren discovered that these kids were more unruly than he had bargained for. Manager (or minder) of the Dolls during the final months before the band's breakup, he came to a quick realization that he was not dealing with professional artists, never mind adults. Recognizing the uncontrollable "id" that was symbolically reflected in their "Dolls" tag, McLaren once called them "a fucking bunch of vain bastards . . . never ever wanting to grow up."[34] Thus, McLaren's curious attempt to transform these boys-who-just-wanna-have-fun into politicized fronts for Communist propaganda was fated for disaster. Dressing the lads in red rubber suits, McLaren had the band perform in front of a red Soviet flag backdrop. Such situationist stunts would enjoy their day a few years later in the more political environs of the Sex Pistols, but they fell flat with the Dolls, whose realm of reality was more heroin and sickness than hammer and sickle.

In the face of the band members' deepening descent into drug addiction, McLaren's last-ditch attempts to revive the pulse of the band with gimmicks were unsuccessful. Their decline and fall in 1975 was somewhat ironic as it occurred just months before the CBGBs scene put underground New York rock—much of it inspired by them—into the spotlight. Instead, the band members would go their separate ways into new projects: David Johansen developed the novelty lounge act alter ego of Buster Poindexter, while Johnny Thunders and Jerry Nolan formed the Heartbreakers. Each would watch from the sidelines as their sound, style, and dumb humor propelled punk rock through the second half of the decade; later, they would inspire hair-metal decadents like Hanoi Rocks and Mötley Crüe through the 1980s. Even today, the sly swagger of the Dolls' glam-punk-metal lives on in the tongue-in-cheek guitar rock of Queens of the Stone Age, Eagles of Death Metal, and Louis XIV, as well as in the re-formed New York Dolls themselves, who, led by surviving members David Johansen and Sylvain Sylvain, recently released their much-awaited comeback disc, *One Day It Will Please Us to Remember Even This* (2006), an album that displays some of the same raw riffs and brash attitude that first distinguished them. On one new song, "We're All in Love," Johansen brings an adult self-deprecation to the child's play abandon of the band's early years, recalling, "Jumpin' around the stage dressed like teenage girls. / Castin' our swine before the pearls. . . . / They go to work. / We go to play."[35]

The incongruous elements of humor always function by virtue of their surrounding contexts, and the New York Dolls were the ultimate contrarians of their era. As musicianship turned more technical, the Dolls went simple; as lyrics aimed for poetic stature, the Dolls wrote childlike doggerel; as costumes were inspired by runway fashion, the Dolls dressed like Halloween street freaks; and as rockers looked to be (pop) stars and artists, the Dolls were the gutter-punk outsider kids, biting (and spitting at) the hands that fed them, just as their bastard offspring would continue to do with punk's more official arrival a few years hence.

Modern Lovers

With their eponymous debut album—recorded in 1973 and released post-breakup in 1976—the Modern Lovers created a new tradition of rock comedy: loser humor. Crafting a caricatured narrator who embodied the quintessential sensitive square with an inferiority complex, lead singer and lyricist Jonathan Richman went geek while his peers were going glam. The sensitive losers that populate the songs on *Modern Lovers* were of a markedly different kind than the tortured poets of the L.A. singer-songwriter school, though. Where the latter's self-examinations offered the often narcissistic reflections of adults, Richman's unreliable narrators were self-deluding adolescents, the pop song equivalents of J.D. Salinger's pathetically lovable Holden Caulfield. Despite never garnering anything more than a cult following, the Modern Lovers—and Jonathan Richman in his subsequent career as a solo artist—created an endearing and enduring rock persona type that prevails to this day.

The lovable loser character had few precedents during the early seventies and before. Although Buddy Holly and Roy Orbison had presented figures of fun with their thick-rimmed glasses and awkward poses, their lyrics never delved into the depths of psychological desperation and self-loathing that Richman was later to locate. Certainly, rock music had long created outsider caricatures who bemoaned their rejection and social alienation; from Eddie Cochran to the Shangri-Las to the New York Dolls, this identity has been simultaneously celebrated and parodied. However, the rebel outsider has romantic power, an inverted superiority status of him/her against the world. Such characters are inspiringly pitiful and heroically pathetic. The Modern Lovers' anti-heroes are pitiful in both senses of the word (sympathetic and just pathetic), deluded romantics who cannot see straight, and thus suffer the confusions, pains, and insecurities of their short-sightedness. Although these Salinger-esque arrested adolescents lacked the aggression and assertiveness that would soon characterize the youths of punk, they became important prototypes for sensitive "arty" new wavers like the Talking Heads, as well as for many subsequent alternative and indie rock acts of the 1980s, 1990s, and 2000s.

It is perhaps fitting that the godfathers of loser humor could find no one to release the John Cale–produced batch of songs they recorded in 1973. Warner Brothers and A&M both showed fleeting interest but then backed off, leaving the tapes to gather dust until finally being put out in 1976. By then the Modern Lovers had disbanded and Jonathan Richman had embarked upon a solo career that, while still displaying his trademark wit, would never revive the lyrical and musical edginess of those early songs. The 1976 release date of *Modern Lovers* had a fortuitous side, however, as the album hit the market during the height of the initial punk explosion, thus benefiting from a more attuned scene than it would have received in years prior. The subtle self-deprecation of the album's suburban angst tales may have gotten lost in the punk sea of urban anger and revolt, but the post-Velvets garage band sound on *Modern Lovers* had all the minimalist charm and ragged amateurism of punk.

Besides John Cale twiddling the knobs, the influence of the Velvet Underground can be felt in many aspects of the album. Musically, it appropriated the simple "jam" style the Velvets had developed in songs like "Sister Ray." Lou Reed's deadpan "flat" singing-speaking style was also an inspiration to Jonathan Richman, who would take that anti-vocal technique to extreme parodic levels. Instrumentally, too, the Lovers, like the Velvets, eschewed conventional playing, avoiding the standard self-aggrandizing guitar solos and symphonic keyboards of the prog-rock of the day. Instead, a rhythm guitar chugs unobtrusively along, accompanied by a simple but evocative atmospheric organ. This backdrop musical style facilitated the emphasis on Richman's bizarre lyrical narratives and idiosyncratic delivery.

Modern Lovers' opener, "Roadrunner," introduces us to the Richman wide-eyed innocent character/narrator type. Over a repetitive two-chord evocation of a road journey, Richman's alter ego suburban romantic speaker takes listeners on a ride around Massachusetts. This speaker is neither "born to be wild" nor "born to run," nor does he indulge in the daredevil speeding of Chuck Berry's restless rebels. Instead, he listens to the radio to ward off his loneliness and wonders at "modern world" marvels like the local "Stop 'n' Shop."[36] A classic contribution to the rock & roll road song tradition, "Roadrunner" is this genre's ironic inverse, devoid of romance or freedom, revealing the crass suburban world that—of course—the idiot-infant speaker of the song sees but cannot comprehend.

After this song's opening glimpse of the environment from its geek's-eye view, Richman takes the listener into the interior, shrinking the world from open roads to the claustrophobia of the character's narrow reality of confined obsessions. Romance (or the lack thereof) is the premier arena of suffocation, where relationships are more imaginary than real, and love is a debilitating prison. "Someone I Care About" and "Girlfriend" represent sensitive guy desires, eliciting sympathetic audience "aahs," but "Hospital" penetrates to the potentially malevolent side of the over-"caring" lover-obsessive. Adapting Randy Newman's stalker caricature from "Suzanne" and prefiguring the Talking Heads' "Psycho Killer," "Hospital" invites us into the darker territories of the self-esteem-challenged. Like Newman and the Talking Heads, the Modern Lovers pursue their psychological examinations with the darkest of humor, enabling a penetration into taboo territory that would otherwise be merely off-putting and disturbing. Richman skillfully misleads listeners in the opening verse of "Hospital," representing an apparent romantic who is transfixed by the eyes of his lover and wants to be back with her when she gets out of the hospital. Soon, though, warning signs enter the narrative, as the speaker loosely lets slip, "I can't stand what you do" and "I've lost my pride."[37] Before long, we learn that he has been stalking her neighborhood at nighttime and unduly obsessing during the day, contemplating ways to repossess her. As the lyric oscillates between the disturbing and the pathetically funny, listeners are left to contemplate the fine line between love and hate and, most significantly, how the girl landed in the hospital in the first place.

"I'm Straight" develops the theme of insecurity by setting our lovable loser against a character called Hippy Johnny. Blissfully ignorant of the cool quotient of the drug-taking rock rebel (represented by Hippy Johnny), the speaker (Jonathan?) attempts to win over the girl of his desires (Hippy Johnny's girlfriend) by nervously boasting of his sobriety. "I'm straight!" he cries, hopeful that his clean-cut ways and clear-thinking personality will prevail. "He's always stoned, he's never straight," he then stutters in an attempted put-down of his rival.[38] Set in the context of an early 1970s rock culture where decadence and copious coke consumption were both chic and standard practice, Richman's innocent proclamations on behalf of "straight"-laced geeks are hilariously incongruous. As he kills two birds with one stone, we end up laughing at both the stereotypical portrait of "cool" Hippie Johnny as well as the sheltered naiveté of the young speaker whose rational thinking might register with the girl's parents but not with the girl herself.

A related theme of Richman's caricature that he develops to subversive ends is generational dislocation. The root rebellion of rock culture has always resided in its generation gaps and its rejection of older generations, old ideas, and just the old. With proto-punk stirring insurrectionary attitudes in the young, and glam and funk provocatively grooving and styling for the new generation, the Modern Lovers, typically, traveled the wrong way up this one-way street. Their "Dignified and Old" presents a bleaker version of the Beatles' "When I'm Sixty-Four," while "Old World" recasts the Fab Four's stab at the counterculture, "Your Mother Should Know." "I still love my parents and I still love the old world," deadpans Richman, committing heresy in the face of rebel-rock conventions.[39] Trying to escape from the cruelties and insensitivities of his peers, Richman's characters attempt to stop time and withdraw into a kinder, gentler (and imaginary) world. His vocal delivery, in a voice aching and itself out-of-time, brings a poignancy to the humor that forces us to empathize with, as well as to laugh at, the anti-hero. Ken Tucker concurs, observing in Richman an oxymoronic "serious naiveté that allows him to deal with whimsical or trivial occasions with enormous gravity and spirit."[40]

In his life as in his art, Richman has always distinguished himself—like the speaker in "I'm Straight"—by his lack of rock image and style. His fixed grin and boy-next-door clothes put him in comic contrast to his costumed times and even to his fellow Modern Lovers, who were often decked out in leather jackets and struck rock poses. As with other elements of his comic arsenal, Richman's anti-rock style has established itself as a subversive (anti-)pose within rock culture, Mark E. Smith (of the Fall), David Byrne (of the Talking Heads), and Eddie Argos (of Art Brut) being three of its more self-conscious practitioners.

Misfit rock has blossomed into a full-fledged subgenre since the trailblazing days of the Modern Lovers in the early 1970s.

Its practitioners have drawn from the same techniques of self-effacement and caricature in setting their geek identities against the rigidities of macho posturing. The Talking Heads and Orange Juice picked up the Lovers' baton in the late 1970s, passing it on to alternative quirksters like King Missile and They Might Be Giants in the eighties, then on to emo godfathers Weezer and indie-pop geeks Barenaked Ladies in the nineties, before landing in the hands of new-millennium nutters like Art Brut and the Rebel.

Despite the enduring legacy and influence of the band, the groundbreaking *Modern Lovers* album, like so many of the most influential rock releases, never received the full critical acclaim it deserved in its day. Even Jonathan Richman himself was content to leave the original demos of the album on the shelf after the band broke up in 1973 and has largely disowned the album since its release. Within the broader artistic community, though, the album has more recently become a touchstone, oft cited and oft sighted. Moreover, Richman's stylized flat delivery and impeccably bad timing continue to resurface periodically and variously within indie-rock culture. His "Greek chorus" singing role in the comedy film *There's Something about Mary* (1998) revealed Richman still working his aesthetic, and *Rolling Stone*'s recent inclusion of *Modern Lovers* in its Top 500 albums retrospective gave a long-overdue hat-tip to the original loser who just refuses to stay down.

THE CBGBs SCENE: BORED IN THE U.S.A.

Initially referred to as the underground, then as punk, and later as new wave, the burgeoning scene that bubbled out of the small, grimy CBGBs bar in New York City's Lower Manhattan district attracted journalistic tags that reflected the yearnings of the mid-seventies critical community in the U.S. for something new and exciting that could be rallied around. What emerged from this battered Bowery bar was less a scene distinguished by a common style and more one with an array of heterogeneous acts united by the general sense of being influenced in some way by the Velvet Underground. Like the proto-punk predecessors, the CBGBs bands were minimalist in sound and decadent in demeanor, and they delivered their rough-hewed sets with myriad forms of cynical humor. Whether representing the city streets (the Ramones, Richard Hell & the Voidoids) or the smart-ass art school set (Talking Heads, Patti Smith), each plundered the depths of irony in forming their variant rock personalities.

In 1974, when these bands first appropriated CBGBs as their staging post, the young, live music scene in New York had all but disappeared. The Mercer Arts Center, which used to play host to the New York Dolls and their ilk, literally collapsed, and Max's Kansas City, ground zero for the Velvets and the Warhol set, was orienting to a more up-market demographic. For new young bands the options were limited. And when Television scoped out CBGBs for a base of operations, few could have predicted that within a couple of years it would be the most notorious alternative rock club on the planet.

Nationally, the rock culture had become a profitable business, but it had grown complacent and bland, as the established hegemony of rock acts (Elton John, the Eagles, Fleetwood Mac, etc. . . .) offered easy-listening fare that lacked challenge or danger. Moreover, for the new generation of youths, mainstream rock was old people's music played by spoiled rich "stars." What had happened to the raw spirit of rock music? Where were the rock rebels? Who was there to relate to? These and other questions soon inspired demands for action to which the CBGBs bands would respond.

The publication of the fanzine *Punk* by two New York scenesters, John Holmstrom and Legs McNeil, did much to draw the new bands under a collective identity. Inspired by their mutual love of the Dictators' *Go Girl Crazy* (1975) record, Holmstrom and McNeil set about the task of documenting the fomenting scene. Their *Mad* magazine satirical approach, complete with comic strip interviews and a predilection for the absurd and silly, connected *Punk* to the irreverent humor of the bands they covered. Yet, despite the unifying symbol of *Punk*, it had become apparent by the time of the CBGBs Festival of Unrecorded Rock Bands in the summer of 1975 that the movement was more a splintered collection of many styles and sounds. Loosely, they divided into the "dumb" humor punk camp (best represented by the Ramones) and the "intellectual" irony of the new wave camp (of which the Talking Heads became the figureheads). Despite their marked differences in background, aesthetics, image, and sound, each were concept humorists, (self) parodists who erased the gap between high and low art. Their observational wit and ear for tongue-in-cheek delivery made the Ramones and the Talking Heads two sides of the same coin.

Though never as overtly anti-establishment as the later British punk acts, the CBGBs bands projected many lines of subversion, some social and some institutional. The very sight of the Ramones, kitted up in biker jackets and ripped jeans, blank expressions staring down from hunched shoulders, presented a comedic incongruity in relation to the hedonistic good times of disco culture and the high living of the West Coast AOR bands. Likewise, the Talking Heads, with their eyes fixed upward to tall buildings and the air that surrounds, brought fresh perception and a philosophical bent to unsung topics, always with the wonder of urban explorers and an irony concerning these peculiar exercises. Not only would such humor reawaken the slumbering rock primate, but it opened the eyes and ears of future performers. CBGBs established a rock underground that has become a permanent facet and asset; it also rooted within rock culture a distinct "punk humor" that has likewise stood the test of time.

The Ramones

The stand-up comedy personas of the Smothers Brothers, Cheech & Chong, Rita Rudner, and Andrew Dice Clay show that "dumb" humor is by no means the sole preserve of rock performers. Nevertheless, this style is naturally amenable to rock artistry—particularly to its more youth-oriented acts. Indeed, both meanings of "dumb"—stupid and silenced—are invoked when the term is used to refer to rock humorists. Systematically called "idiots" as kids and told to "shut up" by an oppressive adult culture, subversive rock humorists have long *acted* out in kind, exaggerating their repressed state in a "dumb" parody that indicts the parent generation with a poignancy that mere words, ironically, cannot fully express.

The street-savvy but less-than-intellectual working-class rock-rebel is a caricature fixed in the foundations of rock & roll history. One thinks of Elvis Presley's inarticulate grunts or Gene Vincent's monosyllabic slang outbursts. Here, repetition, minimalism, and an anti-geek "cool" are the characteristics of the dumb expressions. The humor becomes evident to listeners in the knowing wink of the artist, establishing the space between him/her and his/her assumed character. The challenge of the dumb humorist is to exaggerate sufficiently the dumbness of the persona, such that audiences can clearly distinguish it from the writer pulling the strings. Where that differentiating space is too small, unclear, or insufficient, the act is in danger of being seen as just plain dumb. As with Randy Newman's parodies, the Ramones were playing a role, but for them the significance hit closer to home: These dumb youths were not just experimenting with different cultural characters; they were ironically taking on a persona already attributed to them by their antagonists and adversaries. To be a "punk" was a badge of honor if you were one, but it was a term of condemnation if you were not. Both Randy Newman and Andrew Dice Clay may have sometimes suffered the slings and arrows of a too-ambiguous parody positioning in their work, but with the Ramones, many "outsiders" still do not get the(ir) joke.

The second sense of "dumb" that has lent itself to rock expression is silence, or the muted tongue. Here, the minimalist aspect of the style becomes paramount, representing a youth voice that has been silenced by adult authorities, alienated from decision-making, and ostracized from the world of social communication. It plays to the loner persona of rock, the silent type who has been reduced to that condition. As humor, the minimalist persona speaks words that are loaded guns; a single word or expression can resonate with power and/or multiple meanings; puns and irony can fuel what seem to be the simplest of expressions. Again, this dumb mut(at)ing of conventional articulation has deep roots in rock history, from Bo Diddley's coded slang to the Sex Pistols' inflammatory irony. Little

Richard's "A-wop-bop-alu-bop-a-wop-bam-boom!" outburst in "Tutti Frutti" is perhaps the most famous example of dumb rock expression, its sonic "boom" of non-words and noises energetically expressing palpable release from pent-up youthful frustrations.

The band that mastered the art of dumb humor was the Ramones. For them, dumb humor was not merely a lyrical affectation; it was the essence of everything they did, said, and were. The Ramones spoke dumb, sang dumb, wrote dumb, dressed dumb, performed dumb, and were musically dumb. In the history of rock, none have been dumber, nor for so long. Their artistic skill is registered in how they managed to stay consistently funny within this minimalist and repetitive field. Critic John Rockwell once described the band's repertoire as "one slim joke repeated over and over and over."[41] Yet they never degenerated into a novelty act or, conversely, elevated their aesthetic into arty self-consciousness. Like the best dumb humorists, the Ramones were subversive in purpose, and they never lost the requisite "cool" that sustained the street credibility of their act.

Emerging from a lower-middle-class neighborhood in Queens, New York, in 1974, the band quickly established itself in conceptual as well as musical terms. By each adopting the "Ramone" surname, they symbolically erased the aura of individuality and stardom that pervaded the rock scene of the early seventies. Inspired by preceding dumb rock bands and genres—MC5, the Stooges, the New York Dolls, the girl groups, bubblegum pop—the Ramones set out to crystallize their minimalism and repetition into a conceptual (self-)parody. They wrote songs antithetical to the prevailing trends of fantasy and hedonism, prefixing "I Don't Wanna" to any number of activities. "I Don't Wanna Go Down to the Basement" and "I Don't Wanna Walk Around with You" survived early rehearsals to make it onto their debut release, predictably just titled *Ramones* (1976). However, so as not to be charged with wholesale negativity, the boys expressed their affirmative side by writing "Now I Wanna Sniff Some Glue," an ode to the cheap intoxicant commonly inhaled by street kids at the time.

Such songs established what Malcolm McLaren once termed the "politics of boredom," capturing the condition felt by many adolescents and juxtaposing it in exaggerated form against the out-of-touch self-indulgences of the stadium rockers. The Ramones underscored this caricature humor, too, with songs that clocked in at around two minutes, each featuring the same buzz-saw guitar sound and droning "bored" vocal delivery. Again, these were deliberate musical statements subversively set to challenge the pretensions of rock culture, particularly its proud embrace of technical virtuosity and "high" art ambitions. When the likes of Eric Clapton and Santana ruled rock radio, the Ramones wrote songs that did not even have guitar solos!

The band's dumb humor extended to style and image, also. Again, they set themselves counter to the starstruck glam costumes of their peers, instead gravitating back to the age of the 1950s rock rebel. Their uniform of black leather jackets, ragged jeans, and dirty plimsols evoked images of Marlon Brando's biker character in *The Wild One* (1954) or the greaser urchins of *Blackboard Jungle* (1955), wise-ass kids looking for something to rebel against. In the slick corporate atmosphere of contemporary rock, the Ramones found plenty to resist, and they parlayed their protests through multifaceted dumb aesthetics. For kids and critics bored with mainstream rock and looking for an injection of energy and humor, the Ramones offered an attractive and stark alternative.

Initially, the Ramones' caricature minimalism was an acquired taste. The band found few fans beyond the select rock critics and decadent trendies who attended the alternative clubs of New York. In the mid-1970s, that meant there were few outlets for the band to ply their trade, but with the commandeering of CBGBs by the boys from Television in 1974, the Ramones found the ideal home away from home. Critic Bernard Gendron once described CBGBs as "a dank dive with a notorious bathroom," but its confined space and dingy décor made it the perfect setting for the Ramones' brand of back-to-basics rock.[42] There, they honed their thirty-minute sets as well as their performance gestures: legs astride, heads drooped, hair covering faces, air-pounding fists. These rebel stage poses became as integral a part of the cartoon package as the band's music and lyrics.

By 1976, the band had tightened their set of two-minute-something assaults into a collection of incendiary songs. Signed to Sire, they set about recording their debut album. The resulting *Ramones* cost only $6,000 to make—extraordinarily cheap by industry standards—and it clocked in at about half an hour in total when many albums (and sometimes songs) of the era were twice that length. However, like the proto-punk and punk albums of many (Velvet Underground, Modern Lovers, New York Dolls, Sex Pistols), this debut defined the aesthetic and captured the band's essence as effectively as any of their subsequent releases.

As the first song on their first release, "Blitzkrieg Bop" both introduced the Ramones' sound and announced their intentions. Its title wryly alludes to the novelty dance crazes of mid-1950s rock & roll, but any nostalgia or innocent charm is subverted by the accompanying references to Nazi Germany's "blitzkrieg" battle advances. Together, the words in the title serve as the perfect "mixed" metaphor for the band's style: fast, uncompromising, dangerous, and aggressive. Furthermore, "Blitzkrieg" and "Bop" are juxtaposed for alliteration in such a way that a subversive gesture is humorously advanced—and the music had not even started yet!

In "Blitzkrieg Bop" as elsewhere, Ramones lyrics were minimalist, funny, and deceptively simple. They were deeply rooted in the topics and clichés of rock past, but they were also wholly new and original; they were dumb and repetitive, while managing to be profound and provocative (by being dumb and repetitive). "Beat on the Brat," for example, is the quintessence of succinct lyricism. The song contains only a few lines, sufficient, though, to paint an adolescent scene that is evocative, familiar, and cruelly funny. Rolling the "r" in "brat" with sadistic glee, Joey Ramone undercuts violence with silliness through his choice of imagery and use of rhyme and alliteration. "Beat on the brat with a baseball bat," instructs (or informs) the speaker in a tone that captures the last-resort feelings every boy has sometimes felt toward his antagonist.[43] In this adolescent arena, little needs to be said and communication is often more physical than verbal. The Ramones both describe and act out in this children's playground, their rhetorical techniques (imagery, tone, rhyme) consistently forefronting humor in the reportage.

Most Ramones songs are cocooned in the blinkered world of adolescence, where there are no concerns beyond girlfriends, fighting, and (in their street world) sniffing glue. However, occasionally the band broadened their lyrical scope, tackling unusual topics in their own unusual manner. "Havana Affair," from *Ramones*, is as cartoonish as their other teen tunes, but here the topic is Cuban spies and American imperialism. However, this is no Dead Kennedys or Rage Against the Machine screed against the system. Here, the imagery is Ramones-style quirky, and the delivery is deadpan and mischievous. Speaking in the first person as a Cuban exile, Joey undercuts his character with his strained English, saying, "I used to make a living, man, pickin' the banana."[44] An equally absurdist take on prescient political issues can be seen in the band's 1985 song, "Bonzo Goes to Bitburg," a wry response to President Reagan's (some felt) insensitive visit to Nazi grave sites in Germany.

The Ramones rarely strayed from their initial conceptual mold over their two-decade career. They were a band committed to its narrow scope, and some felt their dogged minimalism to be ultimately limiting, while others hailed them for being able to keep the creative fires burning using such a basic template. By 1996, though, the boys had had enough, both of their limited commercial appeal and of each other. Ironically, since their demise and the subsequent deaths of Joey, Dee Dee, and Johnny, the band has been elevated in status and acclaim. In 2002, they were inducted into the Rock & Roll Hall of Fame and, more disturbingly, Ramones merchandise has become mainstream "hip" today, their famous emblem T-shirts ubiquitous, sported by frat boys and the Paris Hilton–Hollywood set.

Despite such curious incorporations, the real legacy of the Ramones is to be found in the influence their distinct sound, style, and humor have had on subsequent rock bands. British punk first wavers like the Clash, the Buzzcocks, the Damned, and the Lurkers would have sounded markedly different but for the presence of the Ramones' eponymous debut album in their lives.

Indeed, the band's distinction and stature have become such that new subgenres—Ramones-core and cartoon punk—have emerged, their practitioners religiously attempting to replicate the patented dumb humor and bare-bones guitar rock once affected so naturally by those four scruffy Queens kids.

Talking Heads

In the punk chain of causation, the Talking Heads emerged from some unlikely sources, but, by virtue of place, time, and circumstance, their identity is destined to be associated with this musical revolution. The band were regulars at CBGBs between 1974 and 1976, and their stark minimalism and contrarian attitudes to rock formalities put them in good stead with the emerging punk scene. However, their art school intellectualism, pop melodies, funk rhythms, and abstract humor also made them outsiders within the larger outsider set. Tagged as "new wave" by the late seventies to differentiate them from their rebel-yell guitar-buzz contemporaries, the Talking Heads proved to be an incongruity within all contexts—and they embraced that identity with an ironic self-consciousness and subversive wit.

With their core members graduates of the Rhode Island School of Art & Design, it is not surprising that art aesthetics would enter into their methods—just as they had for previous art school rock humorists like the Kinks and Roxy Music. Like those bands, the Talking Heads were visual beings using the rock vehicle. Lyricist David Byrne's observations were invariably distinguished by a cubist's angular quirks; he saw life and its spaces from unusual perspectives and in curious ways. He saw air and paper as engaging topics for lyrical concern, looked at war from ground level, scrutinized towns through their physical structures. Byrne's eye for the everyday betrayed the strong influence of Jonathan Richman, who, in songs like "Roadrunner," had offered prototypical examples of the kind of wide-eyed irony and witty sense of detail that came to define Talking Heads' songs. But whereas Richman brought an ostracized innocence to his narration, Byrne was "a real live wire," electric sparks of neurosis and anxiety coursing through the veins of his lyrical experiences. The resulting songscapes were filmic mise-en-scènes with the action dramatized by the urgent, tense, animated "acting" of Byrne in various speaker roles.

"Psycho Killer" was the band's debut single release in 1977, and though it proved to make little commercial dent, it has become as emblematic of the band's style and humor as "Roadrunner" has to the Modern Lovers. Its jagged, sliced rhythms and jerky vocal enunciation endeared it to the punk subculture of the time; yet, in many respects, the song was also something of an aberration alongside the more deadpan, less threatening numbers in the band's set. Byrne's attempt to get inside the mind of a serial killer led listeners into dark comedic quarters. According to biographer Jerome Davis, the song was an attempt "to combine Alice Cooper with Randy Newman."[45] Like the latter, Byrne gets in character, speak-singing his confessional, vocally acting out his "tense and nervous" condition. As the second verse begins, the narrative perspective shifts from first to second person, the killer addressing himself with an eerie inquisition that reveals his schizoid state. Disturbing though the portrait becomes, elements of levity consistently undercut the proceedings, whether it be the pop cliché "fa fa fas" of the chorus or the occasional pidgin French that adds quirky detail to the characterization.[46] The humor of the fine (art) touches is superseded only by the hilarity of the sheer ambition of, firstly, tackling such a topic, and, secondly, attempting to do so from the inside out. Jerome Davis suggests that Byrne as "psycho killer" was an art exercise akin to Brian Ferry's persona projects, saying, "He knew that he wanted to become an art project, to animate a created character."[47]

Their debut album—which included "Psycho Killer"—*Talking Heads 77*, was successful by CBGBs standards (reaching number 97 on the Billboard chart), but few could have predicted that the band would be rock stars by the decade's end. Even within the New York punk scene, they were perceived as marginal figures. Critics—and even punks—liked the band, but they eluded easy categorization, and their overall "everything" just did not seem to correspond with the street aggression and bombast that defined the subcultural dominant. As the Ramones steered punks to leather jackets and ripped jeans, the Talking Heads dressed like their fashion icon, Jonathan Richman, in square suburban wear. Jerome Davis believes that this was self-conscious subversion on the band's part: "For Byrne, adopting a conservative demeanor was a pretty revolutionary move. Wearing a LaCoste shirt to CBGB was a total contradiction in terms."[48]

The band also pushed against the prevailing winds of the underground in its eccentric stage performances. Whereas punk crowds ordinarily spat and pogoed in tandem with the band onstage, they just stood and stared in disbelief when David Byrne spasmodically jerked around his microphone while straight-laced Tina Weymouth bounced merrily along to her bass grooves. This style was contrived to contrast, of course, to deconstruct the gestures of punk peers who themselves thought that they were the deconstructers. And as their label, Sire, released debut albums by their more conventionally punk acts (the Saints, the Dead Boys, and Richard Hell & the Voidoids) at the very same time that *Talking Heads 77* came out, the practical need for differentiation became all-important.

As if to create further distance between themselves and the rest of the scene, the Talking Heads' post-1977 work became less punk and more art-funk. Teaming up with ex–Roxy Music sound-eccentric Brian Eno for production duties on their next three albums (*More Songs about Buildings and Food* [1978], *Fear of Music* [1979], and *Remain in Light* [1980]), the band ventured into new, uncharted territories of sounds, styles, and lyrical surrealism. Like the oversize suits Byrne was soon to sport onstage, the key feature of the new sound was expansion. Years before Paul Simon was credited as the "inventor" of "world music," the Talking Heads looked to Africa for rhythmic inspiration. Flattening their usually jerky rhythms into slower, funkier patterns, with African percussion and free-form structures, their Eno-period songs opened up (the band) in scope and length, fostering a lyricism of greater freedom and space.

The increasingly distinctive Byrne's-eye-view was soon zooming in on ever more unusual topics, including heaven ("a place where nothing ever happens")[49] and air ("it can break your heart").[50] In "Animals" (1979), Byrne brings comedic inversion to our conventionally sympathetic perceptions of animals as noble creatures in harmony with nature. Here, they are awkward, insecure, and mean-spirited. "Think they're pretty smart, shit all over the ground, see in the dark," the speaker quips.[51]

The Talking Heads were at their most socially subversive in their songs of cultural observation. In "The Big Country" (1978) Byrne surveys the state of modern America. Instead of the sweeping land of open opportunity suggested by the title, he finds a neatly ordered suburbia, convenient and boring. Through an exaggeratedly irate narrator, Byrne protests with mock disdain, "I wouldn't live there if you paid me to." The Luddite caricature that is the speaker is presented as so aggrieved, as he mouths such predictably "bohemian" clichés, that the object of the song's scorn is called into question. "It's not even worth talking about those people down there," says the speaker with turned-up nose.[52] Is the band here satirizing the debilitating dullness of suburbia or the self-righteous cynics who condemn it while enjoying its comforts? Or both?

As if to show that reality is perceptual, that life can be seen from multiple sides, Byrne tackles the same topic—existential crisis in the modern suburban environment—from a new angle in "Once in a Lifetime" (1980). Here, the funk backdrop creates a soundscape for Byrne to interject surrealistic fragments of lyrics, suggestive clichés that capture the confusions of contemporary life. A questioning rhetorical style is employed as the stressed speaker takes us through his (and our) midlife crisis. "And you may ask yourself / How do I work this?" the speaker inquires, suggesting both a material and philosophical meaning to the question. "This is not my beautiful house . . . this is not my beautiful wife," he stresses, merging object with human purchase à la Roxy Music. The "Me" has met the "Mean" generation in this cultural critique, and the speaker cannot find a way to make sense of it or to equate consumerism with happiness. "My God, what have I done?" he cries out at one point, as if glimpsing the loss of youth's innocence. But the refrain, "Same as it ever was," continues unabated, suggesting a fatalistic reality that could never have been averted.[53] Byrne here teases the culture with sardonic suggestions and leaves us discomfited with open-ended questions.

In the later "Road to Nowhere" (1985), mockery is once again applied to modern living, but here the speaker expressly celebrates rather than criticizes his fate. The humor here shifts from the caricature satire of "The Big Country" to the apparent incongruity of enjoying "the road to nowhere." This cheery journey is underscored with a nursery-rhyme-like happy melody and jaunty rhythm. "Maybe you wonder where you are," sings Byrne. "I don't care."[54] This blissful ignorance adds a further twist to the satirical intent, suggesting that free will has disappeared in a "brave new world" where, as Aldous Huxley once prophesized and the Buzzcocks later ratified, "everybody's happy nowadays." At another level, the song is also an implicit critique of the critics, a gentle ribbing of writers like John Updike and John Cheever, whose midlife crisis stories had defined the contemporary "lost generation" in literature. The Talking Heads further illustrate their theme in the highly acclaimed video of the song, where the band and various objects dance in constant circles of abandon.

In the original 1981 video for "Once in a Lifetime," the band took advantage of the then-developing MTV medium with a clip that brought their artistic bents to a visual interpretation of the song. The marionette dance moves of David Byrne—later echoed in the 1985 Jonathan Demme–produced live clip from *Stop Making Sense* (1984)—portray his character as a puppet manipulated by larger forces. The physical humor of the dance is Chaplin-esque in nature, evoking those famous gestures and that silent social commentary. Like Chaplin, too, Byrne, by the end of the decade, was using costume to great visual effect. The excessively big suit he donned for "Once in a Lifetime" created a surreal picture of bourgeois trappings, the "little" man squirming helplessly inside. In the mock self-interview extra feature on the *Stop Making Sense* DVD, Byrne (as interviewer) asks himself, "How did you ever think of that big suit?" to which Byrne (the interviewee) deadpans, "I wanted my head to look smaller."[55] The "Once in a Lifetime" images and costumes have become legendary in the annals of physical rock humor, and they testify to the Talking Heads' adeptness in using lyrical and physical humor with integrated potency. And as testament to their acclaim as representing the intellectual wing of punk rock, "Once in a Lifetime" was recognized by National Public Radio in 2000 as one of the hundred most important American musical works of the twentieth century, while its video has been exhibited in the New York Museum of Modern Art.

It was the reach and resonance of their inventive video work that was most responsible for the Talking Heads becoming international rock stars by the 1980s. By the next decade, though, the band members had splintered off into the various side projects they had each been engaged in for some time. Induction into the Rock & Roll Hall of Fame in 2002 would unite the band one last time, as fitting tribute was bestowed on their visual, lyrical, physical, and sonic contributions to the "art" of rock.

OUT OF THE ASHES

Most rock histories chart a lull at the end of the 1970s, a calm after the punk storm of 1976 and 1977. However, within the by-then-permanent underground, post-punk proceeded with a momentum of creativity, diversification, and innovative humor. The three-chord street side of punk continued with gusto in enclaves of cities across America. L.A.'s "hardcore" punk scene inherited and exaggerated the Ramones' "dumb" punk humor, while the Dead Kennedys, from San Francisco, harnessed progressive, sociopolitical humor with their caricature parodies. New York's "no wave" scene—spearheaded by Lydia Lunch and James Chance—brought avant-gardist deconstruction to post-punk with its combinations of noise brutality and wry allusions.

Punk and post-punk humor made interesting inroads into the mainstream pop market, too, as fusions of present and past styles created some lively and fun(ny) new postmodern hybrids. The Cramps merged punk with rockabilly to produce psychobilly, while the B-52s plundered 1950s kitsch iconography—with what Gillian G. Gaar calls their "wacky tongue-in-cheek image"—as a front for their pop-punk.[56] These new wave, postmodern bands ironically derived a pseudo-authenticity by ironically drawing from past rock genres, while their processes of plunder were always accompanied by an omnipresent self-deprecating humor, thereby softening potential charges of plagiarism. Tom Carson once said of the B-52s that they were "just intellectual enough to be self-conscious about how surreal it is."[57]

The United States witnessed the emergence of the first punk-influenced superstars, also, as the seventies transformed into the eighties. Postmodern feisty females like Madonna and Cyndi Lauper took the lessons they had learned from punk feminism and adapted them to the MTV-propelled world of mainstream pop. The intention of the Sex Pistols and others may have been to put an end to rock music as we know it, but by the early eighties it was apparent that they had expanded its possibilities beyond anyone's expectations or imaginations.

Punk was not the only seventies insurgence to have enduring effects on subsequent rock culture, either. Funk, having restored street rhythms and boast humor to urban America, passed the baton to a new breed of street-beat poets at the end of the decade: rappers. Part of a broader hip-hop subculture, rap would come to represent new possibilities in music-making and humor that would be deeply rooted in African (American) histories, yet articulated in rhythms, rhymes, and dialects formed within the dreams and realities of the urban present.

If the 1960s had represented the high point of rock authenticity, the seventies tricksters of glam, funk, and punk were the revolutionary transformers, clearing space by burning down the past, then leaving the rubble to be recycled into new mutations of what critic Lawrence Grossberg calls "inauthentic authenticity."[58] These eighties postmodern acts would proceed to sample and salvage with a spirit of irreverent wit, mixing deft illusions, bold allusions, and playful ironies for the new technological generation.

THE EIGHTIES:

Postmodern Regenerations

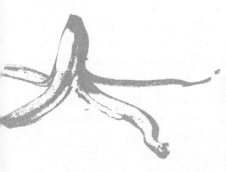

ALTHOUGH NEVER A commercial phenomenon, at the dawn of the 1980s the most dominant artistic influence in rock was punk. With its pride in the primacy of the creative "auteur" and its protestations on behalf of "authenticity," it was essentially the last full gasp of rock modernism, concluding that period of rock & roll from 1950 to 1980 that was forever looking forward, seeking to shed the past and to create the new. Despite going into decline as an active genre, punk was by no means over, as new upstarts like the Dead Kennedys and maturing rebels like the Clash found new targets for their subversive sniping with the incipient Reagan and Thatcher administrations. Nevertheless, as punk mutated into the new decade—refueling as "hardcore" or softening as "new wave"—the fragmentations of the scene and subculture were indicators that structural realignments were afoot in the rock body politic. These reconfigurations manifested themselves in a series of postmodern regenerations.

The old rock modernism that had set a distinct and distinguishable alternative rock culture against the mainstream was challenged as the eighties began to unfold. Whereas sixties and seventies "rock" subversives had set themselves against the "pop" music of their days, critiquing its commercial trappings and manipulative exploitations, many new eighties rock acts were also mainstream pop stars. Using irony as their password to critical acceptance, artists like Madonna, Prince, and Cyndi Lauper playfully toyed with the sign systems of pop while simultaneously undercutting its tenets with subversive humor. These postmodern upstarts were savvy stars playing both sides of the fence; their punk-inspired spirits drove them to expose the processes of pop productions and marketing while they laughed coyly on their way to the bank.

The niche marketing that had comfortably categorized rock genres throughout the 1970s collapsed into a multiplication of subgenres, sub-subgenres, and who-knows-what-genres throughout the 1980s. Terms like "psycho-billy," "hardcore," "cow-punk," "new wave," and "no wave" suggested the myriad mutations of punk proper, while differentiations between the mainstream and the marginal became fluid and uncertain. Madonna was a mainstream act with marginal gestures; REM were a marginal act who attained mainstream success. College radio's expansion and the independent record label revolution carved out new avenues, making the margins more marginal and the rock tent much broader. These realignments were to regenerate rock music, creating new spaces for new manifestations of subversive rock humor.

Developments in areas outside of rock music were essential to these changes. Technological advancements brought about cheap recording equipment and new means of musical production; the emerging rap form would take full advantage of this technology, using two turntables and a microphone as the stepping-off point into high-tech sampling, turning the postmodern recycling process into its own art form. Poor urban kids previously shut out of rock's expensive studios could now take hold of the means of production, thanks to the accessibility of the new technology. With these new voices came new expressions of subversive rock humor, many—as before—deeply rooted in African (American) history.

Alongside technological advances, the launch of MTV in 1981 similarly revolutionized rock music as it shifted the emphasis of rock humor from lyrical expression to visual theatrics. Despised by many rock traditionalists for its objectification of women and for killing audience imagination, MTV became the avenue for many new image-oriented acts and offered new ways of experiencing and consuming popular music. During its early years particularly, MTV became a playground for many rock humorists and aspiring filmmakers. Besides ushering in a new eighties British Invasion of post-Bowie pop pin-ups like Duran Duran and the Human League, MTV also created spaces for marginal but visually conscious acts such as Devo, who used the form to air their experimental mini-movies.

Visual humor had been Devo's devotion since 1972, when the band formed in reaction to the Kent State University shootings, to which founding member Gerald Casale had been a witness. The band's subversive humor started with their name, an abbreviation of the word "devolution" and implicitly an abbreviated way of saying that American/Western civilization was regressing into a dehumanized condition. Putting their art department education to rock use, Devo were soon the cutting-edge visual provocateurs of Ohio's burgeoning avant-garde punk scene of the mid-seventies. With a brand of satire suited to punk's anti-establishment sentiments, the band adapted the abstract humor of surrealism and dada to experimental filmic adventures. Pioneers of the video form, the band had been videotaping their performances as early as 1973. Thus, when MTV emerged at the dawn of the eighties, Devo were there to provide a bridge from punk to the new image-driven genres of new wave and pop. "Whip It" became a breakout success in 1980, its bizarre video imagery bringing mystique and artistic credibility to MTV.

Long known for their use of clothing as commentary, for the "Whip It" video the band dispensed with their usual yellow chemical-protection uniforms (signifiers of imminent nuclear danger) and instead donned red "flower pot" hats (symbols of sexual energy zones, according to the band). To illustrate lyrics that ridiculed the self-help prescriptions of the Reagan administration, Devo deployed sadomasochistic imagery, suggesting the perverse strictness of the new political regime. Set at a ranch corral, its key scenes showed band member Mark Mothersbaugh whipping the clothes from a sophisticated-looking woman while various cowboys and their girlfriends—laughing and drinking beer— looked on as amused spectators. The incongruity of these figurative images made for the kind of quirky—yet disconcerting—comedy that MTV sought in its early years.

Logic and common sense were subverted in the hands of Devo and other video-makers, who used the fast-cut techniques of advertising to serve up surrealistic fragments of weirdness. The Art of Noise, Herbie Hancock, and Peter Gabriel were "cutting" edge video artists in a similar vein. The Eurythmics' "Sweet Dreams" (1983) was one of the most successful and notable examples of avant-garde humor applied to the commercial video form. Its juxtaposition of roaming cows with futuristic high-tech images exploded imaginations rather than erasing them, letting incongruity humor run amok in its barrage of rebellious incoherence. These spectacles of "art-y-fice" soon degenerated into the new/old rock clichés of the "hair" metal videos, though even they, in their excess and exaggeration, often betrayed a self-effacing humor behind their exploitative sexism and bravado.

With its fusion of advertising and art, technology and spectacular imagery, MTV not only ushered in the age of postmodern rock but it also fostered the new queen of postmodernism: Madonna. Her ability to oscillate between contrasting identities (virgin/whore, male/female, gay/straight, victim/victimizer) made her the most intriguing pop star of the day, as well as the most controversial. Her trickster antics and ever-changing modes and moods befuddled critics and engaged all. An "instinctive postmodernist," Madonna played the media as her primary instrument, and with virtuosity theretofore never witnessed.[1] Her parodic allusions to the icons and images of pop culture's past skewered the expectations and categories of her time. Ultimately, she used an arsenal of comedic techniques to challenge social determinations of gender and sexuality, as well as feminist responses within those discussions.

Like her eighties peers, Madonna was a postmodern pilferer of the past. Indeed, the most defining feature of the era's music may well be how often it looked backward in order to strive forward. Whether it was rap artists sampling old James Brown, Chic, and George Clinton songs, or Culture Club and their British ilk's blue-eyed soul stylings, eighties rock was the sound of the past regenerated for the present. For the new generation of youth reared on MTV, this was indeed new music, recycling merely being a new technique of creativity. Humorists became the leading lights of rock's regenerative wave. They used pastiche and parody to comment and call attention to the codes and clichés of popular culture, with all its (implied) rules concerning sex, gender, race, and generation.

Some of the "arguments" the new subversives of eighties rock/pop were making related to issues of identity politics. They challenged conventional representations (in music and beyond) of women, homosexuals, and people of color. It soon became apparent that outlets like MTV and an increasingly emboldened college radio were creating spaces for these new voices. Of course, eighties music did not eradicate racism or sexism; however, it did open up new channels of discourse about them. As such, many of the eighties subversive humorists had much in common with the burgeoning radical stand-up comedians flourishing at the time. Eddie Izzard, Bill Hicks, and Roseanne Barr brought similarly provocative challenges to issues of sexuality, gender, and social class within their field.

While eighties rock changed the music culture with its progressive inclinations, it also stayed the same by persistently looking in the rearview mirror. Nevertheless, through postmodern pastiche that drew from the debris of its history, rock also "regained its memory," welcoming the past into the present and regenerating both in the process.[2] One such scene that looked backward in order to progress forward was the hardcore punk scene, which grew out of Los Angeles before spreading to other California cities and beyond.

HARDCORE

The first wave of punk rock—rooted in New York and London—had for the most part exhausted itself by the end of the 1970s. In the U.K. the form metamorphosed in multiple directions: into avant-garde post-punk, the stylized pop-rock of new wave, and the puristic, more doggedly working-class "oi" subculture. New York punk followed its dominant art school foundations, drifting into the abrasive deconstructions that came to be called "no wave," or, as in the U.K., the more commercially formed alternatives of new wave. As critics and observers were all but closing the casebook on *old school* punk rock, subterranean stirrings emerged from within various pockets of Los Angeles's (sub)urban sprawl. These sounds, faster and more primal versions of punk, and these bands, nastier and more violent, became associated with the subgenre of hardcore. Drawing from its pervasive aura of violence and confrontation, the California hardcore movement boasted some of the most subversive of punk humorists.

Like oi in the U.K., L.A. hardcore was very much an internal musical reaction. Distressed by the "art"ificiality of much post-punk and the emasculated sellouts of new wave, hardcore sought to strengthen its core punk principles. Songs were faster, emotions were intense, and slogans became more combative: "What the fuck, fuck shit up!" was the pithy war cry of Black Flag. Hardcore had no time for the theoretical deconstructions that amused the art school set of post-punk; its humor was learned in the remedial classes at the dumb school taught by the New York Dolls and the Ramones.

Historians often cover late 1970s Los Angeles by concentrating on the various soft rock singer-songwriters that dominated the local culture. Linda Ronstadt, the Eagles, Fleetwood Mac, and Jackson Browne were the L.A.-based international stadium stars of the day, and their introspections were couched in bourgeois terms, set against the sun, sea, and skies of the idyllic California dream. However, even in its pre-hardcore heyday, a punk rock scene was smoldering in the dark recesses of the region. As early as 1977, DJ, promoter, and all-around scene-maker Rodney Bingenheimer was facilitating the arrival of punk rock, first by playing the off-the-presses releases coming from the U.K. and New York undergrounds, and next by opening the Cabaret club as an outlet for local upstarts to play at. The Germs soon legitimized the local punk scene with the release of their raw debut single, "Forming" (1977), on the local What? Records label. Before long, a whole subculture had emerged around small bars and clubs like The Masque, Starwood, Hong Kong Café, Blackie's, and Club 88. They hosted shock provocateurs like Fear and pranksters like the Weirdos.

John Doe, from the city's most popular punk band, X, compared the L.A. first wave to the more arty New York scene, opining, quite simply, "We were funnier."[3] Local scenester Kristine McKenna concurred, stating, "Not enough has been made, in fact, of how funny L.A.'s first-generation punks were."[4] L.A. hardcore humor came from its embrace of its own marginal status in the city, from its scorn for the city's "dream" image and corporate rock apathy. Hardcore humor was born of revenge and provided relief; it reacted to the realities (rather than the myths) of (sub)urban life in L.A.

Much of the humor of hardcore—as with the U.K. punk scene—came from its broader subcultural elements. Within the L.A. scene, artists and writers were particularly influential. The gig flyers and band posters that graced the walls and lampposts of the city were often as confrontational and sardonic as the bands they represented. Matt Groening (later the creator of *The Simpsons* cartoon) cut his artistic teeth in this environment, but it was Raymond Pettibon's shock-graphics that left the greatest mark. His satirical artwork for the Minutemen and his insurrectionary dadaist flyers for Black Flag have become legendary in the annals of punk visual expression. They melded graffiti with comic book stylings and porn images, creating the kind of grotesque advertisements that *Mad* magazine had once pioneered. Kristine McKenna recalls of this band-art that "though the results were often visually crude, they were invariably witty."[5] Grotesque caricatures of new president Ronald Reagan—often in unflattering poses or dressed in punk attire—were particularly popular flyer images among the more politically provocative local acts and artists.

At the extreme end of L.A. hardcore humor were Black Flag, the Germs, and Fear. These bands had little in common with the more politically correct post-punk acts emerging from the U.K. and New York in the early eighties; their modus operandi was equal-opportunity abuse and sarcastic provocations. Black Flag were the primary instigators of hardcore aggression; much of the violence that has been tied to this scene was the byproduct of their incitements. Though Black Flag are popularly associated with the legendary Henry Rollins, he was actually the band's fourth singer and did not join up until 1981. But with or without him, Black Flag wailed and flailed about the alienation of youth culture and skewered the apathetic with such piss-taking put-downs as "T.V. Party" (1982) and "Six Pack" (1981). And with or without Black Flag, Rollins has become renowned for his own contributions to dark, disturbing humor, this keenly illustrated by "Drive By Shooting" (1987), the single he released under the decidedly un-PC moniker of Henrietta Collins & the Wifebeating Childhaters. In recent years, though, Rollins's presentations on the college lecture circuit and on his own TV show have revealed him to be a satirist of (slightly) broader appeal.

Fear were equally un-PC in their offerings and particularly extreme in their offenses, never missing an opportunity to disturb and provoke. Singer Lee Ving's stand-up haranguing of audiences is captured in graphic detail on Penelope Spheeris's *Decline of Western Civilization* (1981) documentary. Songs with titles like "Fuck Christmas," "Fuck Authority," and "The Mouth Don't Stop (The Trouble With Women Is)" employ Andrew Dice Clay–style shock tactics in their grotesque humor. These exagger-hating Fear songs made the Ramones' "I Don't Wanna" titles seem positively innocuous by comparison.

A less tempestuous, more goofy form of L.A. hardcore humor was represented by bands like the Descendents, the Circle Jerks, and Social Distortion. At their most mature, these bands' songs addressed adolescent concerns of alienation and victimhood; at their most childish, they tackled more-frivolous locker room fare. From Manhattan Beach, the Descendents were quintessential L.A. suburbanites, and their juvenile humor supported the pop-punk melodies of their music. The "Fat" EP (1981) contained the song "My Dad Sucks," while the band's subsequent *Milo Goes to College* (1982) album featured the loser humor of "I'm Not a Loser." Silly more than offensive, Descendents hardcore was pitched at a teenage demographic, their offbeat wit sufficiently raw to avoid the tag of novelty band. "Suburban Home" (1982) sarcastically expressed the California state of mind with its lines "I want to be stereotyped. / I want to be a clone," while "Hürtin Crüe" (1986) showed the band cheekily expanding beyond their adolescent identity issues to poke fun at their equally goofy "hair metal" neighbors.[6] The Circle Jerks, a band that took its name from a slang term for group masturbation, were, not surprisingly, also equally at home with teenage dumb humor. Their debut album, *Group Sex* (1980), captured the short and fast dynamics of L.A. hardcore by holding fourteen songs within its fifteen-minute duration. Led by ex–Black Flagger Keith Morris, the Jerks played the kind of catchy guitar riffs that would later inspire a like-minded generation of Cali pop-punks like Green Day, the Offspring, and blink-182.

If dumb humor constituted the core of hardcore, acts like the Minutemen and the Dead Kennedys were aberrations within the scene. Their political consciousness and social satire had more in common with first-wave British punk than with the more self-absorbed alienation anthems of their peers. Like the Circle Jerks, the Minutemen were the embodiment of their name's suggestion; they had a lot to say within very short outbursts. In a career that spanned only five years, they released twelve records, each containing songs lasting barely a minute or two in length. Hailing from working-class San Pedro, thirty miles outside of L.A., the Minutemen brought class consciousness to their hardcore, crafting obtuse and surreal images into suggestively political diamonds in the rough. "The Roar of the Masses Could Be Farts" (1984) and "Political Song for Michael Jackson to Sing" (1984) captured the more absurdist side of their wit, while "This Ain't No Picnic" (1984) offered a sarcastic indictment of racism. In a scene so dominated by white acts (Bad Brains being a rare exception), such social consciousness was welcome relief within hardcore's often limited world. Besides stretching the lyrical reach of the scene, the Minutemen also flirted with hybrid music styles, mixing orthodox punk riffs with free-jazz interludes and psychedelic workouts—all within a two-minute song! Steven Wells regards them as "the most eclectic and avant-garde of all the '80s hardcore bands."[7]

Less absurdist in their political humor were San Francisco's Dead Kennedys. Perhaps the most socially attuned *and* the funniest of all American punk bands, the Dead Kennedys stormed onto the California scene in 1979 with "California Über Alles," a song that unmasked the fascist leanings of the state's "hippy" politicos. Behind his sardonic grin and the intent to maim, lead singer/lyricist/provocateur Jello Biafra resurrected the rhetorical ghost of Jonathan Swift as he took satirical aim at all arms (and other limbs) of the authoritarian system. His band spearheaded American punk throughout the early 1980s, though their sociopolitical predilections were more passionately embraced by the Brits than they were within their own state or country.

Dead Kennedys

Jonathan Swift, Mark Twain, Oscar Wilde . . . Jello Biafra?! The Dead Kennedys' acerbic frontman deserves to be placed in such rarefied comedic company by virtue of the three-minute satirical missiles he fired off during his band's reign of (counter)terror between 1979 and 1986. Showering their targets with blasts of political parody, the Dead Kennedys (or DK, as in "decay") lyrically shamed and maimed with the most subversive strains of moral indictment.

A more geo-specific context for the Dead Kennedys' art is their home city, San Francisco, and state, California. Only a decade removed from the center of the hippy counterculture when they formed, the band was imbued with the freedom-seeking drives of that movement, though they expressed their dissatisfactions in a rather more aggressive fashion. Yet, when one recalls songs like "I-Feel-Like-I'm-Fixin'-to-Die Rag," by fellow San Franciscans Country Joe McDonald & the Fish, we see the same strategies of parody employed in the service of sociopolitical purpose. A few years after Country Joe wrote his song, the use of parody was refined by another Californian, Randy Newman. His adoption of the voices of hypocrites and oppressors in order to shame them ushered in a proto-punk attitude, if not sound. By the late seventies, California (especially Los Angeles) had caught the punk bug, one particularly influenced by the irreverent and sarcastic screeds emanating from the London-based scene. DK both rode the wave of California's early (proto) punk expressions and helped develop the subsequent hardcore scene, invigorating each with their own brand of biting wit.

As with the best satirists, Jello Biafra's writing was born of anger and frustration as much as the desire to entertain. As the Reagan administration brought about a climate of fear and hysteria in its early years, so the Dead Kennedys exposed its political manipulations by echoing them in exaggerated lyrical scenarios, a warbling Orwellian vocal delivery, and a sinister musical backdrop. As he spat through his oppressors' voices, Jello Biafra questioned, provoked, teased, and prodded, all the time with a sardonic, sneering grin reminiscent of Johnny Rotten.

The band's name gave audiences an early indication of the type of humor that was in store for them. Many considered "Dead Kennedys" to be a sick and insensitive moniker; Biafra, though, regarded it as a metaphorical reflection on the death of the American dream. Such (mis)interpretation would prove to be a constant factor in the band's contention-filled career. In order to circumvent the objections of club owners in their early gigging days, the band often played under various pseudonyms, among them the Sharks, the Creamsicles, and the Pink Twinkies. These playfully ambiguous (or ambiguously playful) names hilariously betrayed the harsh satirical barbs audiences were faced with once the band hit the stage. Indeed, those shows were never lacking in the band's patented practical humor. At one gig in 1984, the band came onstage wearing Klan hoods, then removed them to reveal Reagan masks. Such guerrilla performance art alluded to the antics of the sixties Berkeley protest movement as well as to the more theatrical British punk acts of the late seventies.

Releasing music through their own Alternative Tentacles label, the Dead Kennedys established their satirical identity with the striking titles of their first three singles: "California Über Alles" (1979), "Holiday in Cambodia" (1980), and "Kill the Poor" (1980). "I am Governor Jerry Brown," proclaims Biafra in the opening line of "California Über Alles." In character, he then ventures into a fantastical Orwellian vision of a future hippy dictatorship where "zen fascists" dose the masses with "organic poison gas." Besides its primary political purpose, the song also alludes to the ubiquitous religious cults dotted around California in the 1970s. Biafra envisions a small leap from their communal mindset to an authoritarian state overseen by "the suede denim secret police."[8]

The follow-up, "Holiday in Cambodia," has become the band's signature song, though its four-plus-minute length, mid-paced tempo, and echoing guitars make it an anomaly of California hardcore. With a hat-tip to the Sex Pistols' "Holidays in the Sun" (1977), Biafra employs Johnny Rotten's "what if . . . ?" approach to his fantasy satire. What if the rich white kids who claim to be "down" with the poor black underclass were transported from their comfort zones to the rice fields of Pol Pot's Cambodia? Like Kurt Vonnegut, Biafra uses imaginative leaps in order to make sardonic social comments. Here, the targets are the so-called "yuppies" and "wiggers" that would become topics of talk shows over the next two decades. Like the best satirists, DK were prescient as well as pointed.

Single three saw the band return to the speaker-parody mode. "Kill the Poor" is essentially an adaptation of Jonathan Swift's famous "A Modest Proposal" (1729) essay, in which he ironically suggested that the most practical way to solve the starvation problem in Ireland was to eat the children. Biafra calls for similar "efficiency and progress" in eradicating the poverty and unemployment problems of the United States. As the neutron bomb does no collateral damage to property, the speaker-as-politician declares, "Jobless millions whisked away. / At last we have more room to play. / All systems go to kill the poor tonight."[9]

And if these singles (and their album *Fresh Fruit for Rotting Vegetables* [1980]) were not controversial enough, the band followed them up with "Too Drunk to Fuck" (1981) and "Nazi Punks Fuck Off!" (1981). While the former speaks for itself, the latter saw Biafra turning his attentions away from macro political concerns to the escalating violence within the California hardcore scene. By the turn of the decade, a more aggressive "meathead" fraternity had taken over punk crowds, and a disturbing neo-Nazi element was among them. In no uncertain terms, the band eschew their usually comedic approach in telling this faction "Stab your backs when you trash our halls / Trash a bank if you got real balls."[10]

The controversy surrounding DK's output finally caught up to them with the release of *Frankenchrist* in 1985. The band was a regular adversary of the PMRC as they grew emboldened in the early 1980s, and their inclusion of an H. R. Giger poster illustration (the so-called "Penis Landscape") with this album gave the censor-mongers something to act on. Biafra was charged with distribution of harmful material to minors, the lengthy trial ending in 1987 with a hung jury. Embittered by what were becoming daily infringements upon his freedom of speech and equally disturbed by authorities' unwillingness (or inability) to recognize the band's satire and parody at play, Biafra lurched into a Lenny Bruce–like downward spiral and siege mentality. Though internal disputes were factors, too, the Dead Kennedys were laid to rest with their aptly titled 1986 finale, *Bedtime for Democracy*.

Internal fighting has kept both Jello Biafra and the re-formed Dead Kennedys (minus Jello) in the courthouse over the last two decades. Nevertheless, Biafra has continued to ply his satirical trade on the lecture circuit, lashing out at all who would compromise freedom of speech and expression. His perennial targets, the religious right and two-faced politicians, continue to fuel his righteous contempt and anger as he rages into middle age. Indeed, as a candidate for the Green Party in 2000, Biafra sought to infiltrate the political arena, voicing the same slogan he had once used when standing as a San Francisco mayoral candidate in 1979: "There's always room for Jello." It's a modest proposal that fans of his firebrand form of subversive humor certainly second.

RAP BREAKS

Besides being the freshest and the most exhilarating genre of popular music to arrive since punk, rap also (ironically) revealed the most roots. Embodying the concept of "postmodern regeneration," rap dug deep into the past in order to construct a present art form that sounded both new and original. Its ingredients of oral narratives, trickster humor, and musical polyrhythms had their roots in Africa's past and present. Twentieth-century antecedents heard in rap music include the party-playfulness and wordplay of Cab Calloway's swing, the improvisations and cutting contests of jazz, the negative-positivity of blues relief, the oratory certitude of preachers, the put-down "dozens" jab-insults of Muhammad Ali, the political satire and street grooves of raw funk, and the sound system DJ-style of Jamaican dub reggae. These were but a few of the sources rap tapped and regenerated. Set in the context of an African American urban present of struggle and hardship, rap broke out of the New York underground at the close of the 1970s. Though many initially dismissed the form as a fad, it would soon become the dominant genre of contemporary popular music.

Most early objections to rap were made on the grounds that it was little more than thievery, made from stolen samples of others' music set to an electronic drumbeat. Its new recording ethics and proud plagiarism disturbed rock's proud proponents of authorship, authenticity, and creativity. Yet, like other postmodern expressions of its kind, its concepts were hardly new. The blues had long been a tradition in which song ownership and authorship were often unclear; many blues standards had existed in "communal ownership,"[11] passing between artists who contributed only new "versioning."[12] There is clearly an element of African trickster humor in rap's sly regenerations of others' creations, and thus irony in its pervasive straight-faced cries to "keep it real."

As the streets of New York at the turn of the decade were soon to reveal, rap music was but one feature of a broader subculture that included graffiti art on public sites, break dancing on city streets, a street-slang dialect, and a visual style of distinction. Symbolically or literally, each of these forms shared rap's principles: competition, performance, and a critical sense of humor with complex codes of comprehension. Hip-hop scholar Tricia Rose connects these subcultural expressions to the social subordination of African Americans, saying, "Oppressed people use language, dance, and music to mock those in power, express rage, and produce fantasies of subversion."[13]

Rap's subversive humor is largely linguistic, and it often lingers in the subtext of what might appear to be a "serious" address. Rappers' aggressive boasting and threats are too often and too quickly interpreted at straight-face value. Just as the saddest blues lyric can make you laugh and bring you joy with its relief humor, so rap can function similarly. Gangsta rap may be the harshest and most violent of all musical expressions, but it can also be very humorous in the hands of an adept wordsmith. The revenge fantasy that is NWA's "Fuck tha Police" (1988), for example, is also relief humor for a black constituency that feels systematically beaten down by the police system's history of beat downs. The band's detailed "tall tales" of payback subvert the reality of the power imbalance between the police and black youth. In their celebratory exaggerated revenge anecdotes is superiority humor, a chastening of police power, and a welcome fantasy of youth empowerment. Consider the following excerpt from "Fuck tha Police" in which Ice Cube dream-confronts the police: "You'd rather see me in the pen. / Than me and Lorenzo rolling in a Benzo. / Beat the police out of shape / And when I'm finished bring the yellow tape / To tape off the scene of the slaughter."[14] Cube's boasts here are theatrical deliveries, offering humorous incongruity to the known truths of such encounters. By subverting reality, NWA call attention to that reality, and by inverting it, they empower victimized black youth through relief. Such humor is not for everyone, nor does it even register with everyone; as such, it embodies the traditions of trickster humor, where one meaning is meant for one constituency and another for others.

Since its 1979 breakthrough single, the Sugarhill Gang's "Rapper's Delight," rap has stressed its boast style, a variation on the ritualistic dozens insults that had been standard playground practice for generations of black youths. Also known as "woofing," "sounding," or "joning," dozens humor relies on the rhythms of street-speech, the wit of wordplay, and the outlandishness of the put-down.[15] The original fifteen-minute version of "Rapper's Delight" reveled in such humor, setting the bar high for subsequent on-comers. The intertextual dialogue of rap then took off as new "crews" conducted ongoing verbal wars of "signifying" humor with one another. Roxanne Shanté, for example, started her own in-house "beef" by releasing "Roxanne's Revenge" (1984), a response boast to UTFO's "Roxanne Roxanne" sexist boast. As battles raged around the dozens humor, fun puns, and wordplay, rap music began to spread its wings and broaden its palette of sounds and samples. By the mid-eighties it had splintered into many subgenres, each offering different takes on the form.

Born of urban ghettos rife with drugs, gangs, violence, and constant tensions with the authorities (particularly the police), rap understandably grew a strong political arm as it vowed to "keep it real." KRS-One and Grandmaster Flash & the Furious Five had given early indications of how social struggles might provide pertinent topical material for rap expression, but the arrival of Public Enemy took rap polemics to new levels of sophistication and insight. PE brought Black Panther–style rhetoric and stage iconography to their raging raps, ripping into injustices of all kinds and sizes, from the selective protection given to black citizens ("911 Is a Joke" [1989]) to Arizona's unwillingness to recognize Martin Luther King Jr. Day as a national holiday ("By the Time I Get to Arizona" [1991]). Moreover, like Gil Scott-Heron and the Last Poets before them, Public Enemy stressed the importance of black self-determination, using satire to chastise drug addicts for their self-destruction and concomitant community destruction in "Night of the Living Baseheads" (1988), while also viewing the government, police, and media as responsible parties in the crack epidemic. As with other titles like "Swindler's Lust" (1999), "Son of a Bush" (2002), and "New Whirl Odor" (2005), "Night of the Living Baseheads" exhibited the band's penchant for subversive wordplay.

The entertaining comic hijinks and pointed social commentary one witnessed in PE videos—particularly in the one for "Baseheads"—showed visual humor to be another weapon in the band's arsenal. Chuck D and Flavor Flav were the consummate complementary duo, using the contrast of their personalities for comedic effect in the same way that Laurel & Hardy, Burns & Allen, Cheech & Chong, and the Smothers Brothers had before them. Their dynamic worked through juxtaposition, the wacky sidekick set against the straight man, comic relief flourishing from the "serious" setups. Flavor Flav was PE's hype man, its "fool," providing physical humor (in dress and dance) and "light" verbal wit in juxtaposition to Chuck D's "serious" and harsh indictments. The resulting incongruity humor offers an engaging comic relief in tandem with the subversive main content.

The black pride features of Public Enemy's discourse were also projected by other rappers, if in sometimes less radical form. De La Soul and the Jungle Brothers offered a lighthearted Afrocentrism in their "daisy chain" raps, mixing ethnic pride with neo-hippy philosophies and colorful costumes. De La Soul's light-but-serious "Millie Pulled a Pistol on Santa" (1991) employs incongruity humor by using the context of a Christmas song—usually the terrain of joy and goodwill—to tell a disturbing story about a victim of abuse. In this song, De La Soul's use of satire distanced them from the macho bravado of fellow male rappers, such that Tricia Rose would later refer to the band as a "tongue in cheek spoof of rap's aggressive masculinity."[16]

As the decade developed, a darker humor arose on the West Coast, where some rappers sought to articulate harsh realities by using hyperrealism. Their reportage stories of L.A. street life, in all its gore or glory, created the subgenre known as gangsta rap. Less politically correct than the East Coast political rappers (Public Enemy, Queen Latifah, KRS-One), gangsta rappers exaggerated their gang-banging and sexual encounters into comic fantasy. The shock of their controversial rhymes was felt from coast to coast as leading acts like Ice T and NWA came under the scrutiny of the PMRC because of their profane content, and of the FBI by virtue of their anti-police wish-list tall tales. "Power via jokes" was Tricia Rose's explanation of the motivations behind these gangsta rappers' often "sick" humor.[17]

A correlative companion to gangsta rap was "dirty" rap. Evolving in opposition to the emasculating effeminacy of the late seventies disco movement, rap had always exaggerated its macho prowess; by the end of the eighties this had reached often misogynistic proportions. The dirty rap school heralded Ice T and 2 Live Crew as its naughtiest students. Ice T's detailed sexual exploits were generally preposterous in their excess, a comic offshoot of his carefully crafted pimp image. His conquest boasts served to massage his own ego-image as well as to provoke the would-be censors of mainstream white America (as represented by the PMRC). And 2 Live Crew, likewise, had tongues tucked firmly in cheeks (of various kinds) with their X-rated party rhymes. The Crew's self-described "booty raps" pushed the boundaries of crudity, feeding the testosterone-fueled desires of frat-boy America while getting adults' collective knickers in a twist. Their *Nasty as They Wanna Be* (1989) album became the unlikely focus for freedom of speech debates at the end of the decade, as the PMRC and other legal channels sought to silence Luther Campbell and his posse of provocateurs. *Nasty* songs like "We Want Some Pussy," "Throw the D," and "Me So Horny" had critics comparing the band to the then-equally controversial Andrew Dice Clay. Many black people, though, recognized such raunchy (if guilty) pleasures as the latest installment of an African American stand-up tradition that included Red Foxx, Robin Harris, and Moms Mabley.

The pervasive locker room humor of gangsta and dirty rap served to perpetuate the half-truth that rap music was the sole preserve and representative voice of young, urban, black, male America. However, the full truth was that rap had included female voices since its early years (Roxanne Shanté, Queen Latifah, Salt 'n' Pepa). Though rare, white acts, too, joined the rap game during the 1980s. The Beastie Boys contributed a type of frat-boy humor that was different from

2 Live Crew's, one that was bursting with absurdist imagination and cheeky lyrical wordplay. Their long-standing credibility within this largely black genre has been subversive in itself, suggesting that space is available for any artist with the requisite quotients of hip and humor. As the Beastie Boys have matured into the present decade, they have increasingly turned their talent to satirically exposing the hypocrisies and shortcomings of the current Bush administration.

By the end of the 1980s, rap music and hip-hop culture had grown into a broad tent of expressive possibilities. The culture even spawned its own film subgenre through rap-soundtracked (and often rapper-starring) gangster movies like *Colors* (1988), *New Jack City* (1991), *Boyz n the Hood* (1991), and *Menace II Society* (1993), not to mention its own historical mockumentary in *Fear of a Black Hat* (1994). Rap also made itself ubiquitous visually by becoming a mainstay on MTV, a channel that for the first few years of the decade had been reluctant to show black artists. By 1987, though, rap had its own show in *Yo! MTV Raps*, as well as its own in-house VJs. The dissemination of rap infiltrated mainstream culture, making the sound a common feature of everyday life, while new hip-hop-derived terms made their way into dictionaries. Crossovers and cross-pollinations would continue to make rap the premier postmodern music form of our time, while its urban bases would continue to generate new rap subversive humorists into the 1990s and 2000s.

Ice T

He's hip. He's hard. He's a hustler. Call him Ice T . . . or just the Iceberg. The concept of the cool gangster—ice water running through his veins, girls at his beck and call, spouting staccato slang, a posse by his side—long precedes the "gangsta rap" subgenre. Dashiell Hammett, Raymond Chandler, and Jim Thompson penned the hard-boiled crime novels that introduced such characters; though, as both a commentator upon and the living embodiment of the urban gangsta, Ice T has modified and popularized the genre. Like their literary forerunners, the gangsta rappers reflected the less celebrated sections of Los Angeles. Theirs was not the Hollywood-red-carpets (though they would be treading them soon enough) or the sea-and-sunshine L.A., but the South-Central ganglands of Compton and Crenshaw—at night. Here, much African American youth reality revolved around drugs, prostitutes, and gang-banging; it was a far cry not only from L.A.'s glamour spots but also from the rapping, break dancing, and graffiti art that were culturally regenerating the streets of New York. "We weren't livin' in hip hop culture," said Ice T when explaining why he wrote about the harsh realities of his surroundings.[18] By 1982, with "The Coldest Rap," Ice T had given birth to a new subgenre in hip-hop: gangsta rap. It would prove to be rap's most enduring style.

The humor of Ice T—in image and style—is not dissimilar from that which is found in the hard-boiled fiction-writing forerunners. Raymond Chandler's characters were also larger-than-life caricatures, mythical individuals who inhabited their own fantasy-realities; his prose also sparkled with the wit of chopped rhythm and repetition, gritty vernacular, casual violence, and exaggerated cool. Consider the following proto-rap passage from Chandler's *Farewell, My Lovely* (1940), spoken by his most favored narrator/(anti-)hero, Philip Marlowe: "I giggled and socked him. I laid the coil spring on the side of his head and he stumbled forward. I followed him down to his knees. I hit him twice more . . . I used my knee on his face. It hurt my knee. He didn't tell me whether it hurt his face."[19] Such passages are just a backbeat away from being the truly original gangsta raps, and though Chandler may not be commonly cited by gangsta rappers as a primary source of inspiration, his stylistic legacy—as illustrated in film noir and modern gangster films—has been adopted and adapted by artists within hard rap culture.

Ice T, like Chandler, used exaggeration to portray both a gangsta and a parody of a gangsta, a pimp and a parody of a pimp. Anyone who has seen an episode of MTV's *Cribs* featuring a gangsta rapper's home/life will understand that his American dream success is also an ironic comment upon success. It is "symbolized" in his fleet of cars, the gold chains he dons, and the "grill" on his teeth. Gangsta rappers' "hip" is the modern equivalent of swing's "hep," and Ice T is the former's equivalent of the latter's Cab Calloway. Their humor is located in their grandiose excesses, in their unbounded and self-conscious displays of success and superiority. This larger-than-life comedic style could manifest itself in a boast rap, a sexual fantasy, or a new suit. Its deeper psychological purpose, as Tricia Rose has noted, is to provide empowerment to the constituency (young black males) that has been systematically denigrated and emasculated by a long history of institutionalized discrimination. Thus, the gangsta rapper offers "revenge" fantasy inversions around his primary topics of violence and sex; the results are—to reiterate Tricia Rose's assertion—"power via jokes."[20]

Ice T's early albums—*Rhyme Pays* (1987) and *Power* (1988)—established him as a charismatic voice in the rap game, but with his third release, *The Iceberg/Freedom of Speech . . . Just Watch What You Say* (1989), he became an international star, as well as one of rap's more controversial figures. The album's profane language, raw street crime details, and X-rated sex stories were so extreme that Oprah Winfrey even dedicated a show to discussing its contents, complete with PMRC head Tipper Gore and her punk adversary Jello Biafra as panel guests. Today, this album stands as one of rap's most potent expressions of subversive rock humor.

Alongside the omnipresent themes of gang-banging and . . . just banging, *The Iceberg* tackles the topic that was at the heart of the *Oprah* episode: freedom of speech. It was thus fitting that Ice T invited fellow first amendment defender Jello Biafra to guest on a track. From within the crashing storms and ominous heavy metal sustained notes that introduce track one, "Shut Up, Be Happy" (a suggestive rebuttal to the "Don't Worry, Be Happy" pop hit of the time), Biafra assumes his best Big Brother voice to narrate an Orwellian vision of the oncoming totalitarian clampdown. "Do not attempt to contact loved ones, insurance agents, or attorneys. Shut up," the newscaster tool-of-the-state instructs, simultaneously side-swiping at yuppie concerns. Paradoxical *1984*-like orders keep the masses in check: "Do not attempt to think or depression will occur"; "The number one enemy of progress is questioning." This storm of a song abates with the closing, ironic comfort, "At last, everything is done for you," echoing Aldous Huxley's mantra in *Brave New World* (1932) that "everybody's happy nowadays."[21]

With the prologue over, Ice T steps to the microphone, donning the mantle of his pimp-writer hero, Iceberg Slim. Assuming the voices of a "chorus" sidekick and the primary narrator in alternation, the Iceberg relates some tall tales featuring his crew's various sexual exploits, as well as establishing his own place in the hierarchy of his rap competitors: "Time to bleed, slaughter, slice / Tried to say I wasn't nice as we waxed them punks like lab mice. / Dice 'em up, slice 'em up, dissect. / Put you in a boiling pot and let your ass sweat."[22] The humor here emanates from the sheer extremity of the content and imagery, but also from the sonic effects and rhythms of the internal and end rhymes. Such boundless linguistic flurries would provide similar comedic relief to the over-the-top tall tales of Biggie Smalls a decade later.

Equally extreme is the dirty rap "The Girl Tried to Kill Me," an uproarious and detailed story of an encounter with a dominatrix. With self-deprecating hilarity, here Ice is forced into submission, first by the woman, then by her 6'10" husband who inconveniently arrives at the end. The raunchy rhymes within ("Talkin' 'bout legs and lips, mind-blowin' hips / Had to cross my legs just to look at her tits") are of the Red Foxx variety, the kind of X-rated bawdiness most mainstream sex comedy veils in suggestive innuendo.[23]

Concluding the album in the same vein in which it began, Ice T returns to the censorship theme with an all-out sarcastic assault on the PMRC and FCC in "Freedom of Speech." Evoking the age-old irony of censoring rock music, Ice scornfully mocks, "Hey PMRC, you stupid fuckin' assholes / The sticker on the record is what makes 'em sell gold. / . . . The FCC says 'Profanity—No airplay'? / They can suck my dick while I take a shit all day."[24] One can almost imagine 2 Live Crew's Luther Campbell adding a background "hell yeah, tell it like it is" here.

Through his insults and boasts, Ice T has consistently represented both the politically conscious side of hard rap as well as its more fantasy-oriented gangsta side. In his book, *The Ice Opinion: Who Gives a Fuck?* (1994), he attempts to address the sometimes schizophrenic nature of his persona and personality. Though pervasively misogynistic, Ice T has also expressed positions condemning violence against women and gays; a cutthroat go-getter, Ice T has also rapped on behalf of the rights of war veterans, prisoners, and the poor; often charged with celebrating gangsta life, he has also explained the real economic determinants that create the conditions for such a lifestyle. And from a subgenre almost exclusively African American, Ice T has consistently sought kindred spirits from the white worlds of punk and heavy metal and aimed his music (both as Ice T and in his metal-rap group Body Count) across racial lines. Indeed, in an attempt to welcome the uninitiated into his world of hip-speak, he even includes a three-page "Pimptionary" of slang at the end of his *Ice Opinion* book, in which he gives us the 411 on chillin' in the hood with his homies or on gettin' dissed by his buggin' hype bitch back at the crib.

Beastie Boys

Over twenty years and still "rhymin' and stealin'," the Beastie Boys are the quintessential postmodern pirates. Transitioning from hardcore punk to rap in the mid-1980s, the Beasties—like other rappers—were charged by old school critics with being plagiarists, with being talentless thieves whose idea of creativity was to steal (sample) others' work. (Indeed, the prosecution might add that there is nearly as much Led Zeppelin on their debut album as there is on *Houses of the Holy*.) Suffice to say, their subversions of rock's principles of authenticity and originality were rarely greeted warmly. Even within the hip-hop world itself, the band was summarily dismissed as pirates, just one more example of white interlopers "stealing the blues"—and getting rich in the process. Such rap "nationalism" was pervasive in the eighties, if somewhat ironic considering the sampling nature of the form. Another perspective that tagged the band as pirates came from the band itself. In "Rhymin' and Stealin'," the first song from their first rap album, *Licensed to Ill* (1986), the Beasties proudly announced their manifesto of intent in the opening lines: "Mutiny on the bounty's what we're all about / I'm gonna board your ship and turn it on out."[25]

Besides subverting the basic myths and tenets of rock

authorship, the Beastie Boys quickly established their own identity within the rap genre. They were not afraid to play the enemy within, often mocking the macho strutting of harder rappers and stretching the collective imagination of the genre with out-of-the-box rhymes and references. Few thought so at the time, but when one revisits their two eighties albums—*Licensed to Ill* (1986) and *Paul's Boutique* (1989)—today, one hears some of the most revolutionary, original, influential, and hilariously funny music in the history of rap *and* American popular music.

Proud New Yorkers, the Beasties were initially one of many punk-oriented groups who saw and sought a common cause with the city's burgeoning hip-hop culture in the early 1980s. But whereas the Clash and Blondie merely flirted with the new form, these pirates jumped ship from punk. Sounding like Bad Brains in early 1984, after hooking up with producer Rick Rubin, they were sounding like a rap act by the end of the year. Of course, one of the distinguishing elements of the band was that they brought their punk attitude, irreverence, style, and humor with them, such that the early musical results consisted of rap with a discernible punk (and metal) edge. In early shows their punk theatrics were on full display, too. Their first tour (supported by Public Enemy) caused a stir when the band adopted a large inflatable penis as a primary stage prop and when they cajoled their audiences with Johnny Rotten–type provocations. Their label, Def Jam, though, were content to tolerate such mischief, as *Licensed to Ill* stormed the charts, hitting number one on its way to becoming the biggest-selling rap album of the decade.

The centerpiece of *Ill* was the faux-rebel anthem, "Fight for Your Right (to Party)." Its video became a staple of MTV, while the song became a fixture of frat-boy parties around the nation (and beyond). Its *Animal House* mayhem (reflected in the lyrics, music, and video) was (like the Boys themselves) silly on the surface, but quite crafty in construction. Essentially, the song was an eighties update of the kind of generation gap songs once popular in the 1950s from acts like the Coasters, Hank Ballard, and Chuck Berry. Besides its standard parent-child issues of hairstyles and homework, the Beasties spiced up the lyrics with such lines as "Your mom threw away your best porno mag."[26] Such references were just daring enough to create an aura of youth rebellion, and just innocuous and cheeky enough to be subsumed into the mainstream pop world. This capacity to bridge the hip and the wholesome via humor has been a marker of the band's subversive strategies throughout their career.

Elsewhere on *Ill*, the band play out the standard dozens humor of eighties rap but consistently undercut it with unlikely references and ridiculous "disses." "I got more juice than Picasso got paint," they boast in "The New Style," before launching into a series of juvenile boast-couplets that comment more upon their own wimp-persona than on the credibility of their threats: "Girlfriends with boyfriends are the kind I like. / I'll steal your honey like I stole your bike." These lines are more "Weird Al" Yankovic than New York street rap; they are internally subversive, wry comments undermining the tough street rhetoric of the "serious" rappers. The PMRC crowd found the Beasties to be less than innocent, however, pointing to their lyrics of violence and gunplay. But clearly, theirs is the violence of a Three Stooges sketch, and gun references such as the following from "The New Style" are preposterous in context: "I've got money and juice—twin sisters in my bed / Their father had envy so I shot him in the head."[27]

The Beastie Boys have grown increasingly politically conscious in their more recent output—particularly since 9/11. This greater maturity has not come at the expense of sacrificing their sharp humor, though, as their online-only 2003 antiwar song, "In a World Gone Mad," reveals. Besides being one of the few expressions of dissent from within the music industry (or beyond) to the Iraq invasion, the song is unsparing and courageous in its indictments, particularly considering the chilled, almost McCarthyite environment of that time (as the Dixie Chicks can testify to!). "You and Saddam should kick it like back in the day / With the cocaine and Courvoisier," quip the Boys. The song has a neo-hippy "peace and love" vibe that has always been at the band's core; its pleas for reason, restraint, and resistance to fear-mongering were rare at that time on the national stage. Hitting us with a classic malapropism, they proceed to force the following pointed rhyme: "Now don't get us wrong 'cause we love America / But that's no reason to get hysterica."[28]

To the 5 Boroughs (2004) continues in this lyrical vein. The standard Beastie boasts are still in effect here, and disparate pop culture references jump from every groove as always, but throughout, a more serious purpose merges with the wacky and the witty. As the album title indicates, this is New Yorkers talking to New Yorkers in the post-9/11 world. It is also a targeted diss of Dubya and the various political crises his administration has been responsible for in such realms as foreign policy, the environment, and election fraud. In "It Takes Time to Build," they even implicitly charge Bush with war crimes in the couplet, "Is the U.S. gonna keep breaking necks? / Maybe it's time that we impeach Tex."[29]

Now the elder statesmen of hip-hop and one of the few surviving groups of the first wave, the Beastie Boys continue to develop into new terrain while retaining their original identity as surreal "painterly" rappers in both their sound and lyrical scapes. The universe they have created in just half a dozen studio albums over a twenty-year period suggests that such creativity takes time. Their gonzo serio-comic music may not move the units today that it once did, but these Boys have certainly aged gracefully, and their work continues to have the potent clout of the best subversive humor.

METAL ON METAL

There is a scene in the heavy metal mockumentary *This Is Spinal Tap* (1984) in which the band express their confusion as to why the cover of the band's new album, *Smell the Glove*, has been deemed unacceptably misogynistic, while that of their competitor, Duke Fame, is similarly sadomasochistic in its imagery yet has been released. The difference, explains their manager, Ian Faith, is that on Fame's album cover the man rather than the woman is portrayed as the victim, to which band members David St. Hubbins and Derek Smalls famously conclude that "There's a fine line between clever and . . . stupid."[30] This statement has since been quoted on innumerable occasions by the thousands of fans of this cult film. The comment takes on particular relevance when one considers that heavy metal is the primary satirical target of the *Tap* filmmakers. One could argue that metal's inbuilt excesses make it always (self-)parodic to a degree; furthermore, when one surveys the many metal bands that stormed out of the rock underground throughout the 1980s, their indigenous humor might itself be parsed into two general camps: the clever and the stupid.

Put another way, eighties metal humor consists of bands with a knowing sense of humor (those we laugh with) and others unknowing (those we laugh at). Each has its own potentially subversive elements, depending on the perceptiveness of the audience recipient and whether (s)he (mostly he) gave a "dominant," "negotiated," or "oppositional" listening.[31] The two sides of the metal humor coin are represented by two cult films of the period: *This Is Spinal Tap* brings a "clever," knowing humor to its parodies; it uses superiority humor to expose and ridicule the lack of self-awareness of its fictional band members. *The Decline of Western Civilization Part II: The Metal Years* (1988), on the other hand, is Penelope Spheeris's documentary of the Los Angeles "hair" metal scene during the decade. Unobtrusively, Spheeris lets her self-deluded subjects (W.A.S.P., Poison, Vixen) become their own objects of ridicule. These bands' real antics often trump *Tap*'s parodies, such as when Odin's singer compares his band to Led Zeppelin and the Doors, when, at that time, they did not even have a record deal. Like Robert Plant and Jim Morrison, though, Odin's frontman had a penchant for tight leather pants, except he—in the movie—displayed a preference for the assless cut style.

The distinctions of eighties metal humor can be partially explained when one traces metal back to its influential forerunners. *This Is Spinal Tap* serves us with a history—as well as illustrations—of metal's developments. For example, when Tap perform "Heavy Duty," it seems that we are listening to a typical hard rock metal anthem. Then, suddenly, the song takes a turn when a classical minuet is inserted in the middle eight. On the surface, this is just incongruous silliness, but the broader suggestion is that eighties heavy metal still exhibits many of the art rock affectations that more-serious-minded seventies metal bands harbored. Set against the more primal riffs of eighties metal as well as those featured within the song itself, the farcical classical interlude in "Heavy Duty" serves to highlight sonic incongruity humor, but also the band's hilarious blindness to their own rock pretensions; in other words, their delusional stupidity— and, conversely, the filmmakers' cleverness.

This Is Spinal Tap cuts to the heart of how rock bands have the capacity to so divorce themselves from reality that they disappear into fantasylands where they become the self-proclaimed gods that *deserve* our mockery. Director Rob Reiner portrays his film's band in a perpetual cocoon. We learn that the Tap lads' obsession with rock stardom came early, their arrested adolescence stuck in stasis. Growing up in a state of perpetual childhood, they created an insular fantasy world where the truths of failure were not allowed in. Thus, any threats to the fantasy utopia were ignored or spun into positives. The characters indulge themselves in unattractive self-promotion, fooling themselves (while annoying others) with their delusions of grandeur. In a rock world where glam fantasies are required more than encouraged, and where frontmen are expected to be charismatic über-stars, heavy metal acts have always been susceptible to such slips into self-delusion.

As the fictional Spinal Tap and the *real* bands of *Decline* suggest, many eighties metal acts appropriated the theatrical grandeur of Kiss and Alice Cooper, though not always their accompanying self-effacing humor; however, there were some exceptional bands that adopted and adapted the whole package. These more knowing wits of metal included Van Halen and GWAR. For them, fantasy and reality could be kept at arm's length, and each could be used to comment humorously upon the other.

Van Halen, more than any other band of their era, were responsible for dragging heavy metal from cult semi-underground status and into Middle America's living rooms. They were assisted mightily by MTV, who rotated the band's soft porn comedy videos with clockwork regularity. "Hot for Teacher" (1984)—both song and video—may have disturbed adult moral arbiters, but a new generation of ogling adolescent boys were magnetized by its Benny Hill–type saucy images, while girls could also get excited by the charming camp of blond bombshell frontman David Lee Roth. His tongue-in-cheek physical humor slyly satirized more-earnest metal peers, while his lounge lizard persona undercut his prescribed and expected role as "leader" of a heavy metal band. Roth's contextual comedic contributions can be fully measured only when one considers how bland and unfunny Van Halen became once Sammy Hagar replaced him in the singer's spot.

GWAR are one of the most self-conscious heavy metal bands to come out of the 1980s. More performance artists than serious rockers, they hone in on the costumes and stage-acting legacy of horror-humor that had been left by Screamin' Jay Hawkins, *The Rocky Horror Picture Show,* and Alice Cooper. GWAR (God What an Awful Racket) offer the *Spinal Tap* take on death metal. Their song titles alone give an indication of the type of shock-humor they engage in—"Baby Raper," "Fuckin' an Animal," "Fishfuck"—though the real (he)art of the band is in their stage acts. GWAR's theater of the perverse revolves around an array of props, most of which emit various fluids designed to variously s(t)imulate sadomasochism, sex, and scatology. In the name of gore, band members with such aliases as Oderus Urangus, Jizmak the Gusher, and Slymenstra Hymen act out the essence of their names. A GWAR show is a costume party for kids who wish that Halloween was not just an annual affair, but an every-night carnival celebrating the disturbed and the perverse. But it is also—as they say—all in good fun. The band's id mayhem—set against bare-bones metal riffs—satisfies Freud's principal theory of humor: that it resides in our desires to air sublimated energies of sex and violence. A night out with GWAR is a night of escapist release and of comic relief, where one's only concern is the cost of the laundry the following day.

Like other rock genres founded in the sixties and seventies, heavy metal fragmented into multiple subgenres as the 1980s unwound. Indeed, it has continued to gravitate in many directions over the last two decades, sometimes a cult underground and sometimes re-penetrating mainstream rock culture. Contemporary metal-oriented acts like Marilyn Manson, the Darkness, and Dethklok suggest the diversity of the genre and its humor today. However, certain core metal features still remain intact: glam theatrics, fantasy escapism, and distortion-laden guitar riffs continue as mainstays of the form. How those ingredients are portioned, mixed, and cooked still determines the nature of metal's indigenous humor: whether we laugh at or with the artist; whether it be of the knowing or unknowing kind; how it negotiates that fine line between clever and stupid.

"POST"-FEMINISM

One of the more revolutionary trends of 1980s rock involved the roles and participation of women. Often just the submissive faces that fronted male bands in the past, women's involvement in all aspects of rock culture changed with the spaces made available by the punk rock movement; they became musicians, managers, journalists, record company executives—and singers. Seventies female punks like Siouxsie Sioux, Ari Up, and Poly Styrene may not have emerged as superstars, but they offered prototypes from which a plethora of eighties female artists would draw inspiration. Those female punks who did attain success, such as CBGBs veterans Debbie Harry of Blondie and Tina Weymouth of the Talking Heads, continued to thrive into the eighties, delivering their alternative and often wry takes on gender identity to ever-larger audiences. They continued a New York punk legacy that spawned new subversive humorists from within the Big Apple, too, like performance-musician-radicals Karen Finley and Laurie Anderson, or the no wave "beatnik-from-hell" Lydia Lunch.[32] These artists' avant-garde gestures drew from punk's antagonistic approach while adding new injections of eccentric and provocative humor.

Another mostly male-dominated genre that women subverted by virtue of their very presence as well as their subversive humor was rap music. Few genres have so assertively defined themselves through their testosterone levels as rap, and even fewer have been more sexist in their representations of women. Thus, humor in a female rapper's hands becomes a tool of survival and a tool of cool, hip being the ultimate determinant of artistic survival. In countering the kind of misogyny spouted by 2 Live Crew and Easy E, a female rapper *could* adopt a straight rebuttal approach. However, within this "dozens" arena, such a strategy would be immediately dis(mis)sed with an unceremonious "b" word. But if she counters with humor, as Salt 'n' Pepa do with their mockery of male "tramps," then the males' boasts and abuses are disarmed and trumped. The game-playing involved here is often linguistically esoteric to the out-crowd, but it is the humor that makes possible the assertions of female rappers, and it is the humor that empowers these trickster underdogs.

One type of humor that has been particularly employed by female rappers is that of the bawd, a style that blues women of the past, such as Bessie Smith, Millie Jackson, and Big Mama Thornton, used so subversively. Tricia Rose explains: "Similar to women's blues, [female raps] are caustic, witty, and aggressive warnings directed at men and at other women who might be seduced by them in the future."[33] Some of the more bawdy and bold women rappers have arisen from the genre's most macho subgenre—gangsta rap. Hoes Wit Attitude (HWA), Boss, and Bytches With Problems (BWP) are female rap acts who have recognized the power of their sexuality and have used it in often humorous fashions for their gorily detailed subversive revenge fantasies. Often appropriating the words "bitch" and "ho" as badges of honor (much as gays have done with "queer" and African Americans have done with "nigger"), these women steal the thunder of male offenders through strategies of rhetorical disarmament (of men) and rearmament (of themselves). BWP's "Coming Back Strapped" (1991) offers a classic female revenge fantasy, while "Two Minute Brother" (1991) is a "slight" put-down of a somewhat different kind. These songs suggest that this is not your mother's women's movement, and that the liberal era of consciousness-raising is being bypassed by a new kind of feminism.

These strategies of 1980s feminism—as exercised by its pop heroines—were tagged by some as "post"-feminist by virtue of their differences from previous feminist approaches and as a reference to their connection to the cultural condition of postmodernism. Post-feminism had its leading practitioner and cheerleader in pop's first female superstar: Madonna. With a sense of humor never off-duty, Madonna has commandeered all media outlets—music, videos, magazines, books, TV, film—as means to express herself. In a process that continues to this day, she has subverted (if not transformed) conventions of gender, race, and sexuality that, prior to her, had stood firm and secure in the face of criticism.

Madonna

The "Queen of Pop" is also the chameleon of pop. And as much as Madonna has changed the stripes of her music and style over the last three decades, she has also drawn variously from a broad history of humor in facilitating their execution. The "bawd" and the "bitch" are the two principle *types* of humor that Madonna employs, and comediennes Mae West and Bette Midler, as well as comedic actresses Carole Lombard, Judy Holliday, and Marilyn Monroe, have been her primary influences. Through them, Madonna learned the art of put-on humor, how to pose for the masculine gaze in a way that undermines its objectification. Like the screwball female comics of Hollywood's "golden age," Madonna learned the skills of the subversive trickster: exaggerating, parodying, and pretending.

Madonna is the principle postmodern icon of the video age; her music is largely irrelevant next to the enormity of her persona and image. Her twenty-five year masquerade ball has seen her "toy" with gender archetypes with such sustained ingenuity that she has become the most discussed (and argued about) figure of modern feminism. Some have seen her highly sexualized images as semi-pornographic, perpetuating submissive roles for women. Others have seen her as a libertine, breaking down the constrictive roles that patriarchy has historically assigned to women. Whoever you spoke to about Madonna during the 1980s, they were sure to have an opinion (or two). Her protean transformations have fascinated and flabbergasted, eliciting extreme reactions of love and hate. Furthermore, her ongoing world of controversy—a byproduct of her trickster antics—continues to this day. Like other tricksters before her, Madonna is a savvy, one-step-ahead maverick who tweaks the nerves of the cultural subconscious, creating by deconstructing, regenerating by subverting. The most successful female recording artist of all time is also its craftiest humorist.

The most provocative period of Madonna's career was her early "virgin" years. Though her initial work caused rumblings in disco quarters, her sophomore effort, *Like a Virgin* (1984), established her as the most important female figure in the pop world. The title track offered the initial shock, its lyrics and video ambiguously oscillating between images of a sex kitten and a coquettish innocent. Both were submissive "acts," as well as parodies of conventional male desires. Susan J. Douglas adds, "Madonna was posing both as a sex object and as someone ridiculing the passivity that usually goes with being a sex object."[34] Young girls were particularly intrigued by Madonna's combination of strength and seduction. They related not so much to the sexuality as they did to her control of that sexuality, and they demonstrated their adoration by becoming "wannabes," copying every detail of their pop heroine's wardrobe and gestures.

Feminist critics, too, were quick to note that Madonna provided a new representation of female empowerment, one that sacrificed neither independence nor femininity. She seemed to straddle (among other things!) previously designated categories of masculine and feminine, straight and gay, serious and comedic. This boundary-blurring facilitated different readings from different audiences (or different readings from the same person); it destabilized our binary thinking and simultaneously satirized all "fixed" thinkers in the process.

The postmodern revolution of gender consciousness was no accident. Madonna-the-trickster was not only one step ahead of the game but she was also perfectly cognizant of the strategies and effects of her provocations. Her early style is illustrative of this point. The navel-exposing blouses (now mainstream fashion), crucifix earrings, and "Boy Toy" belts were all skillfully selected items designed to elicit a reactionary response. Was she a slut? Sacrilegious? Submissive? For Madonna, her accoutrements were tease-(s)a(t)tire, representing the right to rebel, to dupe, and to be playfully irreverent. "Everything I do is sort of tongue in cheek," she once admitted.[35] And of the controversial "Boy Toy" belts, she explained, "They [the critics] didn't get the joke. The whole point is that I'm *not* anybody's toy."[36]

Amid the firestorm that greeted "Like a Virgin," Madonna released "Material Girl" (1984), with its equally provocative video. At one level this song seemed to represent Madonna coming clean with her critics, conceding that her skills were in marketing, not art. The admission "We're living in a material world / And I am a material girl" appeared to be a confession of her own shallowness.[37] Again, though, Madonna was playing to established prejudices by ironically mocking them. Exaggerations, stereotypes, and intertextual allusions are all comedic techniques on display in the "Material Girl" video, and the song's lyrics serve a supporting role with their "low" humor puns and double entendres.

The video transports us to the "material world" of the classic Hollywood comedy *Gentlemen Prefer Blondes* (1953) (itself an adaptation of the 1925 Anita Loos novel of the same name). A comparative mode is established as the "Diamonds Are a Girl's Best Friend" sequence is recreated as pastiche for "Material Girl." The original "Diamond" scene had featured Marilyn Monroe in a role that parodied gold-digging materialism, showing her as submissive to the men holding the purse strings. Madonna, oft tagged as a Monroe wannabe, replayed this famous scene over the "Material Girl" musical backdrop. An intertextual dialogue then unfolds as we are forced to compare the respective texts. Madonna does not merely offer a pastiche, though; rather, she pushes her interpretation into parody by exaggerating Monroe's sexual gestures and by commanding the camera's gaze with sly glances and wry smiles. The nod and wink that she brings to the performance stresses a put-on knowingness; the video thus not only seconds the parody of materialism intended by the original, but it also parodies the movie itself because we (the audience) and she (Madonna) share a tacit understanding that Madonna would never be on the submissive side of any situation. The assertive independence that Madonna had established in the public sphere by the time of this video positioned her as a postmodern feminist in contrast to the Monroe film's earlier representations of female identity.

Over the years, Madonna has continued to serve as a touchstone for cultural debates around issues of gender and sexual identity. And she has continued to respond with ever more outrageous acts and gestures of provocation. Like most artists of the 1980s, she learned the art of media-tion from punk rock, with its "cash from chaos" situationist insurrections. Even as recently as 2003, Madonna, a mature wife and mother in her mid-forties, rejuvenated the slumping sales of her *American Life* album by kissing Britney Spears, then Christina Aguilera—each former wannabes—at the MTV Video Music Awards in a mock-ceremonial passing of the Sapphic torch. The trickster has been no less controversial in her recent videos: "What It Feels Like for a Girl" (2000) was pulled due to its graphic violence (courtesy of director-husband Guy Richie), and "American Life" (2003) was rejected by many outlets because of its strident antiwar message. If Madonna's subversive instincts are mellowing with age, they have clearly not disappeared. When she does hang up her final costume, history will look back on Madonna not only as the "Queen of Pop" but also as the queen of trickster humor.

NOVELTY UPDATE

Novelty songs have been a fixture in popular music since before the birth of rock. During their fifties heyday, they functioned in tandem with children's cartoons and comic books, as silly ditties like Sheb Wooley's "Purple People Eater" (1958) captured the hearts and imaginations of preadolescents. Soon after, folk singers like Tom Lehrer and Roger Miller and country artists like Ray Stevens and Homer & Jethro made novelty songs staples of their respective genres, appealing to kids of all ages. Sometimes their good-natured buffoonery had a sly subversive edge to it, but for the most part, their songs were innocent responses to current events and fads. Though the novelty craze continued into the sixties and seventies, sustained by a parade of one-hit-wonder bubblegum bands, it became a dominant force again in the eighties pop charts, courtesy of the most unlikely new source: rap music.

Since its teething years at the turn of the decade, rap had prided itself on being a musical genre of serious intents, capturing the sometimes brutal realities of African American urban street life. It quickly gained a reputation for its harsh, often profane language, and where it exhibited humor, that was harsh and "black," too. Such a character (and caricature) made the more radical rap artist persona non grata on MTV (at least, for the first half of the eighties) and on most mainstream radio outlets. In response, certain emerging rap artists turned their pens to writing more accessible rhymes, trimming (or masking) the sex and violence in their product. These acts appealed to younger demographics that had been excluded by rap's adult themes, while earning themselves an entree into the premier outlets of the mass media.

Physical humor was an integral part of many of the novelty rappers, the more portly characters transforming themselves into self-designated sex symbols with their tongue-in-cheek boasts. Heavy D & the Boyz were the leading lovers of large, recording songs like "Mr. Big Stuff" and "The Overweight Lovers in the House" for their 1987 album *Living Large*. Likewise, the Fat Boys exploited their physical "attributes" for novelty effect, taking their collective 750 pounds to the stages of America and beyond. Their 1987 album *Crushin'* promoted their gimmick to full effect while introducing Darren Robinson's human beatbox to adoring fans. Overall, though, neither the Fat Boys nor Heavy D shook the world of rap, even if their physical charms were sufficient to engage the interests of the preadolescent set.

Tone Loc and Biz Markie used the gimmick of their novel voices to become novelty successes. Songs like "Pickin' Boogers" (1988) suggested the juvenile quality of Biz Markie's lyrical wit, but it was his outrageously out-of-tune, off-key voice that endeared him to the masses. "Just a Friend" (1989) may be the worst-sung hit in the history of rock, and its incongruity humor is only furthered in the video where "the clown prince of hip-hop" assumes the role of Mozart, complete with powdered wig, thus hilariously conflating high art with vocal artlessness. Tone Loc, too, stamped his identity on his songs through his unmistakable voice; its deep, gravelly quality alluded to like-sounding sex-crooners such as Barry White and Isaac Hayes, but it bore the "tone" of parody in its exaggerated raunchiness. Tone Loc ruled pop rap in 1989 with his two slightly saucy novelty hits, "Wild Thing" and "Funky Cold Medina."

Many eighties rappers were also savvy businessmen, and as such they were fully conscious of the marketplace and their demographic reach when constructing their songs. One can assume that the "class comedians" of novelty rap were studying fifties acts like the Coasters and Chuck Berry when they set about writing their own slyly and slightly subversive generation gap anthems. DJ Jazzy Jeff & the Fresh Prince introduced Will Smith to popular culture long before he lived in Bel-Air or defended the earth against aliens. However, his opportunism was clearly well honed as early as the mid-eighties as he and his partner crafted a series of bubblegum hits for the kids. "Parents Just Don't Understand" (1988) was an update of the Coasters' "Yakety Yak" (1958), playing coyly to young people's burgeoning rebellious instincts. Few found the theme controversial in the 1980s, though, as MTV made the song's video—an even more innocuous brew of slapstick and bright kiddie colors—a regular on its limited rotation schedule.

Kid 'n' Play were another rap comedy duo who pitched their rhymes at the lowest demographic constituency. Like the Fresh Prince, Kid 'n' Play parlayed their toddler appeal into broader media, as the *House Party* movies and a Saturday morning cartoon show were created to showcase the lovable lads. Their 1988 album, *2 Hype*, was perhaps ironically titled, as Kid's six-inch-high hair construction was certainly the act's most creative asset.

The clever kid of the school joker rappers was Young MC. Besides writing many of the other novelty hits of his era (e.g., Tone Loc's), Young MC had bona fide rapping skills. His articulate speed-style flow was everywhere during 1989, then nowhere the following year. By Andy Warhol's measurements, Young MC enjoyed about 1.5 minutes of fame, though that was long enough for him to leave behind some classy bubblegum hits with "Bust a Move" and "Principal's Office," the latter a regeneration of the Chuck Berry–Coasters oeuvre.

Novelty songs are not built to offend, but as some of the above examples suggest, they can sometimes offer crafty commentary that might be deemed light rebellion. Perhaps the most controversial of the novelty rappers was Sir Mix-a-Lot. His 1992 "Baby Got Back" hit sparked debate across the land about the offensiveness of the lyrical (and video) content. Was it sexist objectification in the 2 Live Crew vein, as some feminists claimed? Or was it celebrating the virtues of the black woman's derriere, as many defenders claimed? Or was it an implicit critique of the media's privileging of "white," tight behinds, as others alleged? As voices raged over this crude but good-natured novelty song, sales grew to over two million copies. Mix-a-Lot's attempt to capitalize on his riches with the 1994 follow-up "Put 'Em on the Glass" failed, while his follow-up to the follow-up, "Big Johnson" (2003), constituted an attempted penance of sorts, as the knighted one switched gender and concerns and poked some fun at male boasting. His apparent attempt to spark his own "Annie" or "Roxanne's Revenge" response chain, however, ultimately interested no one but himself. Nevertheless, Sir Mix-a-Lot, unlike many of his novelty peers, was far from a one-trick pony, despite suffering from the genre's common one-hit wonder fate. His sex-lite provocations and conscious lampooning of gangsta rap made him one of the more radical pop rappers. His exaggerated parody-of-a-pimp image deflated the self-importance of the new gangsta rappers, while he released comedic songs like "Square Dance Rap" (1988) and socially conscious ones like "One Time's Got No Case" (1992) (about racial profiling) on his own Nastymix label. Collaborations with the punk-novelty outfit the Presidents of the United States of America showed that Sir Mix-a-Lot aimed to stretch the artistic consumption of the kids, rather than merely empty their pockets.

If rap music perpetuated the one-hit-wonder tradition of novelty pop, "Weird Al" Yankovic has proved to be the most notable exception to this rule. His "nerd" parodies of the trends and musical trendsetters of his time—coupled with his own humorous originals—have taken Yankovic's career on a long and winding road from 1979's "My Bologna" (a parody of the Knack's "My Sharona") to his most recent and most successful (to date) album release, *Straight Outta Lynwood* (2006) (a hat-tip reference to NWA's controversial *Straight Outta Compton* [1988]). Oscillating between the silly and the subversive over his twenty-seven-year career, "Weird Al" Yankovic has become the most famous and successful novelty act in the history of pop music.

"Weird Al" Yankovic

By the time "Weird Al" released his debut 1979 single, the music industry had become a bloated monolith. And his subsequent success and staying power owed much to what mainstream American music had in large part become by the dawn of the eighties: an arena for self-important egotists offering up excessively grandiose product. Setting his sights on the worst offenders, "Weird Al" deflated the pretensions of modern rock, knocking the stuffing out of its pomp and circumstance. His parodic technique was to leave the music intact but to change the lyrics, making them comically incongruous to the original. The result was a form of superiority humor, whereby the earnest seriousness of a song was implicitly mocked when replaced with the absurd alternative. With his keen eye for the topical and the typical of his society, Yankovic's parodies have served as watchdogs for the (rock) culture, subverting pretensions and undermining narcissists.

Known primarily for his parodies of others' songs, "Weird Al" has also written original songs that allude to a particular artist's style ("Dog Eat Dog" [1986] on the Talking Heads) or to a specific genre ("Good Enough for Now" [1986] on country music). Sometimes, as in his accordion-based polka songs, he flips his conventional approach of replicating the music and changing the lyrics. Here, original lyrics are used while the music functions as the comedic incongruity. A great number of his songs are novelty in nature but are originals. In many of these songs a satirical element is evident, though the songs do not necessarily use parody. His most popular and subversive songs remain the parodies, though. Here, his lyrics pack an extra punch by virtue of their altered context, in comparison to the original.

Yankovic's catalogue is far from being full of subversive material, though, and his albums contain as many comedic duds as gems. Moreover, he is driven neither by the anger of Jello Biafra nor the intent to maim exhibited by Randy Newman in his writing. In fact, most of Yankovic's songs are quite tame, and he takes great pride in being a family-friendly comic whose songs can be comfortably consumed by pre-adolescents and old-timers alike. Indeed, one of his few instances of public outrage occurred when he discovered that "offensive" Al–style songs, falsely attributed to him, were floating around the Internet. His songwriting and comedic methods—for the most part—are geared toward eliciting laughter rather than a shock reaction.

Nevertheless, many of "Weird Al" Yankovic's songs do contain commentary as well as comedy, and this is reflected in the type of songs he chooses to adopt and adapt. Michael Jackson's early-eighties hits have the kind of fake bluster and melodrama suited for Yankovic's satirical pen, so it is no coincidence that Jackson has been a go-to artist for Weird Al over the years. Both "Bad" (1987) and "Beat It" (1983) have undergone commercially successful Al treatments. For both, he used one of his favorite topics, food, to parody the gang machismo of the originals. In "Eat It" (1984) he adopts the pseudo-aggression of the original, but here it is redirected into the context of a parent instructing his child to eat his food. Michael Jackson's originals already verged on self-parody and were therefore amenable to comedic treatment. Al returned to the same well for "Snack All Night" (1999), a take on "Black or White" (1991). In this instance, Jackson—usually a good sport about Al's tamperings—was less than amused, requesting that the parody version not be released for fear that the original's "serious" message be undermined.

Acquiring permission to adapt pre-released material has been a constant headache for Yankovic. Even though the "Fair Use" section of U.S. copyright law gives him the right to parody without consent, Al has made it a personal policy of good manners to obtain the artist's authorization prior to parodying his/her songs. Most have happily obliged, regarding an Al rendition as a badge of honor, though a few have refused. Prince and Paul McCartney have both waved the red flag, while Eminem's denial received much publicity when Al, on one of his TV specials, spliced new questions into an existing Eminem interview. The result was to show the Slim Shady up as both a hypocrite and a spoiled brat—even more than his initial refusal had done. In a recent incident, Atlantic Records denied Yankovic permission to parody "You're So Beautiful" (2006), when the artist, James Blunt, had already given the thumbs up to proceed. In retaliation, in addition to posting the song online, Al included a scene on his "White and Nerdy" (2006) video that showed him adding "You Suck" to the Wikipedia page for Atlantic Records. Seeing this, a geek-gang of Al fanatics headed for their computers and, in a copycat gesture, actually carried out the defacing. These fallout incidents indicate the larger subversive potential of Weird Al's work. When artists or companies object to his generally inoffensive comedy, they only reveal themselves to be the self-important prigs that got them targeted for lampooning in the first place. For Al, the practical humor of such extracurricular activities becomes an additional strategy of his publicity and marketing.

Rap music, with its exaggerated macho boasting and strutting, has been a suitably prime target for Yankovic's parodic censures over the years. Coolio, like Eminem, revealed himself to be a humorless hypocrite when he complained about Al's hit version ("Amish Paradise" [1996]) of his own hit ("Gangsta's Paradise" [1995]). Coolio apparently saw little irony in the fact that his song was an almost wholesale copy of Stevie Wonder's original "Pastime Paradise" (1976). Chamillionaire was less "objectionable" when Weird Al recently re-recorded "Ridin'" (2006) as "White and Nerdy" (2006). Setting his geek persona against the street context of the original, Al raps, "My rims never spin, to the contrary / You'll find that they're quite stationary." He then boasts of how he's "fluent in Java Script as well as Klingon."[38]

Whereas "White and Nerdy" is self-deprecating in its satire of contemporary geek culture, Yankovic is at his most subversive when he explicitly targets the foibles and idiosyncrasies of the artists he covers. "It's Still Billy Joel to Me" (1980) plays upon Joel's reputation, at the time, as a Jack-of-all-trades, an artist who blithely plunders myriad musical styles while giving his songs no personal stamp of distinction. Equally below the belt is "This Song Is Just Six Words Long" (1988), which ridicules George Harrison's bubblegum-like lyrical repetition in his too-chart-friendly, pandering-to-the-masses comeback hit, "Got My Mind Set on You" (1987). One of Weird Al's biggest hits came at the expense of Nirvana in 1992. "Smells Like Nirvana" not only made fun of the incomprehensible lyrics of "Smells Like Teen Spirit" (1992) but it also implicitly suggested that Kurt Cobain was feigning his slurred vocals in order to posture as a rebel-rocker. "We're so loud and incoherent / Boy, this oughta bug your parents," screams Al-as-Kurt.[39] Cobain, far from offended, expressed his feeling of privilege at being one of Yankovic's chosen few.

Besides his chastening superiority humor, Yankovic was also aware of the relief humor he was providing for his audience. On hearing of his own parents' shocking deaths from carbon monoxide poisoning in 2004, Al chose to perform that night's show, saying, "Since my music had helped many of my fans through tough times, maybe it would work for me as well."[40] For Al, and for all novelty humorists, comedy is not about condemnation, though it may have a critical side; primarily it is about entertainment and the capacity to bring laughter to the belly and sustenance to the heart.

THIS IS RADIO COLLEGE

Critic John Street estimates that in the U.K. in 1982, there were 1,500 independent record labels, and they accounted for 40 percent of that year's releases.[41] A similar situation existed contemporaneously in the U.S. as the independent scene consolidated into an established underground. Sometimes this world functioned in antagonistic opposition to mainstream corporate rock, and other times it just operated as a shadow reality.

In this broadening of the subaltern rock base, the indie labels were not alone; they were supported and sustained by the expansion and increasing reach of U.S. college radio. Rad(io) college stations would prove to be the sole outlet for the post-punk genres soon to be tagged as alternative rock, and, later, as indie rock.

Many of the new acts proved to be as independent of the old punk sounds and attitudes as they were from mainstream rock. Processed through the middle class, intellectual environs of college radio, the new bands often satisfied the clever-seeking eccentrics among the more alienated college kids. In this process, punk-style class struggle became a less pronounced lyrical concern, and previous musical formulas exploded into a fragmented array of sounds and styles. This diversity was encouraged by the college radio system itself. Because every major college town had its own student-run station by the 1980s, post-punk production spread beyond the old New York–L.A. nexus, taking in soon-to-be celebrated rock cities like Athens, Georgia, and Minneapolis, Minnesota.

The key transitional band between hardcore punk and alternative college rock was the Replacements, from Minneapolis. They would also prove to be a pivotal forerunner of the subsequent slacker rock and grunge of the 1990s. Between 1981 and 1991, the Mats (as they were often affectionately called) transformed themselves from the raging hardcore of *Sorry Ma, Forgot to Take Out the Trash* (1981) to the sophisticated alt-country of their later work. Through it all, the Replacements were conscious humorists, exuding a loser persona a few six-packs south of Jonathan Richman & the Modern Lovers. Their middle-class angst, literate lyricism, and self-deprecating anthems endeared the band to the college radio crowd, who embraced them as kings of the losers.

The Mats' "don't-give-a-shit" image provided a witty counterpoint to the shameless fame-seekers of mainstream music. Their slovenly poses—beers in hand—coupled with their obstreperous attitudes to rock shows, recording, and videos, showed a band resistant to the rules of the game; they celebrated carefree arrested adolescence with abandon, and, in return, the indie rock underground celebrated them. During one band meeting, the band decided to title their just-recorded album after the next song that came on the radio; this turned out to be the classic "Let It Be" (1970)/*Let It Be* (1984). Pressured to make a video for their breakthrough hit "Bastards of Young" (1985), the band provided a three-and-a-half-minute single fixed shot of an amplifier speaker. Onstage, their irreverent practical joking became legendary, shows inevitably degenerating into drunken jam sessions covering the most unlikely songs. "I guess you could say we're a sloppy rock & roll band that tries to straddle the line between comedy and tragedy," frontman Paul Westerberg once explained with typical wry understatement.[42] Besides putting Minneapolis on the map as a city of alt-rock activity, the Mats offered a model of honesty and self-deprecation that was deeply appreciated by a college rock community increasingly cynical about the manipulations of the mainstream; furthermore, at a visceral level, their adolescent antics provided their audience with vicarious opportunities for free-spiritedness and primal pleasures.

Another Midwestern band that steered Jonathan Richman's loser humor into eighties indie rock was Milwaukee's Violent Femmes. Their take on Richman's innovations was quite different, though, stressing bitterness over resignation. In songs like "Gone Daddy Gone" (1983), "Kiss Off" (1983), and "Add It Up" (1983), singer Gordon Gano spewed angst and anger with such venom and coarseness that the tragic themes lurched into the realm of comic self-parody. The Femmes played a quirky acoustic folk-punk that provided a playful soundtrack to Gano's incessant whining. As with the Replacements, college listeners lapped up these cynics' miserabilia with an empathetic gleeful joy.

The decidedly art school–intellectual branches of post-punk also flourished within college radio's academic halls. Jonathan Richman and the Talking Heads provided the most immediate inroads here, but more avant-garde approaches were also fostered by the noncommercial determinants at play. New York's King Missile developed within the experimental traditions of their native city, while they adopted Richman's deadpan delivery style for their own quirky storytelling. It would be 1993 before the band enjoyed their moment in the sun with the minor breakthrough hit "Detachable Penis," but throughout the late eighties they wowed college audiences with their eccentric topics and absurdist musings. Singer John S. Hall explained why "Jesus Was Way Cool" (1990) and told us the tale of the "Cheesecake Truck" (1990). He even prescribed some practical subversion in "Take Stuff from Work" (1990). With King Missile, one could never predict what would come next, but it was invariably—as their 1990 album title proclaimed—"mystical shit."

On the geekier side of the intellectual wing of college rock were They Might Be Giants. Bostonians like their guru Jonathan Richman, the Giants were quirky and bizarre but never less than literate. The imaginative scope of their lyrics was matched by the eclectic range of their music styles. Incorporating sounds ranging from Tin Pan Alley to punk, they introduced unhip-then-hip instruments like the accordion into unpredictably catchy songs with such nonsense titles as "Birdhouse in Your Soul" (1990) and "Youth Culture Killed My Dog" (1986). Even less could be decoded from their lyrics, which were usually free associations. Band leaders John Flansburgh and John Linnell proved their mettle as "practical" jokers, too, when they set up a dial-a-song system on their answering machines to promote their songs and get a record deal. This bizarre experiment proved successful, and the band have been cranking out their idiosyncratic brand of geek rock ever since.

A harder-edged manifestation of TMBG's surrealistic absurdism was put forth by Camper Van Beethoven. The violin was to Camper what the accordion was to TMBG: an instrumental quirk that took the band a little astray of the conventional new wave sound. Like TMBG, too, Camper drew liberally from various music styles, regenerating them in a unique brew. From their California roots the band inherited a sarcastic—often cutting—lyrical point of view as well as the Valley-boy vocal clip of singer David Lowery. Incongruity was the nature of Camper Van Beethoven's humor, as revealed in "Eye of Fatima, Pt. 1" (1988), a song about giving acid to cowboys, and "Take the Skinheads Bowling" (1985), the nonsense-sense sing-along number that became a cult hit on college radio from coast to coast.

While Camper Van Beethoven were skewering the skinheads, another college radio cult band was satirizing frat boys, plastic punks, the paisley underground scene, and the British goth-dance set: the Dead Milkmen. Spearheaded by singer Rodney Anonymous and guitarist Joe Jack Talcum, the band graduated into immaturity from their Temple University foundations. The lovable flipside of the Dead Kennedys' school of mockery, the Dead Milkmen were college wise-asses of the most sophomoric kind. Their 1985 underground hit "Bitchin' Camaro" established a colorful lyrical palette, while their 1986 album *Eat Your Paisley*—which included "The Thing That Only Eats Hippies"—established the band as the premier provocateurs of the in-crowd in college rock. As adept at gross-out humor ("The Puking Song" [1990]) as they were at cute 'n' cuddly satire ("Punk Rock Girl" [1988]), the Milkmen brought a cutting edge to novelty punk rock. And when it came to their own likes and dislikes, they celebrated fellow outcast eccentric wits like Mojo Nixon with the same openness and enthusiasm that they put into mocking the pretentious self-importance of subcultures like the California paisley set and the English doom-and-gloomers. "Instant Club Hit (You'll Dance to Anything)" (1987) was their shout-down to the latter.

The punk-centered satirists of college rock represented by the Dead Milkmen included kindred spirits such as blues-country "redneck" ironists Mojo Nixon and Jon Spencer and funkier pioneers like the Red Hot Chili Peppers. Fronted by the dynamic comedic duo of singer Anthony Kiedis and his bass-slapping sidekick Flea, the Chili Peppers brought a carnival spirit to eighties indie rock. Part punk, part clowns, somehow the band have taken their George Clinton chops and minimalist stage costumes (strategically placed tube socks!) to the international stage, attracting many copycats in their wake. Their current worldwide fan base continues to pay homage to these pied pipers of silly-funk, following their carefree, irreverent party-parade as it dances into its third decade.

The Red Hot Chili Peppers, Mojo Nixon, and Jon Spencer illustrate how the innovative college-radio bands were also—like the other postmodern acts of the era—drawing from genres past. As unlikely as it might have seemed at the end of the seventies when punk was at its peak, even the sixties hippy movement was being integrated into the post-punk world by the early eighties. Early practitioners of this curious punk-hippy paradox were the Flaming Lips. Maybe their Oklahoma base made them less susceptible to national trends, but since 1985, Wayne Coyne has led his band of renegades through new worlds of whimsy as eccentric as any Syd Barrett produced. Delving into the surreal, the trippy, and the psychedelic, the band has continually amazed with striking sounds that oscillate between harsh noise and melody, the abstract and the celestial. With a straight-man but melodramatic delivery, Coyne has crafted oddball epics with such wacky titles as "Pilot Can at the Queer of God" (1993) and "Yeah, I Know It's a Drag . . . but Wastin' Pigs Is Still Radical" (1991). The resulting incongruity between the earnest and the absurd plays games with our senses, not to mention our common sense. To this day the Lips continue to leaven the pervasively cynical tone of indie rock with off-kilter childlike whimsy, but in their ruptured deconstructions of craft, their wi(l)de-eyed innocence has proven no less challenging to our receptive expectations.

X-TREME HUMOR

As alternative rock stretched its imagination into new corners of creativity, there emerged a number of bands that were too hot even for college radio to handle. These bands inhabited the outer edges of the rock body and often tested the tolerance of its most ardent supporters. These were the bands mentioned in hushed tones in specialized independent record stores, where their records were passed along—like forbidden porno mags—in brown paper wrappers. Inspired by the anarchic impulse of punk as well as by antecedent eccentrics like the Velvet Underground, Captain Beefheart, Iggy Pop, and Hasil Adkins, the extreme artists of the eighties were often offensive, sick, and painful to even the most open-minded listener. In pursuit of the harshest anti-aesthetic, these bands ventured down dim and dangerous paths, where the humor was darker and more extreme in its excesses. From GG Allin and the Butthole Surfers in the United States to the Macc Lads and Throbbing Gristle in the U.K., eighties extreme humor was trangressive, provocative, and sometimes very *un*funny; its "sick"-ness proffered its relief, its anti-aesthetics served as an anesthetic, and its incongruity with all basic social and/or musical mores forced constant subversion of the limits of our freedom of expression.

Developing in parallel to the extreme rock humorists of the decade was the "sick" stand-up comedy revolution. Inspired by Lenny Bruce's provocative and combative satire in the fifties and sixties, the eighties sick comics bypassed conventional manners and political correctness, offering up a raw, profane form of assault humor that sought to awaken the social sleepwalkers of Reagan's America. Among these loose-cannon comics were Bill Hicks, Sam Kineson, Andrew Dice Clay, and Roseanne Barr. Though hardly one and the same, they shared an "anti" attitude that aimed to shake up conventional thoughts, beliefs, and behaviors. Their instincts were libertarian, and like their extreme musical counterparts, they often served up a brand of humor that was as ugly and disturbing as it was amusing.

The musical roots of extreme rock humorists can be found in hardcore punk. L.A. hardcore bands like the Germs and Fear were primary forerunners of the new extremists of subversive humor. Next to the Germs' Darby Crash, Iggy Pop's stage antics seemed choreographed, while Fear's Lee Ving perpetrated offensive humor and humorous offenses that made the Sex Pistols seem like voices of reason. Exaggerating the primal (if not the subhuman), these hardcore acts were uncaged beasts of mayhem, providing a circus for the depraved in which the bands continually performed a high-wire act.

The bastard child of extreme hardcore punk was GG Allin, though he was subversive by essence as much as by design. He was an anti-artist who upped the ante on being anti; his rebellion was *in extremis*, with transgressions of pathological proportions. His subversions of any and all conventions produced "art" of the most incongruous kind; it was painfully hilarious through its sheer audacity. Darby Crash and Sid Vicious may have been his models, but GG Allin took their abject aberrations into the abyss of degradation. The very embodiment of Freud's "id" concept, Allin set free his inner child in a wholesale purge. Sex and violence, the two primary sublimated human forces according to Freud, course through his perverse songs. "Kill Thy Father, Rape Thy Mother" (1993), "Expose Yourself to Kids" (1986), and "Suck My Ass It Smells" (1993) are but a few examples of his "psycho"-sexual predilections. Allin's scatological potty-humor was the calling card of his stage shows, too, where blood, piss, and shit would all emanate from his body to the stage. Between swigs of Jack Daniels, Allin shoved the mic stand up his ass or assaulted (or was assaulted by) his audience. His Marquis de Sade–like transgressions came to a close in 1993, when the man christened Jesus Christ Allin died of a drug overdose. Whether GG Allin was a funny but troubled man (i.e., we laugh at him) or a scheming subversive humorist (i.e., we laugh with him) is a debate that lingers. Whether he was rock sicko or sick comic, his physically grotesque humor lingers in the minds, hearts, and intentions of all new punk bands that plan at their outset to be the most offensive, shocking, and disturbing *act* of all time.

More (un)natural successors to extreme hardcore—and to an extent heavy metal—came from a subgenre of eighties alternative rock that one might call the "underground underclass." Like extras from the *Texas Chainsaw Massacre* films, these rocking "rednecks" mixed humor and horror to concoct expressions of the grotesque. Unlike heavy metal horror humorists GWAR and White Zombie, these underground slasher merchants seemed less theatrically contrived. Texas's Butthole Surfers were the frontiersmen of this grotesquery, their "twisted circus" of "killer clowns" attracting those in search of danger.[43] Their depraved cultural observations came in the form of "noisious" songs with hilarious titles like "The Revenge of Anus Presley" (1983) and "The Shah Sleeps in Lee Harvey Oswald's Grave" (1983), and on albums called *Brown Reason to Live* (1981) and *Rembrandt Pussyhorse* (1986). Chief freak Gibby Haynes stalked stages with genuine menace as nude dancers, fire-eaters, and sex change movies provided supplemental visuals. Music journalist Michael Azerrad described the Butthole

Surfers as "creepy and dark and ugly and weird" and said they "seemed like they were from another planet."[44] He recalled an early instance of their distinctive sick humor, when Haynes and his cohorts produced a Texas fanzine called *Strange VD*. The zine featured the most horrific pictures of medical deformity the band could find, paired with funny tag lines. Sick indeed.

Strangely enough, the Surfers were not alone in their grotesque travesties of "white trash" degenerates from the heartland. The Birthday Party, Flipper, and Mojo Nixon all indulged in such fare, though to differing comedic degrees. Mojo Nixon was the motor-mouthed Hunter S. Thompson of extreme underground rock. His gonzo rants targeted then-celebrities ("Debbie Gibson's Pregnant with My Two-Headed Love Child" [1989], "Don Henley Must Die" [1990]), social exploitations ("I Hate Banks" [1986], "Burn Down the Malls" [1986], "Jesus at McDonalds" [1985]), and other pop culture paraphernalia of note (or not). Some regarded Nixon's X-rated tribute to MTV VJ Martha Quinn, "Stuffin' Martha's Muffin" (1986), as crossing the "good taste" line, while distributors refused to handle his ode to corporate rock, "Bring Me the Head of David Geffen" (1995). His absurdist blue-collar celebrations evoke the spirit of Kinky Friedman, and they are still held in reverence by the PBR-drinking cultural slummers of alternative rock culture.

Steve Albini noise-casted from within musical constructs more conventionally rock, though his guitar experiments were often as dissonant and jarring as those of the post-hardcore herd. Another advocate of the no pain, no gain school of provocation, Albini's band, Big Black, set dentist-drill guitars against a drum machine pulse. Not content just to test his audience's eardrums, he then sang lyrics on such taboo topics as rape, murder, and incest—without a point of view discernibly sympathetic to the victim. Like Randy Newman, he often sang his songs "in character," but unlike Newman he was never concerned when they were "misread" or when he was condemned for the ambiguity of his positions. Michael Azerrad and other Big Black critics have questioned whether Albini was an "unabashed bigot or a merciless satirist."[45] Some have argued that he was both.

EXTREME TAKEOVER

Many of the trends established in 1980s rock continued into and throughout the 1990s. The incorporation of technological advancements, the fragmentation and multiplication of genres, and the referential recycling of the past were all postmodern trends central to both decades. However, the most surprising legacy came from the most unlikely source: extreme humor. Despite the extremists' presence in all the cracks, margins, and netherworlds of eighties rock culture, few could have predicted their rise and dominance in the next decade, and that this once "alternative" sensibility would so forcefully penetrate the mainstream. Sex and violence—the two fundamental forces underpinning all rock rebellion—would become even more explicit in the nineties, and identity politics would become more extreme.

The new extreme performers pushed the outer limits, not only of musical conduct, but of humor, too. Cynicism became the prevailing disposition of the new era, its grunge, riot grrrl, rap, and metal humorists articulating this mood through the critical humor of sarcasm, irony, and parody. These humor forms became ingrained in most genres of rock music in the nineties, making for a dark (if not golden) era of rock humor. As the virus of marginal extremism infected the larger rock body, the pervasive cynicism led to a brand of humor much harsher than had been witnessed in prior decades, though one no less pointed and subversive in intent and practice.

THE NINETIES:
Rock in Flux

HUMOR BECAME A coping mechanism for many in the nineties, a zone of relief in the face of fast-changing circumstances. Many of the transformations were rooted in the previous decade, when notions of artistic credibility, musical legitimacy, and identity politics had been thrown into flux. Contrasting trends emerged during the nineties as practitioners of fragmented genres attempted to define their roles and purposes in rock culture and beyond. Resulting tensions were often played out on the battlefield of humor, with factions firing satirical missives at one another. Grunge artists mocked the sexist machismo of hardcore and heavy metal, the two styles they had most directly appropriated; the riot grrrls felt that grunge and hardcore were still boys-only clubs and struck back at them with often venomous parodies; lo-fi acts became ironic antagonists and traditional country the symbolic antithesis to mainstream rock trends; hippies and punks retreated into the roots of their respective subcultures, each reliving their mythologies in mutual opposition to one another; and the cash cow rewards of gangsta rap encouraged its parodists and practitioners to push the envelope of misogyny further, while a simultaneous surge of female artists throughout the period propagated various shades of feminist thought. Such contrasting and often combating forces revealed a rock culture in flux.

As much as the story of nineties rock (and) humor is about factional alignments, it is also about the blurring of genre boundaries and the hybridization of previously distinct styles. Hybrids such as Body Count's rap-metal, Ani DiFranco's folk-punk, and Splitlip Rayfield's punk-bluegrass amount to more than just genre-blurring, though. Hybrids evoke two (or more) distinct voices in the music, each implicitly commenting upon the other(s). Marilyn Manson's fusion of metal riffs with punk attitude, for example, was instrumental in altering both genres, politicizing metal and adding a more sinister edge to punk. Similarly, Eminem's credible involvement in the predominantly African American rap form and Bikini Kill's adoption of the male-dominated punk style augmented rather than diluted the respective genres, creating new possibilities, involvements, and meanings. John Leland recently discussed how such hybridization has become the essence of the most progressive modern music, saying that "hip thrives in the hybrid, the hyphen."[1] It is no coincidence that the hybrid artists of this era are also mostly humorists; they erase demarcations as acts of subversion, playfully provoking the closed-minded and testing the limits of conservative presumptions.

Hybrids not only reflected rock in flux but also the increasing diversity beneath the rock tent. The inherent antagonism between the mainstream and the margins—a war fought in previous decades—continued and expanded in the 1990s. However, often it was the hybridizers who crossed over, outsiders Eminem, Nirvana, and Marilyn Manson becoming the most unlikely of mainstream rock stars. Some, like Nirvana, were embarrassed by their riches and attempted to shore up their marginal "dignity" even as they were being accommodated into the mainstream rock body. These issues of authenticity and selling out continued to dominate rock infighting as before (at least within white rock culture). Such discussions became complicated as independent record companies merged with majors or served as subsidiaries. The cynicism in the holier-than-thou quarters of indie rock lingered and was often voiced in sarcastic asides and thinly veiled jibes.

The subcultural arena in which many of these debates took place was popularly known as "Generation X." A concept spanning many artistic genres—as well as describing a cultural condition—Generation X became the designated term for the new youth culture. It served to explain and differentiate nineties youth from their baby boomer parents. Variously tagged as slackers, twentysomethings, grunge kids, 13ers, or busters, Generation X was not so much a catchall group for modern youth as it was a description of a particular group of white, middle-class, young people. This demographic seemed to embody the traits represented (or heralded) by the emerging Seattle grunge bands of the late eighties/early nineties: alienation, skepticism of the media, and broad cultural cynicism. They were seen as sarcastic, self-absorbed, and impotent; as lazy, delusional, and clueless; as immature, drug-addled, and rebellious (without a cause). Many of these defining terms, not surprisingly, were leveled by the parent generation, who were perplexed by the ennui of their offspring and by their carefree dismissal of the American go-getter spirit. Some so-called Gen Xers fought back, blaming the inheritance of debt, divorce, and dysfunction that their parents had bequeathed them. Others reveled in the denigration, (ironically) acting out a slacker persona, withdrawing into their own stereotypes, and wearing their "loser" identifications as badges of honor.

Nirvana became the celebrated icons of slacker culture, but the phenomenon extended beyond rock music. A youth-oriented literature that had been gaining momentum since the early eighties was conveniently incorporated to represent the new "lost generation." Writers like Bret Easton Ellis (*Less Than Zero* [1985] and *American Psycho* [1991]) and Jay McInerny (*Bright Lights, Big City* [1984]) created characters with just the right combination of blankness and solipsism to be associated with the Gen X phenomenon. Their prose was ironic and cynical, their youthful characters alienated and lost, such that each new book was predictably marked as "the new *Catcher in the Rye*." Critics remarked on the constant pop culture references, the video-speed scenes, and the sarcastic clichés of dialogue that seemed to mirror the realities of the new blank generation. Douglas Coupland's *Generation X* (1991), from which the demographic drew its designation, particularly reflected their short attention spans and cynical spirit. "Our Parents Had More," "Dead at 30 Buried at 70," and "Quit Your Job" were not just chapter headings in the book but generational slogans, while "McJob," "Occupational Slumming," and "I Am Not a Target Market" were among the many sarcastic margin(al) statements that embodied the novel's dystopian outlook.

TV and film, too, were quick to jump on the Generation X bandwagon, creating product specifically targeted for the in-vogue subculture. *Reality Bites* (1994) and *Singles* (1992) caricatured then-established X-themes and styles, while MTV's *The Real World* offered "real" guides to X-lingo and X-cruciating illustrations of X-whining and X-hedonism.

By the mid-1990s, Generation X was everywhere. It had its own uniform (flannel shirts, backward baseball caps), its own slang ("not!"), its own literature, film, music, and TV niches, its own festival (Lollapalooza), its own politics (strictly PC), its own issues (divorce, gay rights), and its own expressions of rebellious humor (cynicism, sarcasm, and parody). These subcultural features would dominate the rock culture of the decade, as they would inspire those uninspired by them to react in opposition. The resulting tensions made for some angry articulations on all sides, fueling a dark, self-conscious humor as the primary means by which artists tried to make (non)sense of it all.

SLACK ATTACKS

The musical wing of Generation X had its own caricatured personality in the form of the slacker. This "type" would be cited with regularity by critics intent on mocking nineties youth, but so too would it be embraced by Gen Xers themselves, as they often celebrated the figure in self-mockery. The latter is particularly evident in the Sub Pop flyers for their roster of grunge-oriented bands. Created by cartoonists like Frank Kosik and Raymond Pettibon, veterans of the hardcore heyday, their poster images played to and perpetuated crass stereotypes of the slacker in grotesque ways. Nirvana, too, both embodied and satirized the slacker persona that imprisoned them. Both in real life and in art, Kurt Cobain levelled sarcastic assaults on his generation's impotence while simultaneously exuding sympathy for this condition. Beck, another icon of Gen X, had a similarly ambivalent relationship to the slacker persona. His breakthrough single, "Loser" (1994), became the anthem of the slacker sensibility, its (self-)mockery as biting as that of Nirvana's "Smells Like Teen Spirit" (1991) and "In Bloom" (1992).

The slacker musical style as exhibited by the likes of Nirvana and Beck was not an invention of the early 1990s. Its antecedents, as Michael Azerrad has assertively argued in his book *Our Band Could Be Your Life* (2001), reside in the 1980s alternative underground so often overlooked by rock historians. The key bands in the formation of this mode were Dinosaur Jr. (with its proto-slacker frontman J. Mascis) and Sonic Youth. Toiling in the trenches of indie rock since 1981, Sonic Youth wryly named their 1991 filmed tour of themselves and Nirvana *1991: The Year Punk Broke*. During the decade prior, the band had developed a slacker groove and quirky eccentricity that would fundamentally influence many of the subsequent Gen X bands. When not indulging in esoteric abstractions, Sonic Youth (particularly in the songs written and sung by Kim Gordon) often directly addressed gender issues both within and beyond the rock industry. Gordon's deadpan sarcasm on numbers like "Kool Thing" (1990) established a PC feminism that both Nirvana and the riot grrrl bands would inherit. Elsewhere, songs like "Mariah Carey & the Arthur Doyle Hand Cream" (2004) and "Into the Groove(y)" (1986) (the latter performed under the band name Ciccone Youth, in reference to Madonna's birth name) showed the band's willingness to fire some satirical shots across the bow and into the heart of mainstream (rock) culture. Musically, too, there is a charm and wit to the chaos and dissonance of the Sonic Youth sound that Pavement and others would later invoke. Their colliding guitars and off-kilter effects were the legacy of New York's no wave scene, which used deconstructive humor to comment upon the surrounding sounds of slick, corporate rock.

In the hands of Pavement, such avant-garde strategies thrust the music into amusing slacker disarray. Frontman Stephen Malkmus expanded Sonic Youth's penchant for wry, laconic lyrics delivered in a dry, deadpan vocal. His deceptively lazy articulation perfectly complemented the band's shambolic, lo-fi, colliding-guitars interplay. One could never be sure of the seriousness of Pavement's endeavors, or whether, as the British would have it, they were just "taking the piss." The band fostered their mystique, keeping the media at arm's length as they created messes from their madness. Their sloppy early songs did not sound amateurish so much as they seemed to circumvent conventions and common rock sense. Lyrically, they were equally impenetrable, eliciting "is he or isn't he kidding?" questions from curious but intrigued listeners. Even when the lyrics appeared straightforward, Malkmus would often pop up to disavow interpretations. A case in point was "Range Life" from *Crooked Rain, Crooked Rain* (1994), a song that appeared to be a put-down of then-indie darlings the Stone Temple Pilots and the Smashing Pumpkins. While referencing the latter, the song's lyric goes, "Nature kids, they don't have no function / I don't understand what they mean / And I could really give a fuck."[2] When Pumpkins frontman Billy Corgan reacted with outrage to this apparent "diss," Malkmus responded that the lines were intended as parody and were spoken through a contrived hippy character's point of view. This may have been what Michael Azerrad had in mind when he stated that Pavement was writing "indie rock about indie rock . . . where nothing was revealed and all could be denied."[3] Pavement's in-house parochial satire was evident in other songs, too, such as in their minor hit "Cut Your Hair" (1994), which made fun of image-consciousness as a prelude to selling out. "I don't remember a word," Malkmus (or his speaker?) deadpans. "But I don't care . . . did you see the drummer's hair?"[4]

With a less accusatory poison pen, Rivers Cuomo of Weezer also engaged issues of "rockism" and ego identity in his often self-effacing songs. Inheritors of the grunge sensation, Weezer mixed pop and metal with an alchemy that favored the former. Their geek rock evoked the self-flagellating ghost of Jonathan Richman as well as the "loser" consciousness of Generation X. Wearing thick-rimmed glasses ("just like Buddy Holly"), Cuomo fashioned himself into a geek with the requisite irony that made him cool.[5] His awkwardness was played out in celebrations of faux innocence, as in "In the Garage" (1994), which describes the joys of rock music possible for a band before it gets big enough to sell out. His guilt-riddled ministrations were less angry than Cobain's, but they were equally self-deprecating in humor. In "Pink Triangle" (1996) Cuomo's speaker bemoans his unrequited love for his lesbian crush, quaintly inquiring, "If everyone's a little queer / Can't she be a little straight?"[6] Although the band's consistently lighthearted and child-friendly videos kept a smile on the faces of Weezer fans, a darker self-loathing and insecurity always lurked beneath Rivers Cuomo's witty tales of woe. Their comic videos, one might add, set the band in sharp contrast to the more humorless grunge whiners of the day, while their empathetic personal(ity) crisis humor provided relief to the growing constituency of what appeared to be equally troubled Weezer fan-disciples. The band's loser humor was popular in the mainstream as well as in the margins throughout the decade, and they enjoyed a renaissance at the end of the decade as the emo movement embraced them anew.

Another band that engaged the angst of their age with an ironic and nerdy smart-assness was Ben Folds Five, a three-piece that chose their misnomer because—they claimed—it "sounds better."[7] If Weezer's stadium rock sound was in part a parody of traditional "cock rock," Ben Folds Five's guitarless ensemble deconstructed the favored formats of (alternative) rock. Folds described the results as "punk rock for sissies."[8] Distinguished by Folds's always-clever witticisms, the band transcended the slacker template, and as outsiders they were not bashful in offering insights and opinions on the Gen X phenomenon. "Underground" (1995) gives an account of the hip indie scene as seen through the eyes of a wannabe who would "love to mix in circles, cliques, and social coteries,"[9] while "Battle of Who Could Care Less" (1997) charts a nihilistic struggle among assorted slackers. The latter employs caricature humor delivered in the deadpan reportage style once popularized by Squeeze. "Call to see if Paul can score some weed," quips Folds-as-slacker, playing to one of the type's more common stereotypes.[10]

Sublime were another celebrated Gen X band associated with the slacker persona, though their perspective was not always marked by the irony of their more self-conscious peers. From Long Beach, California, Sublime embodied the surf/skate punk aspects of the slacker image. Their hybrid songs drew from ska, reggae, funk, punk, and hip-hop, the end products being classic party numbers for hedonistic beach "dudes." Like their peers No Doubt, the Mighty Mighty Bosstones, and 311, Sublime projected a positive humor of celebration and social irreverence. Their third-wave ska combined the sophomoric aspects of punk rebellion with the stoner-humor of the slacker nation. Although their adolescent fun may have lacked the more serious purpose of some of their contemporaries, their pot songs, party beats, and in-crowd slang did provide escapist comic relief for their much-maligned subculture.

As the 1990s unfolded beyond the immediate buzz of Generation X, the slacker persona lingered on in other emerging music scenes, such as with the neo-hippies seeking solace in the stoned romanticism of the Grateful Dead and on the alternative outskirts of the traditional country music revival. Both represented symbolic and literal retreats from the anxieties of the "accelerated culture" all around. In the music of Nirvana and Beck, though, total retreat was not an option, but then again, neither was a comfortable identity within the present. These two key artists employed various types of humor in order to negotiate the inherent contradictions and paradoxes of their confusions and circumstances.

Nirvana

After long laboring in the wilderness of underground obscurity, alternative rock pushed its way onto the big stages and into mainstream culture with Nirvana. In terms of the trends and tenor of the times, Nirvana were a rocking perfect storm; they invoked punk's attitude, metal's riffs, and pop hooks that would feel at home in a Beatles songbook. Hollywood could not have scripted their heavenly rise any better, though the band were far from willing participants in the process. Hailed as the voice of his generation (X), Kurt Cobain focused much of his songwriting attention on pouring scorn and sarcasm on the band's predominantly slacker and head-banger following; embraced and propelled by the financial and media clout of Geffen Records and MTV, Cobain likewise mocked these institutional forces with a venom and disdain not witnessed since Johnny Rotten sang "EMI" in 1977. Unlike the Pistols and punk, though, Nirvana reneged on the "us versus them" subcultural contract; for Cobain, "we" were the pawns of "them," and "he" was as trapped in the corporate machine as anyone.

The zeitgeist moment for Nirvana, alt-rock, and Generation X came with the release of "Smells Like Teen Spirit" in late 1991. Though peaking at number six on the U.S. national charts, the single hit the number one slot in many other countries. Nirvana crashed the national stage with an anthem, centered on a guitar riff of which Boston (the band) would have been proud, that spoke against their generation as much as it spoke for it. "Here we are now, entertain us," demands Cobain, mercilessly mocking slacker apathy and self-centeredness. Through a first-person point of view and a slurred voice emoting part-boredom and part-rage, Cobain implicated himself as victim/point-man of this "teen spirit," establishing the line between the authentic and the phony but unable to locate himself in either camp. Using a series of paradoxical lines to establish the schizoid struggle, Cobain provided both a sarcastic take on teen rebellion and an endorsement of it. As with Bob Dylan's early "anthems," Nirvana captured the tortured mood of their time, and just as Dylan's "answer" was "blowing in the wind," Cobain's sarcastic conclusion to his own tortured position as consumer and dupe was "Oh well, whatever, nevermind." There is self-deprecating resignation to this line, as language itself denies him a satisfactory resolution. The conclusion of the song traces Cobain in his descent into a Samuel Beckett–like void. "A denial," he screams, over and over and over again.[11]

The video representation of "Teen Spirit" (a clip as responsible as the song itself for thrusting Nirvana to rock stardom) provides clarity to the obfuscations of Cobain's lyrical abstractions and marbled vocal wailings. Set at a high school pep rally, a stereotypical suburban scene is established with Nirvana performing their song for the seated students. Signs of dissent come into view, though, as the camera pans in on the cheerleaders, who are all sporting anarchy symbols on their outfits. As the song progresses, the student body grows restless, ultimately erupting in a spontaneous riot. Beneath its self-consciously tongue-in-cheek "rock 'n' roll high school" codes, the video countered the assumption that contemporary youth is doomed to ennui. Within even the most apparently staid middle-class kid, it suggests, resides a simmering cauldron of outcast rage just waiting to boil over. Nirvana, apparently, can provide the necessary precipitant heat.

If "Smells Like Teen Spirit" established Nirvana as the voice of, about, and against Generation X, the album that followed, *Nevermind*, solidified that designation. Replacing Michael Jackson's *Dangerous* at the top of the charts in January 1992, *Nevermind* made a symbolic and literal statement in dethroning the King of Pop. Some in the underground rock community were thrilled by the breakthrough, optimistic that it might usher in a new era of meaningful rock in the mainstream; others were more skeptical, aware that success can precipitate a sellout of a different kind. Both schools of thought were partially right, and Cobain was front and center, attempting to negotiate the possibilities and perils of his band's new stature. As many of the songs on *Nevermind* suggest, Cobain had already been musing over the consequences of fame and fortune before their arrival. "I hope I die before I turn into Pete Townsend," he had once presciently written in his journal.[12] Indeed, the cover of the album illustrated the dilemma, with its image of an "innocent" baby underwater, reaching out to claim a dollar bill from a fishing hook. It was not necessary to show who was holding the rod at the other end of the line. In "Stay Away" Cobain wonders, "I don't know why I'd rather be dead than cool,"[13] while "In Bloom" foresees the adoring masses that would soon leap onto the Nirvana bandwagon. "He's the one who likes all our pretty songs," Cobain sings, sneering at the average "everyfan." "But he don't know what it means," he concludes.[14] *Nevermind* even had a working title of *Sheep* prior to its release, a further indication that Cobain was pointing his satirical stick squarely at the hands that fed him.

By the release of *In Utero* a year later, Nirvana were international rock stars. In response, the band raged with even greater sarcasm against their now-mainstream fan base. "Serve the Servants" sets the tone with its ironic opening lines, "Teenage angst has paid off well / Now I'm old and bored."[15] The darkening mood (both musical and lyrical) and (self-)loathing are further developed in "Radio Friendly Unit Shifter," the title of which invoked pat industry-speak with icy sarcasm. "Rape Me" constituted Cobain at his most stark and cynical. The opening notes echoed the "Smells Like Teen Spirit" riff note for note, signifying (in the context of the new title) that that milestone song had since become the band's millstone. "I appreciate your concern," Cobain sneers, mocking the self-interested helping hands of the media, corporate establishment, and rock community.[16] "Rape Me" is one of many primal screams on *In Utero* that evoke the kind of raw, candid, and scornful songs that John Lennon wrote after the Beatles' breakup. Both artists employ black, self-deprecating humor as a kind of survival mechanism, a lifeline against the mounting internal and external pressures and expectations. If, as some have suggested, *In Utero* was Kurt Cobain's official suicide note, it was not expressed without a modicum of gallows humor.

Despite the torment and pain (physical, mental, and psychological) that Cobain undoubtedly endured during his two years under the spotlight, he was not averse, like his doppelganger John Lennon, to periodic retreats into the most juvenile forms of prankster humor. As a kid, Cobain had garnered a reputation for such humor by spray-painting GOD IS GAY on random pickup trucks in his hometown of

Aberdeen, Washington, mocking the local narrow-minded "rednecks" (he would later redeploy this phrase sarcastically at the close of "Stay Away"). Such a penchant for gender/sexuality subversions would prove to be an integral part of Nirvana's public displays, too. While his heavy metal peers kitted themselves out in scary costumes for the 1992 MTV Headbangers Ball, Cobain showed up in full drag. A serial cross-dresser (as were bandmates Krist Novoselic and Dave Grohl), Cobain often donned women's clothes for both videos and stage appearances. At their legendary Reading Festival performance in 1992, Cobain provided a comic response to the rumor that he might not perform that night due to (much-publicized) health and heroin problems by arriving onstage in a wheelchair and hospital gown; then, like Lazarus, he proceeded to spring into full animated rock star mode. For their 1992 debut *Rolling Stone* cover shot (seen as a career pinnacle by many an aspiring artist), Cobain offered his gratitude by sporting a T-shirt that he had inscribed with the words CORPORATE MAGAZINES STILL SUCK, alluding to the "Corporate Rock Still Sucks" indie slogan of the time. A year later, the band would turn the sartorial satire back on themselves, recognizing their newfound fame by wearing formal Brooks Brothers suits for the same magazine's follow-up band cover shot.

As songs like "Rape Me" and the above gender-bending pranks suggest, Nirvana were a band concerned with issues of identity politics. As a teen, though Cobain had been drawn to the masculine sounds of heavy metal and hardcore, he had been scornful of the misogynistic elements that often characterized these genres' respective subcultures. His feminist sympathies were further concretized through his friendship with Bikini Kill's Tobi Vail and Kathleen Hanna, who introduced a more politicized framework to Cobain's thinking. Certain early Nirvana songs see Cobain deconstructing patriarchal language with pointed humor. "Never met a wise man; if so it's a woman," he wryly opines in "Territorial Pissings."[17] In *Sex Revolts*, writers Simon Reynolds and Joy Press suggest that Cobain was essentially a mama's boy. His rejection of rock's traditional sexism, they further argue, made him one of the more progressive of modern subversives, part of the "queer straight" revolution of today. In its broad contemporary context, these authors posit that "alternative rock has begun to replace racial envy with gender tourism," and that Kurt Cobain was one of the trailblazing "soft" warriors.[18] One might point to self-deprecating "relationship" songs like "Heart-Shaped Box" (1993) or the resignation anthem "All Apologies" (1993) as rare illustrations of a male rebel artist open to accessing and admitting his frailties and inadequacies. The vulnerability, soul-baring, and self-effacement in these songs have few precedents in the male rock pantheon, with perhaps the notable exception of John Lennon.

On April 8, 1994, Kurt Cobain was found dead from a self-inflicted gunshot wound to the head. His suicide note referenced Neil Young's mock-heroic line "It's better to burn out than to fade away," suggesting that his black humor continued to serve as an existential buffer until his final moments.[19] The posthumous surge in sales of *In Utero*, as well as the money-grubbing circus that has persisted since his demise, provide sadly ironic postscripts to his suicide and offer prescient validation of many of his lyrical predictions. "If Kurt could see the canonization that accompanied his demise it would kill him," quipped the authors of *Generation Ecch!* with more than a little gallows humor.[20]

Beck

The early 1990s were intense times for Generation X. The Nirvana-led Seattle grunge explosion brought out expressions of misery, self-destruction, and self-indulgence not witnessed since Joy Division exported their "grey skies" rock from Manchester in 1979. By 1993, self-loathing was the prevailing mood in U.S. indie circles, and many were seeking alternatives to the increasingly dour alternative rock. Beck arrived—made-to-order as the desired light at the end of the tunnel. As had been the case with Cobain, Beck was quickly embraced as the latest voice of his generation, perceived as the ubiquitous slacker personified. However, also like Cobain, Beck proved to be less the expected novelty representative and more a parodic satirist of Gen X. Unlike Cobain, though, who channeled punk's sarcastic impulses, Beck addressed his constituency with a sense of humor more aligned to hippy whimsy and irony. At the musical level, Beck has embodied and deconstructed his era of musical flux with a collage style of genre juxtapositions that has been nothing less than audacious.

.Beck's bright, lighthearted humor provided collective relief after the dark satire of grunge, though his expressions were not without their own subversive edge and sensibility. Reared in an artistic family (his mother and grandfather were both practicing avant-garde artists), Beck projected their imaginative and experimental spirit into the next generation. Strains of surrealism have been omnipresent in his lyrics, videos, and song collages, though never to the extent that accessibility has been sacrificed. Beck has been the quintessential postmodern artist of his times, mixing high art aesthetics with pop "junk culture," fusing multiple genres of music into inventive hybrids that echo down to pre-rock eras without ever losing their sense of the new and original. Raised in multicultural Los Angeles, Beck has been a cross-pollinating artist by nature, a sponge soaking up the eclectic music and culture of his home city. (As if to recognize as much—and to pay tribute to these geographical resources—Beck titled a recent album *Guero* [2004], which literally translates as "white boy.") His reconfigurations of old forms, cut-and-paste samples, and free-association lyrics have been the constant ingredients of his dizzying and innovative songs, while his absurdist—sometimes smug—sense of humor has conditioned the tone and spirit distinguishing his artistry.

Beck developed his subversive consciousness after moving to New York in the late 1980s. There he adapted his catalogue of folk, country, and delta blues songs to the insurgent "anti-folk" movement then in effect. Soon his hybrid experiments were underway, as he began to integrate hip-hop beats into these roots-rooted songs, lacing them with his idiosyncratic, wacky lyrics. "MTV Makes Me Wanna Smoke Crack" (1993) was an illustrative song from these early sessions, but it was "Loser" (1994) that proved to be the momentous recording.

With its cool, slacker beat sitting behind a lo-fi delta blues groove, Beck offered up what would become the catchphrase of the times when he sang, "I'm a loser baby, so why don't you kill me?" Though "Loser" was intended as a parody of the slacker persona, both the song and Beck were received as its very embodiments. Ironically, little was made of the many other bizarre images beyond the key chorus line. Yet, in the stoned ramblings of the song's verses, one finds the full effects of Beck's imaginative quirks, nonsense-sense wordplay, and surrealistic whimsy. The song opens: "In the time of chimpanzees I was a monkey / Butane in my veins and I'm out to cut the junkie / With the plastic eyeballs, spray-paint the vegetables / Dog food stalls with the beefcake pantyhose."[21] Such obtuse lines, unfamiliar within the conventionally narrative folk context, disrupt listener expectations and provoke questions. Is the song (a parody of) the sophomoric ramblings of many a Bob Dylan wannabe? Is it (a parody of) the neo-beat exercises of any number of pothead slackers? As with his indie rock peer Bob Pollard (of Guided by Voices), Beck's lyrics allude to a sense of meaning rather than to meaningful sense. The recipient's satisfaction lies less in cogency and more in the journey into the imagination upon which the listener has been invited to embark. Such an aesthetic relationship with the listener—with its give and take and supply and demand—was the mark of the best psychedelic whimsy of the sixties, as well as of the avant-garde subversions of the surrealists and dadaists before that.

The bidding war that followed the success of "Loser" saw Beck packing his bags in indie-land and joining Geffen Records, home to that other margins-to-mainstream success story, Nirvana. Skillfully eluding charges of sellout, Beck signed a deal that enabled him to put out independent side-projects as well as "major" releases. His debut album, *Mellow Gold* (1994), dispelled any lingering notions that Beck was a one-hit-wonder novelty act. This album fleshed out the kaleidoscopic ambitions that had thus far been concentrated into the three-minute "Loser" hit. *Mellow Gold* established Beck as the premier minstrel of the sonic landscape. Hopscotching among various sounds, styles, and genres—both between and within songs—Beck provided comedy by mixing and (mis-)matching the most unlikely of sources in sharp juxtaposition. Whether it be the country of "Nitemare Hippy Girl," the thrash of "Mutherfuker," or the abstract whimsy of "Fuckin' with My Head (Mountain Dew Rock)," *Mellow Gold* demonstrated playful eclecticism, fluid fusions, and—as the titles suggest—a curious penchant for idiosyncratic spelling. The album offers the portrait of an artist laughing in the face of all rules and boundaries; it was as if Beck saw his only competition as himself, and his sole challenge as outdoing the audacious imagination he had displayed on the previous track. An achievement without precedent, *Mellow Gold* managed to capture the entire history of American popular music while still retaining its cultural modernity and relevance.

His major label follow-up, *Odelay* (1996), established Beck as the most innovative and rooted performer of the decade and saw critics fawning to valorize the artist some had dismissed previously as a novelty act. Less sweeping in scope than *Mellow Gold*, *Odelay* accentuated Beck's hip-hop leanings courtesy of the production of the Dust Brothers, whose prior projects had included the Beastie Boys' trailblazing *Paul's Boutique* album. Drifting increasingly to geeked-out ironic dance grooves, Beck followed *Odelay* with his most genre-specific album in *Midnite Vultures* (1999). Channeling his inner Prince, Beck made *Vultures* his most obviously comedic record and showcased the dumpster diver of pop digging into the bawdiest quarters of the funk and soul traditions. From its fluorescent green and purple cover to the sprightly Stax productions within, the album took listeners on a funky ride through songs of silly sexual innuendo that mutated somewhere between genre parody and reverence. Less clever and more pleasure-principled, *Vultures* saw Beck reinventing himself as a horny lover-boy R&B frontman, whose inherent incongruous humor emanated from the fact that we all knew him as a white boy geek (and thus ironically cool in the process). The album's opener, "Sexx Laws," saw Beck-as-Prince taking a stand against perversion restrictions, while "Get Real Paid" witnessed our (anti-)hero mock-teasing with such lines as "Touch my ass if you're qualified."[22] "Debra" alluded to the Purple One's sex-epic, "Darlin' Nikki." "I met you at JC Penney," coos a bawdy Beck, later enticing his lady to his lair with the invite to "Step inside [his] Hyundai."[23] "Hollywood Freaks" externalizes the cheeky sleaze dynamic with some slick wordplay in a lyric mocking the pre–Paris and Britney set: "People look so snooty / Take pills that make them moody / Automatic bzooty / Zero to tutti frutti."[24]

Via its videos and accompanying tour, Beck used the party vibe of *Midnite Vultures* as a springboard to showcase his natural physical humor. Like the Beastie Boys before him, Beck managed to defuse his musical-racial envy through gestures of self-deprecation. His attempts to slide across the stage like James Brown or spin on a dime like Michael Jackson were always effortlessly flawed and sufficiently stiff, revealing him less as an arrogant soul wannabe and more as a geek dreamer. Like that trailblazer of geek humor, Jonathan Richman, Beck allowed indie white kids to dance vicariously to his R&B fantasies, while the obvious irony of the endeavor registered its own cool and clever factor. On tour, when a bed descended to the stage during "Debra," audiences laughed, not just at the gimmick itself (as one might have had Prince staged it), but at the *allusion* to Prince-like practices contained in the prop/antic itself.

The Beck of the twenty-first century has shed some of the more adolescent tricks of his trade. Instead, a more mature artist has emerged, this particularly illustrated by his low-key breakup album, *Sea Change* (2002), which was notable more for its painful introspection than for any expressions of humor. Some have suggested that his recent albums, *Guero* (2004) and *The Information* (2006), have signaled a return to his early endeavors, but though the whimsical wordplay is still on display, the juvenile zip and reckless risk-taking of his formative work appear to have waned. With these developments—along with the aging of his core audience—Beck has lost much of the youth-cool cachet he built up throughout the nineties. One suspects, however, that this human sampling machine will not retreat into a permanent background, and that his boundless imagination, audacity, and historicity will soon return in a new comic (dis)guise to test the listening habits of future generations.

THE YEARS OF THE WOMAN

The term "The Year of the Woman" has been periodically mass-marketed by the media to describe increased female involvement in the rock industry ever since the late 1980s. Since then, this slogan has become increasingly redundant, a testament to the fact that the involvement of women in rock has become commonplace and taken for granted. Indeed, when surveying the nature of that involvement during the 1990s, one witnesses a great diversity of female artists expressing themselves in multiple ways. Among this cast of characters are some of the most engaging humorists of the era, artists who use their wit to reflect upon personal and public issues of gender and sexual identity. Today, many of the more progressive and subversive rock humorists are women. This is a far cry from their diminished and delimited roles and representations during prior decades.

Of course, the recent rise of women in rock does not mean that they now share equal billing with men on rock's stages, nor behind the scenes in industry boardrooms. The rock business in the 1990s was still largely a boys' club functioning around an all-boys network, and many of the same stereotypes and objectifications persisted in both men's and women's music. This sexism—sometimes outright misogyny—has made the rock industry a battleground for modern female artists, who have often used a caustic wit to draw issues of inequality and exploitation to their audience's attention.

Within nineties female rock itself, feminism was in flux. Madonna's radical post-feminist provocations in the 1980s changed women's attitudes toward issues of empowerment and femininity, both within and outside of music circles. These in-house developments led to debates about the roles, identities, and points of view women should assume in their music. Such discussions were raging outside, too, particularly around provocative texts like the 1991 movie *Thelma and Louise* and Susan Faludi's book *Backlash* of the same year; the latter warned of the dangers of post-feminist humanism in a culture where the feminist project was far from complete. Within this state of flux, female artists from both mainstream and underground music worked through their concerns via lyrics, images, performances, and music. Their dynamic contributions would make the 1990s a decade in which female-inflected humor would not be just a novelty or token, but a dominant force front-and-center stage.

For all the flux and innovations in women's music over the decade, some of its greatest accomplishments came from some of its more conventional artists. Spearheaded by Sarah McLachlan, female folk underwent a renaissance in the early nineties. Capitalizing on the gains made by prior acts like Tracy Chapman and Suzanne Vega, McLachlan gathered the folk strummers of her era together for their very own so-called "girlapalooza": Lilith Fair. A low-key affair in 1996, the festival picked up steam in 1997, gathering a vast cast of all-female (and some mixed-gender) acts. Despite Lilith being dominated mostly by traditional stylists in the Joni Mitchell mold, its success struck a symbolic chord that proclaimed female power and strength through interdependence.

With female folk dominating the mainstream, alternative and anti-folk artists developed in the margins, extending and mutating the form and sometimes reacting against it entirely. The genre's more subversive humor originated with these folk innovators. Liz Phair brought a breath of fresh air for folk(s) when she released *Exile in Guyville* to critical acclaim in 1993. The album's melodic songs, acoustic strumming, and sweet vocals marked Phair initially as another folkie, but because of the lyrics, all those elements were recontextualized. Sarcastically inverting the title and spirit of the Rolling Stones' "male" classic *Exile on Main Street* (1972), Phair appropriated Mick and Keith's sexual candor and braggadocio, producing bawdy songs of wily wit and wisdom. Sex, love, and relationships were certainly the standard topics of conventional female folk, but Phair brought fresh perspectives, multiple voices, and blunt, bawdy humor to them. Proclaiming herself the "blow-job queen" in "Flower" (1993), her innocent delivery was unveiled as ironic. "I'll fuck you and your minions, too," she deadpans shamelessly.[25] The ghost of Mick Jagger lingers in songs like "Fuck and Run" (1993), too, though Phair recognizes the lonely underside of sexual conquests (for women) when she coyly asks, "Whatever happened to a boyfriend?"[26] Darting between bragging voices and those of insecurity, Phair offered a postmodern female identity in flux. Her role-playing inhabited female archetypes and stereotypes only to parody them with wry or bawdy humor. Her droll, matter-of-fact delivery exasperated listeners, some of whom found her sexy, others immoral, and others, like fellow Chicagoan Steve Albini, "a pandering slut."[27] Her sexy-funny style was the folk underground's equivalent of Madonna's trickster multi-positioning.

Ani DiFranco was another folk-rooted singer to emerge from the underground during the 1990s. Her dogged independence and self-sufficiency were as ascetic as Ian MacKaye's was within punk. Through her own Righteous Babe Records label, formed in 1990, DiFranco has released about an album a year, each showcasing harsh acoustic guitar thrashing, forceful singing, and personal-as-political lyrics. Her debut album title, *Not So Soft* (1991), described the type of folkie she intended to be (or not to be), and set her in counter-juxtaposition to the Kate Bush wannabes of the mainstream. Like with many of the Gen X acts of the day, authenticity and self-reliance were principles, not aspirations. She mocked big business practices in "Blood in the Boardroom" (1993), major label head-hunters in "Next Best Thing" (1991), artists who compromise and sell out in "Napoleon" (1996), and her own "righteous" hard-headedness in "The Million You Never Made" (1995). In the latter, the major labels are the enemy "you" set against Ani's "I" as she revels in the possibility that "I could be the million that you'll never make."[28] With the luxury of having no one looking over her shoulder, DiFranco let freedom reign/rain, projecting a provocateur look (shaved head, nose ring, black boots), proclaiming her bisexuality (in "In or Out" [1992]), and pouring scorn on the short-sighted, closed-minded, and greedy, whether they be women or men, rockers or "civilians."

A new breed of mainstream female stars began to "pop" up in the 1990s, beneficiaries, if not advocates, of the feminist groundwork that had been laid before them. African American girl ensembles had been a fixture of popular music since the early years of rock & roll, but nineties upstarts like TLC and Destiny's Child indicated that these groups were no longer willing to be mere puppets objectified and coerced into singing submissive love songs. Walking in the pathways paved by Salt 'n' Pepa and Queen Latifah, TLC combined sassy with sexy to produce success. *CrazySexyCool* (1994) was both their sophomore album release and their statement of purpose.

Renouncing the suffocating glamour of gowns and heels, TLC wore baggy pants and T-shirts, accessorizing politically by pinning condoms to their clothing, or, in the case of Lisa "Left Eye" Lopes, to her eyeglasses. Their message was "we're no pushovers" and "we don't suffer male fools." "Creep" (1994) and "No Scrubs" (1999) employed street vernacular to ridicule jobless and classless (and carless) men. Their tough-gal soul-pop was picked up by Destiny's Child at the close of the decade, who recrafted the message of "No Scrubs" into "Bills Bills Bills" (1999); both songs—not coincidentally—were penned by the same writer, Kandi Burruss.

Even more exaggeratedly consumer-driven and feisty were the "hard" female rappers that rose up from the "hood" to the heights of pop-ularity during the second half of the decade. Mainstream manifestations of eighties bawdy gangsta-gals like Bytches With Problems and Hoes Wit Attitude, successors Foxy Brown and Lil' Kim brought ghetto-parodies to the masses at the same time that male "G"s like Notorious BIG and Snoop (Doggy) Dogg were doing likewise. Just as these men comically exaggerated gangsta stereotypes into outrageous fantasies (or versions of reality), so Foxy Brown and Lil' Kim offered the female equivalents. Kim appropriated male bravado with "Queen Bitch" (1996) and sexual boasting with "Fuck You" (1996). Foxy Brown's provocative lyrical sex romps recalled the dirty raps of 2 Live Crew, while her sexy diva excesses played with "ho" stereotypes just as Ice T had played with "pimp" ones. Such hardcore ghetto imagery was controversial, to say the least, particularly when so many (white) female (and male) artists of the era were being so self-consciously politically correct. The comic excesses of Foxy Brown and Lil' Kim went beyond merely subverting conservative cultural values, though, as if to say that real freedom for women means that *no* rules any longer apply, a principle long applicable to male rock rebels but only recently so for female ones.

Missy Elliott

The rise of gangsta rap during the 1990s changed the face(s) of the genre in relation to black female identity as much as black male identity. The predominant and recurring images of submissive women in states of undress, passively waiting to be acted on, became almost required features of rap lyrics and videos. For female artists, also, the industry's "sex sells" mantra created a squeeze such that sex kittens like Lil' Kim and Foxy Brown became the role model "types" of choice where the dignified Queen Latifah and MC Lyte had once stood proud. If someone had predicted mid-decade that a plus-size woman who rapped *and* wrote *and* produced would soon become the biggest-selling female rap act of all time, one might have reacted with natural skepticism; if someone had further suggested that her songs would be about female empowerment and independence, one would have concluded that either the prophet was a fool or that a revolutionary was in the midst. The latter proved to be the case, as Missy "Misdemeanor" Elliott emerged as the most groundbreaking and innovative pop star since Madonna.

Like Madonna, Missy is as smart as she is sassy, as serious as she is silly, and as sexy as she is sarcastic. Within African American music history, her primary antecedents are bawdy blues belters like Bessie Smith, Big Mama Thornton, Ruth Brown, and Etta James. These women were as sexual and shocking (in their days) as modern rappers, but they applied an uproarious humor to their outrages that accentuated rather than diminished their identities as empowered and self-sustaining women. Missy Elliott's classy and classic raunchiness also recalls "old school" hip-hop women like Roxanne Shanté and Salt 'n' Pepa, while her futuristic outlook has led to her trailblazing new paths for mainstream hip-hop. In the context of a male-dominated rap culture that has been, for the most part, treading water and bottom-feeding from the same tired clichés of gangsta-machismo, Elliott's historical achievements can be fully appreciated and measured only in comparison to achievements beyond rap, alongside Prince during the eighties or the Beatles during the sixties.

Although the Beatles might not be the most obvious comparison to invoke when discussing Missy Elliott, the two actually have much in common. Firstly, neither could have done it alone. Just as producer George Martin was instrumental in bringing the whimsy to the psychedelic soundscapes of the mature-period Beatles, so Timbaland has been the behind-the-console visionary complementing Missy's adventurous endeavors. His dense and wild arrangements of junk samples and sound gimmicks are behind much of the postmodern frenzy that constitutes a Missy song. His playground mixes of rhythms and effects offer amusement for the ears and the mind, his sci-fi visions implicitly boasting that these songs are light years ahead of the competition. Like Martin on *Sgt. Pepper*, Timbaland has shown that subversive rock humor can be a practice of the producer as well as the artist.

Missy, of course, has brought the inspiration and perspiration for Tim's creative knob-twiddling. Furthermore, she has recently become the main producer of her own work. With her background as a writer and arranger for other artists (including Aaliyah's double-platinum-selling *One in a Million* [1996]), Elliott spent years learning the tricks of her trade before bursting on the scene with *Supa Dupa Fly* in 1997. That debut release revealed her artistry and humor as multifaceted and holistic; and, again, as with Prince's work, it suggested a mind and imagination never off-duty, but in constant search of new means and ends. Nowhere is this more apparent than in Missy's own voice, which is chameleon-like in its ability to morph into multiple characters and styles. With the nuance of a comic-impersonator, Missy skips between accents effortlessly, whether exaggerating her Southern drawl or assuming a Jamaican persona; she assumes different points of view, too, by gender-bending from woman to man or age-bending from adult to child; baby-talk, babble-talk, sexy-talk, and even robot-talk (through vocoder effects) are all in her repertoire, while moans, coos, and screams abound; her sultry, Snoop-like stoner-purr also makes a cameo on such songs as "Izzy Izzy Ahh" (1997) and "Pass da Blunt" (1997). Through vocal timbre and elasticity, Elliott creates a comedy of role-playing, the starlet headlining each part. That said, few artists are as collaborative in their song-craft as Missy Elliott. Each of her albums features a veritable "who's who" of cutting-edge hip-hop, creating an aura of communal inclusiveness in which artists are rooting for each other rather than seeking out the next "beef."

Positivity is the essence of Missy's music and the soul of her humor. Rarely does she "diss" other acts, and when she boasts (as she frequently does), the tone is always good-humored and often self-deprecating. Her humor seeks to unite rather than separate, to empower rather than scapegoat. Party songs like "Get Ur Freak On" (2001) function like the hippy sing-alongs of the 1960s; celebrations against seriousness, they exude a positive vibe and joyful humor, and call on all parties to "come together." Such idealism has its own pointed purpose in an arena where conflict and gunplay are no longer confined to just artistic expression.

In "Wake Up" (2003), Missy makes explicit what is mostly implied in her party songs: that hip-hop society needs to call a collective ceasefire and return to "keeping it real." "I got the Martin Luther King fever," she proclaims, before embarking upon a socially conscious rap. Using lines of comic inversion, she deflates the gang-bangers, drug-runners, and self-absorbed materialists of the modern rap game: "If you don't got a gun, it's alright. / If you makin' legal money, it's alright. / If you gotta keep your clothes on, it's alright. / If your wheels don't spin, it's alright."[29] "She's a Bitch" (1999) also provides a counterpoint perspective to G-rap, here addressing the prevailing misogyny of the subgenre and its choice put-down term, "bitch." Instead of preaching her objections, Missy ironically reclaims the word, transforming it into a feminist badge of honor that designates a strong, self-reliant woman. "See I got mo' cheese / Back on up while I roll up my sleeves," she boast-warns in full-throttle "bitch" mode.[30]

A nonideological feminist edge is apparent elsewhere, too, particularly in relation to Elliott's songs of female empowerment. Injecting the personal into the political, "Pump It Up" (2003) sees Missy in Big Mama mode, comically deflating her weight issues, asserting, "I love my gut, so fuck the tummy tuck / Shake my gut like 'Yeah, bitch, what?'"[31] Couched in the context of our skinny-waif world, these sentiments assume a broader satirical clout. Missy turns her female-centered relief humor to the issue of relationship dependence in "Toyz" (2003). In what is principally a "dild-ode" sung in the guise of a romantic love ballad, the narrator informs us, "Now I've got my toys / I don't need none of you boys." With a hilariously back-handed slight on men's worth, she continues, "How could I miss you baby? / I didn't even know you was gone."[32]

As "Toyz" illustrates, Missy Elliott is in her comedic comfort zone when she is playing the bawd. Asserting the sexual without being prey (unless she wants to be that way), saucy Missy is her most favored persona. *Miss E . . . So Addictive* (2001) is particularly populated with raunchy raps. Opening songs "Dog in Heat" and "One Minute Man" establish the sex theme as well as the voracious appetite of our heroine. "One Minute Man" finds Missy and guest Trina protesting that they do not want one, while second guest Ludacris declares that he is not one. Later in the album Missy gets to practice her vocal gymnastics on "Scream (a.k.a. Itchin')," as she boasts that she will make her lover "sing high sopran-ah."[33]

"Work It" (2002) and "Meltdown" (2005) are often cited as songs that showcase Missy Elliott at her bawdy best. Here, witty euphemisms are employed, not because they were required by the censors (as they were in the days of the original bawdy blues-women), but for the sheer hilarity of the double entendre vernacular. "Call before you come, I need to shave my cho-cha," she informs in "Work It," before instructing her lover to "Go downtown and eat like a vulture." Timbaland provides sonic euphemisms along the way, inserting elephant sounds in reference to the man's "trunk."[34] In "Meltdown," the hot and heavy narrator speaks longingly of her man's "magic stick," while offering the following uproarious details: "Juices runnin' like a river / Slowly down my kitty litter."[35] In both songs, the use of euphemism, simile, and metaphor only serve to make the content (and the bawdy humor) more—not less—explicit. Unlike in the 1950s, when innuendo served as a mask to befuddle the would-be censors, here, the practice is a comment upon itself, an in-joke that recognizes that although there is no longer a necessity to hide, we can still revel in the imaginative joys of the elusive language and gestures.

The 2006 release (outside of the United States) of her greatest hits collection, *Respect M.E.*, has prompted fans to pause and reflect on Missy's decade of dominance. Good mainstream pop music may be as rare today as it has ever been; thus when one considers her achievements, it seems she has few contemporary peers worthy of a comparison. Experimental without losing the pop connection, trailblazing but rooted in tradition, humorously subversive without alienating, Missy Elliott's larger-than-life presence transcends hip-hop even as she is one of its most universally admired practitioners and advocates. If sixties Motown pop, the Beatles, and prime-time Prince could be combined and condensed into a single artist, one might call that hypothetical figure Missy "Misdemeanor" Elliott.

A RIOT OF THEIR OWN

By the early 1990s the expanding women's rock movement had generated a subculture that came to be known as the "riot grrrls"—a loose, catch-all term used to describe a number of new, angry female artists. Many who came to be so-designated either disavowed the expression or leveled discomfort at the media caricatures that came to surround it. The tag was first coined by musician-writer Tobi Vail, an activist in the feminist rock in-crowd of Evergreen State College, in Olympia, Washington. In the spirit of subversive humor, the term indicated women reclaiming the patriarchal put-down term "girl," then infusing that word with some angry onomatopoe(t)ic "r"s. The semiotic recontextualization also alluded to feminist writers of the 1970s who would sometimes alter spellings (such as "women" to "womyn") to suggest new ownership of the concept. And just as the Clash had written "White Riot" in 1976 in tribute to the black uprisings in London's Notting Hill district, so these new, young, female rebels were similarly calling for "a riot of [their] own," twenty-five years later.

Centered in Olympia, the riot grrrl movement developed in the shadows of the male-dominated, Seattle-based grunge scene. Kurt Cobain and others had close relations with many of the key players associated with riot grrrl, and clearly the rising tide of grunge and Sub Pop records elevated all boats in the harbor (both male and female). However, although the media glare on Generation X was sufficiently bright to highlight the parallel riot grrrl movement, the two subcultures had markedly different philosophies and praxes. Whereas the slacker types of Gen X exhibited a largely passive, cynical persona, the riot grrrls were strident activists, and as grunge sonically retreated into mid-tempo metal "impotence," the riot grrrls put the "punk" back into alternative rock through their styles, attitudes, and attendant humor.

Like most subcultures, riot grrrl was not defined by music alone. Indeed, the term was initially used as the title of a fanzine (or "zine") put out by Tobi Vail and Kathleen Hanna. The zines became primary communication tools of the movement, outlets for the dissemination of information, ideas, and practical suggestions regarding the involvement of women in rock (and the larger) culture. *Girl Germs* and *Malefice* were among the other regional feminist-oriented zines that sprang up during the early nineties. The zine scene harked back to the fanzine outbursts of late-seventies punk; its feminist component also had deeper roots in the independent magazines of the early twentieth century that had served as forums for women to express their concerns and interests.[36] The riot grrrl zines parodied the pen pal style of contemporary (pre-)adolescent "girl" magazines, their pages used as springboards to satirize the sexism inherent even in the PC zones of alternative rock culture. They countered male rock bravado with exaggerated child-speak slang and crafty masks of innocence. Writers developed the distinctly feminine diary mode to reject conventional concepts of cool, replacing them with celebrations of dorkiness and geekiness. In sarcastically inverting standard rock imagery, the riot grrrls rejuvenated feminism as the new cool at a time when many were writing it off as passé. Essentially, they echoed the sentiment expressed by the bumper-sticker slogan I'LL BE A POST-FEMINIST IN THE POST-PATRIARCHY.

Riot grrrl also parodied conventionally girlish style. In the past, women rock rebels often felt that they needed to copy male iconography in order to communicate their subversive intents. Figures like Joan Jett, Chrissie Hynde, and Patti Smith were recognized forerunners of riot grrrl, but there was a sense that these trailblazers had been obligated to compromise their femininity. In reaction, key figures like Kat Bjelland (Babes in

Toyland), Courtney Love (Hole), and Kathleen Hanna (Bikini Kill) developed what became known as the "kinder-whore" look. An alternative take on Madonna's virgin/whore dichotomy, these women's style presented grotesque parody through paradox; they wore cute "doll" dresses but ripped them; they wore their hair in pigtails but smeared excess makeup across their faces. The innocence of "girl" was tarnished in the process and morphed into the experience of "grrrl." Furthermore, the look had disturbing punk components that darkened the humor. Sartorial images of defiled innocence accompanied the lyrical content of their many songs about issues like rape, incest, and abuse. Bikini Kill and Bratmobile members took to fake-tattooing (often in lipstick) words like "bitch," "slut," and "whore" on their bodies, graphically satirizing everyday male attitudes and put-downs of women and girls. As with early punk rock, riot grrrl was cognizant of the power of the provocative image and, in the hands of the humorist, the potential bite of parody as methodology.

Early punk also provided the template for riot grrrl's predominantly raw sound. Three-chord guitar punk, lo-fi production, and loose musicianship were the honored calling cards of much riot grrrl music. Their amateur minimalism not only reflected a lack of training, though. As with early punk, DIY (as philosophy and practice) aesthetics celebrated an "anyone-can-do-it" attitude that created spaces in which women could operate independently. Male judgment and expertise became both unwelcome and irrelevant, as female artists felt liberated to create according to their own criteria. Again parodying gender "types," these riot punks seemed to be saying, "So you think I can't play because I'm a woman; well, you ain't heard nothing yet!" Particularly influential prototypes for the riot grrrl sound were first-wave punk feminists like X-Ray Spex and the Slits. These London bands were satirists of form and content, using their voices in new and unusual ways to speak on topics previously ignored or taboo. However, whereas those bands focused on female exploitation within capitalist constructs, the riot grrrl acts—though expressing a comparably rabid sarcasm—personalized the political, tackling topics of abuse in their physical, mental, and psychological manifestations.

A more immediate subversive humoristic forerunner to riot grrrl was Kim Gordon of Sonic Youth. While Gordon's band was one of the strongest influences on all nineties alt-rock developments, her contributions were particularly significant for her era's female rockers. Kim Gordon brought a cool, deadpan delivery to the songs she sang, a style that had long been regarded as the property of male rockers. Indeed, Gordon has always been a vocal chameleon, sometimes assuming male voices or personas in her songs. Her perpetual mask-wearing has made her a gender-trickster of modern rock, one flirting with multiple identities, a (wo)man in constant flux. John Leland describes her stage persona as "a woman playing a man playing a woman."[37] A playful sarcasm oozes through Gordon's vocal delivery in "Kool Thing" from *Goo* (1990), as she calls out progressive rappers on their ideological inconsistency. Exchanging lines with Public Enemy's Chuck D, Gordon asks in her patented deadpan, deep-toned voice (one suggesting a woman playing a man playing a woman), "Are you gonna liberate us girls from male, white, corporate oppression?" "When you're a star I know that you'll fix everything," she continues, simultaneously mocking male sellouts and parodying the wait-and-see passivity of the "star-ry-eyed" female "type."[38]

Gordon's fluid gender persona mirrors the identity elasticity operating within the riot grrrl broad church in general. While her postmodern fluidity enabled her to enter, embrace, and play with the "feminine" as Bikini Kill, Bratmobile, and Hole did, Gordon's fascination with the "masculine" mystique of rock rebellion was also adopted by nineties rebel grrrls like L7 and PJ Harvey. Both schools harnessed and expressed power, and both employed sarcasm and parody as mechanisms to ex(er)cise pent-up anger over gender-related issues.

The self-conscious femininity of riot grrrl, as mentioned, was developed in ironic reaction to the identities that have traditionally imprisoned "girls." Band names like "Babes in Toyland" and "Bratmobile" humorously played with childlike innocence, but they also suggested a regressive yearning for the pre-adolescent state of unconditional female friendship and unity. The warped girl-speak of titles like *Pottymouth* (Bratmobile) and "Kiss Curl for the Kids Lib Guerrillas" (Huggy Bear) invoked the natural rebellion of the girl-child yet to be processed by superego socialization. Their renditions of "girl power" may seem unrelated to the Spice Girls' light gestures or the Lilith Fair folk confessionals, but they all sought strength in femininity and strategies of sisterhood.

Bikini Kill were particularly adept at tapping into the idealism of wild youth, mixing natural innocence with disturbing punk ruptures. Their "Rebel Girl" (1996) song-manifesto shares the sisterhood sentiments of the Spice Girls' "Wannabe" (1996), while other titles like *Pussy Whipped* (1994) and "Suck My Left One" (1992) playfully use puns and innuendo to celebrate feminine power and subjectivity. Kathleen Hanna constantly inhabits various feminine types (innocent children, warrior rebels, angry victims), representing them through assortments of screams, whines, and cries, and often uniting them in vengeful anger and sardonic retribution.

If Bikini Kill channeled their inner rebel girl, L7 were the tomboys of early-nineties angry female rock. Some critics have dismissed (or simplified) L7's leather-clad faux-macho poses and three-chord punk-metal as mere imitations of male style, but they surely miss the parody of the poses and the power such parody bestows. There is a strident feminist agenda behind their irreverent (lyrical) gestures, aimed "squarely" (L7 is 1950s slang for "square") at passive females and exploitative males. In "Fast and Frightening" (1990) the band offer their idealized version of Bikini Kill's "rebel girl." Hilariously inverting the gender of the classic rock-rebel archetype, they paint a portrait of a woman who has "so much clit she don't need no balls." She goes about "popping wheelies on her motorbike" such that "straight girls wish they were dykes."[39] Sex and gender identities are uproariously uprooted through such defamiliarized clichés. L7 pushed their bad girl persona on many fronts, most famously in an incident at England's Reading Festival in 1992, when guitarist Donita Sparks threw her tampon into the crowd. Such an agit-prank provided a distinctly female spin to traditionally male stage behavior of gobbing, confronting, and phallocentric body posturing. L7's adventures in deconstruction, reconstruction, and gender flux provided challenging and radical humor throughout the decade, establishing prescient precedents for those future female upstarts about to rock.

URBAN R(H)APSODIES

Rap broke big in the 1990s. A decade prior, the genre was still largely a subcultural phenomenon, operating out of the dark enclaves of select urban spaces. Many critics and rock fans had been waiting (and some hoping) for the fad to end; however, by the early nineties it was apparent that their wait would be a long one. Showbiz caricature MC Hammer became an international superstar by commercializing the novelty features of eighties rap, while Snoop (Doggy) Dogg and Tupac revealed that even the most extreme forms of gangsta rap had international success-potential. Rap's subversive humor in the nineties revolved around the established movements of gangsta realism and progressive Afrocentrism. These parallel, sometimes opposing, trends were pushed to new extremes of expression in the new decade, and while each used the techniques of parody and satire employed by their predecessors, those techniques sometimes (inadvertently) lurched into self-parody and/or plain silliness.

Technology changed the face of rap music from its first decade. Long gone were the days of two turntables and a microphone as innovators like Public Enemy crafted painterly sound-scapes and Notorious BIG released albums with the dense sound effects of a film soundtrack. In the hands of producers like Dr. Dre and Sean "Puffy" Combs, rap songs were transformed into urban rhapsodies, impassioned, multitextured, and epic. Rap videos, too, expanded the form into mini-movies that pushed the sex and violence to new graphic extremes. In an era that witnessed rock music pushing limits, rap came closest to breaking them.

Ice T and NWA had shown in the 1980s that gangsta rap could be a viable commercial style, as well as one that captured (and symbolized) the tough realities of black ghetto life. The second wave that followed harnessed the anger, cool, and boast humor of their predecessors and delivered big production versions to America's mainstream culture. The key "playas" in this transition were Ice Cube and Dr. Dre, two ex-members of NWA. Cube enjoyed huge success with his solo release, *AmeriKKKa's Most Wanted* (1990), while Dre revolutionized the sound with his G-funk, "West Coast" style on *The Chronic* (1992). These albums brought gangsta rap to the white suburbs, and *The Chronic* also became known for introducing the world to the laid-back cool of Snoop Doggy Dogg, who guest-rapped on a large portion of the album.

Snoop Doggy Dogg (who later eliminated the redundancy and became simply Snoop Dogg) was the embodiment of the gangsta rap prototype. Exploiting the territory paved by fellow Los Angelian Ice T, he detailed sex and crime scenes with a detached drawl and unfazed, deadpan tone. Snoop imaginatively walked in the sociopathic footsteps of folkloric criminals like Staggerlee, testing extremes, refusing limits, and enjoying the rewards of wine (or gin and juice), women, and song. His fantasy raps and boasts may have bordered on realism, but they were also played for laughs, just as his pimp furs and "hoes in tow" were intended to elicit amusement when he paraded them at public events. Snoop brought personality to the gangsta game, such that today he is regarded as the lovable "doggfather" of the genre. Who else could be a proud and avowed gang member (of the Crips), a felon who has do(d)(g)ged murder accomplice charges, a peddler of pornography, and a public pothead, yet still be so broadly beloved in the 'hood and on talk shows alike? The answer: only a trickster with the skills of Snoop D-O-double-G, that's who. His endearing charms are in part a product of his obvious hustling savvy, but they are primarily due to his natural comedic antenna. When the gangsta (rap) world got too "real" in the mid-nineties (with the murders of Tupac and Biggie Smalls), Snoop survived the backlash to the subgenre by introducing novelty features that gave his music wider appeal. Today, his crafted slang-speak—an updated version of 1970s street jive—has kids of all ages parroting "Fo' shizzle, ma nizzle" at one another.

Although Snoop has been the most enduring of the nineties gangsta rappers, this is partly due to the fact that he managed to avoid the inevitable slings and arrows (and bullets) along the way. Christopher Wallace, a.k.a. Biggie Smalls, a.k.a. the Notorious BIG, was not so fortunate. Cut down in his prime in 1997, Biggie boasted one of the most unique voices in rap history. His debut album title, *Ready to Die* (1994), was prescient, forecasting the details of his ultimate demise. Nevertheless, what is most overlooked in Biggie's raps is that ingredient that makes them so inviting: their sense of humor. Set in relief to his bleak storytelling and fatalistic visions was BIG's funny-cool, grumble-voiced flow. At once loose, easy, and articulate, he used the sonic humor of internal multi-rhyming and onomatopoeia to bring a smile to one's face in the midst of the darkest (gang-)banging tale. The title track of *Ready to Die* features his patented rhythm-rhyming in couplets like "In a sec I throw the tec to your fucking neck / Everybody hit the deck, Biggie about to get some wreck."[40] As harsh as this content is, relief humor emanates from the excesses of assonance and from the sheer barrage of the sonic flow, as though the "Big Poppa" is pitching his own warped nursery rhymes at his constituency of wayward youths.

Gangsta rap during the 1990s came to dominate the music scene and the media to the extent that many forget it was not the only game in town. For every self-engrossed, individualistic gangsta-pimp spouting and boasting "I," "me," and "mine," there were other rap acts in the shadows following the progressive or "righteous" cause that had been trailblazed by the likes of KRS-One, A Tribe Called Quest, and Public Enemy. This school of rap had its role models not in film-noir outlaws, but in teachers and preachers; for them, prophets were prioritized over profits. They proclaimed "we" before "I" and chose to follow the mature, middle-aged model of Malcolm X rather than his youthful, hoodlum example. The righteous rappers often espoused Afrocentric ideas and imagery, such as those once put forth by pioneers like Queen Latifah, Sistah Souljah, and De La Soul. Unlike the inevitable dead-end trips of violent gangsta rappers (symbolized in the homicides of Tupac and Biggie), progressive rappers looked for a way out, not only for themselves but for their brothers and sisters, too. Motivated by a yearning for freedom just like their gangsta peers, these socially conscious rappers—like Martin Luther King Jr. and Malcolm X before them—saw their individual freedom as inextricably tied to universal emancipation. These were serious missions with serious ideas. Yet, as with the gangsta rappers, when one surveys the progressive rap acts of the 1990s, it is apparent that those who drew most from humor to articulate their intrinsic messages were both the most effective and the most engaging.

The Pharcyde exhibited the kind of relief humor that was popular among the progressive rappers of the 1990s. An Afrocentric rap act drawn to the P-funk sound, the Pharcyde were as playful and bizarre as any rappers in the decade. Inheritors of the spirit of the "daisy chain" posses, the Pharcyde moved between pointed satires like "Officer" (2001), with its take on the Driving While Black phenomenon, and "Ya Mama" (1992), a playground dozens-fest of put-downs and absurdist one-liners. The band's spirit and whimsical wit were irreverent without laboring in negativity or anger.

The uplifting exuberance that propelled the positive rappers of the 1990s spread beyond rap's usual New York–L.A. axis, too. Dead Prez, from Florida, and Outkast, from Georgia, both conveyed alternative retro-sensibilities. Outkast, particularly, brought a goofball humor and parody approach to their "dirty South" hybrids of jazz, blues, psychedelia, funk, and techno. Like Prince before them, Outkast were racial bridge-builders and unifiers by nature, and humorists by instinct. Their 2003 hit single, "Hey Ya," with its video parody of the Beatles on *The Ed Sullivan Show*, is one of the more uplifting releases of modern pop music, a testament to the power of Prince's concept of "positivity."

As the nineties drew down, the various strains of rap music showed no signs of diminishing. On the contrary, heading into the new millennium, rap was the most dominant and influential genre of modern rock. Righteous rap continued with black nationalists like Mos Def, Blackalicious, and the Coup keeping the radical spirit alive—often combining the whimsical and the absurd with militant or progressive messages. This strain of rap has also been bolstered and altered by the rising presence of socially conscious female artists like Erykah Badu, Macy Gray, and Eve. The gangsta realm has continued unabated, too, revitalized with the arrival of 50 Cent. However, the most trailblazing, revolutionary, and humorous rap music of the decade arrived from a most unlikely source: a white kid from the streets of Detroit with the tag Eminen.

Eminem

"I am the worst thing since Elvis Presley / To do black music so selfishly / And use it to get myself wealthy," Eminem wryly admits in "White America" from *The Eminem Show* (2002),[41] seconding John Leland's assertion that he is the latest in a long line of "white boys who stole the blues."[42] Eminem's mega-success as a Caucasian artist within the predominantly African American rap genre has always been the "white" elephant in the room. How he has negotiated this situation and status tells us much about the trickster humorist's artistic means of survival and subversion.

Whereas institutionalized segregation and industry demarcations between R&B ("race music") and rock & roll generally protected Elvis from charges of appropriation and from challenges to his authenticity, Eminem's position has been more precarious. Of course, being the (almost) sole white rapper within mainstream hip-hop culture has hardly been a curse; as he concedes in "White America," "If I was black, I woulda sold half."[43] However, being the biggest-selling rap artist of all time has made him the inevitable target of critics both within and beyond the rap game. Eminem has responded to his various naysayers with the craft and guile of the trickster humorist. Allaying potential charges that his lyrics lack the street credibility of his peers, Eminem created the persona Slim Shady, who reflected a fantasy hypermasculinity without peer. Cast as the alienated white underdog in the often cruelly competitive world of rap dissing, Eminem has used superiority humor to cut down detractors or to preemptively strike at a vast cast of selected targets. He has employed dozens humor to stun and daze (perceived) antagonists with a venom and wit few of his contemporaries have mustered or mastered. Unlike Vanilla Ice (to whom he was often compared early in his career), Eminem has not been fingered as an interloper or as a black-rapper-wannabe because he has credibly competed as a street rebel with the black rap elite, while never denying—indeed, while provocatively calling attention to—his white cultural foundations. Shoving in the collective face of mainstream America extreme images showing how "bad" a white boy can really be, Eminem has managed to shock and subvert that culture even while its sons and daughters have purchased his records in the millions. Creating both antagonists and allies along the way, Eminem has stayed in the eye of the storm, reveling in the melodrama while laughing all the way to the bank.

An authentic working-class biography has been as essential to Eminem's sustained success within hip-hop as his self-protective humor. Whereas the Beastie Boys' middle-class background always made them outsiders to rap's inner sanctum, Eminem's "trailer park" roots—much cited in song and visually represented in the quasi-documentary film *8 Mile* (2002)—have given him lyrical license to his own "ill" rhymes of struggle and strife. This street-sanctioned acceptance has served not only to give Eminem leverage within hip-hop, but to establish him as a role model—or at least representative—of a young, white, proletarian demographic sorely lacking in legitimate icons and idols. Armed with a gritty vernacular and lyrical dexterity—peppered with fashionable dashes of syntactical faux pas—Eminem has increasingly used his voice for subversive ends, whether to ridicule the conveyor-belt parades of modern pop products, to expose the hypocrisy of the bourgeois "adult" moral police, or to satirize the reckless war-mongering of the Bush administration.

Like that fellow Michigan trickster, Madonna, Eminem has courted controversy as his means to an end. Whereas gender-bending and sexual candor provided Madonna's vehicles to mass media furor, Eminem's have been his representations of women and homosexuals. Violence, misogyny, and homophobia have long been staple ingredients in hard rap songs, though Eminem has upped the ante in terms of the extremes of their representations.

Many nuanced arguments have been made concerning the potential influence and effects of these lyrics on young listeners. Critics claim that Eminem's graphic celebrations of violence only encourage real hate crimes, or at least desensitize youths to the realities of rape and assault. Defenders often cite first amendment rights or state that individuals—not the representative artists—should be held responsible for any irresponsible acts. Others point to the fantasy and cartoon elements in Eminem's depictions of violence; they highlight the graphic exaggerations, arguing that the artist is merely parodying preexisting conventions or that he is just playing the trickster, deliberately trying to provoke and annoy his critics. These divergent points of view each have their merits, though they all recognize the powers of language and humor as potentially life-denying or, conversely, freedom-affirming. As such, humor is a flexible—if not uncontrollable—weapon in Eminem's hands. Whether the real effects and outcomes of his humorous provocations have mirrored his artistic intentions will remain an issue to assess and ponder.

Eminem discovered the power and protection of humor as a young teenager when he first entered the fray of Detroit's battle-hardened rap circuit. Here, wits and wit were requisite tools of survival, especially for a skinny white kid. After graduating from the streets, he released his debut album, *Infinite* (1996), to little critical fanfare and charges of unoriginality. In a subsequent effort to create a more distinctive and personalized voice, he then formed his own Mr. Hyde alter ego in the form of Slim Shady, thereby unleashing his id for free-style explosions of outlandish raps that loosely combined raw truths with fantasy fictions. On the *Slim Shady EP* (1997) and follow-up *The Slim Shady LP* (1999) Eminem reintroduced himself to the rap world via his new persona. "Just Don't Give a Fuck" was both a song-statement of principle and an early excursion for the Slim Shady doppelganger. Waving "bye-bye" to Eminem, Shady declares himself "a naughty rotten rhymer," while outlining his trickster philosophy: "Pathological liar, blowin' shit out of proportion / The looniest, zaniest, spontaneous, sporadic impulsive thinker."[44] "Guilty Conscience" (1999) further investigated his new schizoid split consciousness with a good-versus-evil morality play, casting his producer Dr. Dre as the voice of reason (!) and Slim Shady as the devilish provocateur. His early breakthrough hit, "My Name Is" (1999), continued the name-games as Eminem vented and ranted about sex, drugs, and violence from beneath the shadow of Shady. "97 Bonnie and Clyde" (1999) proclaimed an artist with a noir sensibility and an even blacker sense of humor as details of a husband's murder of his wife rained down with gratuitous gore. In their sick excesses, such songs were simultaneously disturbing yet uproarious, graphic yet cartoonish. Stunned listeners could only ask "Is he serious?" then "How can he follow this?"

Hopscotching back to his birth name for his next album title, Eminem released *The Marshall Mathers LP* (2000). Though the album's title seemed to promise a new point of view, and though the personal is here more pronounced, Slim Shady's psychotic perspective is still omnipresent. "Kill You" and "Kim" offer more murder fantasies about his mother and wife, respectively, begging Freudian interpretations of our em-asculated narrator. New punching bags are created, too, as Shady seeks to settle old beefs and to create a few fresh ones. Lashing out with lacerating insult humor, he skewers pop icons Britney Spears and 'N Sync in "Marshall Mathers," then Will Smith, Christina Aguilera, and Britney (again!) in "The Real Slim Shady." Though seemingly begging to be hated with his vitriolic attacks, Eminem was ironically incapable of quelling the embrace of critics high on his verbal gymnastics or the uncritical love of his ever-expanding fan base (who consumed two million copies of *The Marshall Mathers LP* in its first week of release). "Don't you wanna be just like me?" he had once sarcastically asked on "Role Model" (1999).[45] The answer for many (and for his Stan character) was a resounding "yes."

Perhaps suggesting the artist wresting back control from the persona, the title of the next album was *The Eminem Show* (2002). "Without Me" announced his return with characteristic comic bluster and a new roster of targets ripe for ribbing. With a machine-gun barrage of harsh one-liners, Eminem leveled his critics—the Cheneys (Dick and Lynne), the FCC, MTV—before picking off his latest antagonists-of-choice, Limp Bizkit and Moby. Casting Dr. Dre as Batman and himself as Robin in the accompanying video, "Without Me" presented our fearless fighters as the (ironic) saviors of a youth culture lobotomized by mainstream pop fluff.

Behind the ever-present comic theater, indications of social concern became increasingly apparent on *The Eminem Show*. No longer as self-absorbed or as preoccupied with anti-homosexual and anti-women shock-attacks, Eminem has recently wielded his humor weapons for more progressive purposes. "Sing for a Moment" (2002) finds the rhyme fighter at his articulate best, defending rap music against those who would scapegoat it to explain social ills: "They say music can alter moods and talk to you / Well, can it load a gun up for you, and cock it, too? / Well, if it can, then the next time you assault a dude / Just tell the judge it was my fault and I'll get sued."[46] Such publicly pointed satire continued on *Encore* (2004), led by its centerpiece "get-out-the-vote" song "Mosh." Here, Eminem calls on his not inconsiderable youth support to "disarm this weapon of mass destruction that we call our President." Elsewhere in the song he pours scorn on the "psychological" warfare waged by the Bush camp against the American people, ironically thrusting back at George Jr. with his own pop-Freudian counter-jab: "Strap him with an AK-47 / Let him go fight his own war / Let him impress Daddy that way."[47]

One senses in Eminem's recent work an increased cognizance of his earned power and potential, reconstituted to serve the subversive purposes for which his intelligence and sharp humor are undoubtedly built. And many will no doubt welcome a lyrical mockery aimed more frequently at legitimate adversaries than at the perpetually put-upon gay community and female constituency. Eminem will likely never be the PC satirist that some would like him to be; for that perhaps we should be grateful, as his impulses may serve alternatively progressive ends. His raw raps are subversive, not only because they remind us to heed Ice T's paradoxical warning, "Freedom of speech, just watch what you say," but because they also provide a frustrated youth culture with an outlet of relief. Freud saw humor as our way of venting the suppressed. Thus, in a society that disallows certain natural urges and that censors particular means of expression, Eminem serves as our representative id, emitting the raw materials repressed in the collective unconscious. His saucy wordplay, juvenile puns, and dozens put-downs are the dirty jokes we want to, but dare not, say at the dinner table; aired out vicariously through the trickster, they symbolically represent our desire to overcome our deepest repressions. Or, as Em puts it in "The Real Slim Shady" (2000), "I'm like a head-trip to listen to, cos I'm only givin' you / Things you joke about with your friends inside your living room. / The only difference is I got the balls to say it."[48]

NIGHTMARES ON METAL STREET

The paradox of heavy metal in the 1990s is that the more it changed, the more it stayed the same. In sound and structure, its form was in flux, part of the hybridization wave that swept across many of the era's genres. In the case of metal, this ushered in a multitude of subgenres: nu metal, art-metal, prog-metal, funk-metal, punk-metal, goth-metal, industrial metal, black metal, death metal, and stoner rock (to name but some). Many of these styles embraced the sonic options made available by new technology, though distorted guitar riffs, a deep bass sound, and cracking drums remained as the mainstay metal sound.

With regard to band image and perspective, metal stayed somewhat in stasis. The theatrical legacy of Kiss and Alice Cooper lingered over the new/nu acts just as it had over eighties bands, with masks, face paint, and costumes continuing as the de rigueur metal fashion. Invariably, the world of horror was evoked, as comics, cartoons, carnivals, and clowns offered a smorgasbord of comedic sources from which bands could draw to project their "dark" fantasies. This visual humor—as before—oscillated (sometimes uncontrollably) between knowing, intellectual commentary and dumb self-parody. However, whether one laughed with or at the theatrical extremes that characterized these bands, their outlandish displays served metal's traditional purpose: relief humor for angst-ridden, white, male kids. Unlike the slackers of the grunge subculture (who internalized their frustrations for the most part), metal bands offered an escape route into fantasylands of utopian subcultures or fun-filled dystopian gore-festivals. And as with contemporary gangsta rap, nineties metal broached all prior limits in providing dreamscapes of subversion to satiate the alienated but hungry souls of nineties youth. Like gangsta rap, too, the more the new metal acts pushed the envelope of shock, the more successful they became; thus, there was little incentive to tone down or compromise, and an awful lot of inducement not to.

The rough and tough working-class city of Detroit had been the incubator for seventies metal pioneers like Alice Cooper, MC5, and Ted Nugent, and it proved to be the spawning ground for some of the more notorious new metal acts like Kid Rock and Insane Clown Posse (or ICP). The latter developed from rap foundations to become—along with Limp Bizkit and Slipknot—leaders of the incipient nu metal movement. Nu (or nü) metal designated a style that added rap vocals to conventional metal riffs and structures. In what was less a fusion than a union, verses were usually rapped against hip-hop backbeats and muted guitars until the explosive chorus unleashed the hard rock attack and familiar primal vocal screams.

ICP, like other nu metal bands, learned from rap the importance of subculture and territory in fostering a loyal following. Rather than gang affiliations or turf, ICP's Violent J and Shaggy 2 Dope created a fantasy playground (the "dark carnival") for their young fans ("juggalos"). The juggalo identity was based on Violent J's "juggla" alter-ego, a psychotic carnival juggler. By wearing his "evil clown" mask and corpse makeup, hardcore fans paid homage to the band. Throughout the nineties, ICP developed their darkly comic subculture, incorporating the subversive instincts of traditional carnival parades and developing their own (s)language of the streets. There was initially little concern over the misogyny and dark forces that the band, an underground youth cult, were tapping, but by the mid-nineties it became clear that ICP had become a formidable national force with a vast army of rabid young juggalos and juggalettes. Suddenly, the band that was releasing songs with titles like "Santa's a Fat Bitch" (1997) and "Fuck the World" (1999) had a teen demographic demanding to see the accompanying videos on MTV's *TRL*. Adding to the unfolding media frenzy, the Disney-owned Hollywood Records caved in to the onslaught of complaints from right-wing religious groups and decided to sever ties with the band in 1997. Not surprisingly, this only fueled the mystique and popularity of ICP as other record companies started a bidding war comparable to the one waged for the Sex Pistols after they were dumped by EMI in 1977.

Less enamored with the shock-humor of ICP was Eminem, himself a Detroit-boy-made-good with a penchant for provocative wit. He lured the band into an ongoing war of words, wits, and songs of which he could hardly declare himself the winner. In response to Slim Shady's threats and taunts, ICP released the parodic "Slim Anus" (2000) followed by the put-down "Nuttin' but a Bitch Thang" (2001). Despite this ongoing "beef," by the end of the decade Insane Clown Posse had established themselves as pop stars in the nu metal world order, mirroring Alice Cooper's career path with their declarations of born again Christianity and following Kiss's merchandizing journey into comic book adolescent adoration.

Cooper and Kiss can claim another nineties descendent in Rob Zombie and his rocky horror band, White Zombie. Like ICP, Zombie drew from comic books and cartoons in crafting his horror persona. He used his sinister, gruff voice and an industrial metal backdrop to create a nightmare wall of sound that stormed the charts during the mid-1990s. "More Human Than Human" (1995) became one of the most successful heavy metal hits of all time, and the accompanying video established its creator (Zombie himself) as a worthy craftsman of visual shock humor. He would later develop his directorial skills and love of schlock horror B-movies into a second career. His films, *House of 1000 Corpses* (2000) and *The Devil's Rejects* (2005), combine slapstick violence with the camp relief of the *Texas Chainsaw Massacre* and *Nightmare on Elm Street* movies.

The social outcast has always been a key motif in heavy metal, reflecting the feelings of ostracism suffered by many working-class male fans and functioning as the ideal protagonist in the escapist horror shows envisioned by metal artists. From this subterranean imagination has developed the subgenre of sleaze rock, a form represented by Jon Spencer, the Cycle Sluts from Hell, and Boss Hog in cultlike seclusion during the 1980s. Nashville Pussy pushed this innately parodic style to new extremes with their AC/DC-inspired paeans to white trash culture. Culling their name from the song "Wang Dang Sweet Poontang" (1978) by the King of Sleaze, Ted Nugent, Nashville Pussy announced their arrival with the debut album title/proclamation, *Let Them Eat Pussy* (1998). With a style unlike the horror-humor of most metal, they channeled the sexual sleaze of the Cramps and dirty rap for their shock humor. With two scantily clad women rocking the band, Pussy moved between the wasted porno-kitsch of the Plasmatics (in songs like "All Fucked Up" [1998]) and the down-home proletarian imagery of Mojo Nixon (in "Fried Chicken and Coffee" [1998]). As with their predecessors, the outcast sleaze of Nashville Pussy would never penetrate the mainstream metal world. However, their trailer park roots-rock would find a diluted representative in Kid Rock, whose marriage of redneck simplicity (on albums like *Grits Sandwiches for Breakfast* [1990]) to celebrity charms (a marriage made literal in his union with Pamela Anderson) made him America's most recognizable white, proletarian pop personality in the process.

Despite heavy metal's long-standing association with outcasts, misfits, and the alienated, the genre has rarely brought any sociopolitical awareness to its largely working-class constituency. Instead, it has used grotesque representations to caricature (or to symbolize) the socially excluded. Although these often extreme representations have not necessarily been derogatory in intent, they have suggested little more than sympathy for the devils. This apolitical attitude was challenged and underwent changes during the nineties as the genre morphed through hybrids into other cultural territories. Rage Against the Machine imported the social consciousness of punk politicos like the Clash into their rap-metal outbursts; Mr. Bungle introduced the absurdist abstractions of Frank Zappa to their innovative soundscapes; System of a Down drew from Bungle's provocative art-metal models to craft Armenian American protest music; Korn brought angst and torment to lyrics more familiar from therapy sessions than from the fantasy forums of heavy metal, giving *realistic* voice to teenage torment; and Tool established themselves as the anti-conformists of nineties metal, even dedicating *AEnima* (1996) to late comedian Bill Hicks, who had raged with similar satirical venom and anti-establishment confrontation before them.

The above acts contributed art-intellectualism and engaged realism to the heavy metal genre, but it was Marilyn Manson who most directly—and under the glare of the public eye—transformed metal from a fantasy-only field into a sociopolitical one. More than any of his peers, Manson put metal in flux, turning satirical social comment and polemical protest into fixtures of the genre as welcome as fantasy horror and subcultural theatrics had always been.

Marilyn Manson

As exhibited in his chosen moniker (as well as his songs and images), Brian Hugh Warner—more familiarly known as Marilyn Manson—investigates, exposes, and teases at the ironies that surround society's designations of good and evil. His dualistic perspective has been expressed and articulated through various means of subversive humor: a lyrical superiority humor unmasks the hypocrisies of institutions, a grotesque visual humor dramatizes the alienation of society's ostracized and excluded, while witty wordplay and double entendres highlight the double-think, double-speak, and double standards of the system's so-called "common sense." The "anti" prefix Manson has been fond of adopting in his songs functions as more than just a gesture of rebellion: It embodies his vision of the world, a philosophy in which ironic inversion is the strategic in-road to outing wrongs, celebrating rights, and holding them both up for public scrutiny and judgment.

Manson became the pied piper of alienated white teenagers during the mid-1990s in much the same way that Alice Cooper did during the 1970s. As a result, Manson has been treated by adult society not just as an example of novelty grotesque, but as a dangerous inciter of youth rebellion and deviant thinking. On the receiving end of everything from record boycotts to protests by religious groups to Senate hearings and denouncements, Marilyn Manson has shown that subversive rock humor has the potential to provoke the powers that be, as well as to engage and embolden the powerless.

With Alice Cooper and Kiss for his prototypical role models, Marilyn Manson (the man and the band) tapped into the traditions of shock-rock once pioneered by those seventies icons, the bogeymen of their own era. Indeed, through his combination of macabre visual iconography with provocative lyrics and delivery, Manson positioned himself in a tradition of rock horror-humor that dates back to the schlock excesses of fifties trailblazers like Screamin' Jay Hawkins, who similarly combined visual theater with melodramatic lyrics to titillate the kids and petrify their parents. In homage to this camp tradition—and specifically to Hawkins—Manson covered "I Put a Spell on You" for his *Smells Like Children* (1995) album.

Although heavy metal has long set itself in opposition to mainstream mores and has reveled in the kind of escapist fantasies that characterize Manson's concepts, his accompanying sociopolitical critiques have separated him from most metal peers. His vitriolic attacks on organized religion and on behalf of free speech place him in the company of satirists like Frank Zappa and Jello Biafra more than any artists from the metal school; indeed, his scathing sarcasm, raw language, and taboo-broaching topics are more inspired by punk traditions than by metal ones. It is his adeptness at drawing from multiple sources—to hybridize and be in constant flux—that has given Manson his distinction. Each album signifies a reinvention of image and music, and a conceptual development, enabling him to avoid the "fifteen minutes" limitation beyond which so many shock-rockers have been unable to extend.

Early releases *Portrait of an American Family* (1994) and the aforementioned *Smells Like Children* (1995) saw the band forming their commercially viable industrial-glam-metal sound while reaching for shocking lyrical material. Sometimes the band settled for adolescent sexual innuendo—as in "My Monkey" (1994) and

"Snake Eyes and Sissies" (1994)—while other times a cartoonlike horror quotient was strategically inserted. *Smells* songs like "Kiddie Grinder," "Everlasting Cocksucker," and "Shitty Chicken Gang Bang" suggested that Manson had opted to take the more inaccessible road to rock stardom.

Fame he found, though, with his darkly ironic rereading of the Eurythmics' "Sweet Dreams (Are Made of This)" (1994), and the grotesque video enjoyed regular MTV rotation. *Antichrist Superstar* (1996) capitalized on Manson's burgeoning public image as public rock enemy number one. "The Beautiful People" featured the zombie groove, possessed vocal hiss, and sinister intent that came to characterize his general oeuvre, while the song's lyrics portrayed a ragged cast of mindless and threatening subhumans, by-products of a warped Darwinism on the verge of an impending cutthroat fascism. Horrified parents found little beauty in "The Beautiful People" and went tattling to their nearest congressional representatives, while hordes of fascinated (pre)teens were drawn like proverbial moths to Manson's brightening flame. The band's high-budget videos rolled off the production line, bringing grotesque imagery, dystopian themes, and nightmare visuals to the living rooms and bedrooms of the rock-attuned world. With a paradoxical pizzazz befitting a band called Marilyn Manson, the song "Irresponsible Hate Anthem" underscored the trickster charm at the core of the phenomenon with its opening ironic boast, "I am so all-American / I'd sell you suicide."[49]

Shelving metal horror for glam sci-fi, Marilyn Manson next appeared as a doped-up androgynous alien on the cover of *Mechanical Animals* (1998). Stealing liberally from *Ziggy*-period David Bowie for his new Omega persona and from Pink Floyd's *The Wall* for his vision of social alienation, Manson added pathos to the satire of his social critiques. Its singles, "The Dope Show" and "I Don't Like the Drugs (but the Drugs Like Me)," were not only guaranteed to disturb and annoy the vigilant would-be censors but they also reflected the resigned withdrawal of Manson's alien persona in the face of a world of greed and exploitation. Manson used various types of wordplay to add comic flavor to his otherworldly album concept.

For example, the neologisms "neurophobic," "phenobarbidoll," and "manniqueen" introduced wittily skewed details to the warped psychodrama of the album's title track.[50]

The wordplay continued with the title of his next release, *Holy Wood (In the Shadow of the Valley of Death)* (2000). Principally an album responding to the mass hysteria that surrounded the 1999 Columbine High School shootings—and the complicit role some claimed Manson's music had in the incident—America's favorite scapegoat offered up his own targets for blame, impaling each with caustic wit. "Some children died the other day . . . You should have seen the ratings that day," he sarcastically states in "The Nobodies."[51] Resurrecting his Omega guise (as the primordial Adam Kadmon), he scrutinizes and lambastes social institutions from family to media. Manson sets up a spoonerism in "GodEatGod" to charge organized religion with the competitive cruelties of capitalism, while the double-negative paradox "I'm not a slave to a God that doesn't exist," from "The Fight Song,"[52] further illustrates the wordsmith's skills in fusing linguistic wit to his broader thematic satire.

Never sacrificing either fantasy or realism for his subversive humor, Marilyn Manson shifted from space to time travel with *The Golden Age of Grotesque* (2003). Inhabiting the pre-Nazi era of the 1930s Weimar Republic, Manson celebrates the decadence of this vaudevillian swing era while forecasting the ominous forces of the impending fascist state. Again, language is twisted and turned into bleak humor, an Orwellian aura infusing punned titles like "mOBSCENE" and "(s)AINT" and neologisms like "gloominati" and "scabaret sacrilegends" (from the title track).[53] Inferring parallels between the mass-produced thinking of Hitler's Germany and contemporary America, Manson mocks the new pop punks as "The Bright Young Things" who "rebel to sell."[54] He combines parody with self-parody in "This Is the New Shit," the lead single that ridicules formulaic hit songs as well as the audiences that maintain such fodder. The chorus offers the prototype: "Babble babble, bitch bitch / Rebel rebel, party party / Sex sex sex, and don't forget the violence / Blah blah blah, got your lovey-dovey, sad-and-lonely / Stick your stupid slogan in / Everybody sing along."[55]

History has provided many examples of bands that have focused on fantasy or politics or history in applying their techniques of radical humor; few can boast that they have embraced all three fields—sometimes simultaneously—in their work. Within the sometimes one-dimensional arena of heavy metal, such eclecticism is even rarer. Yet when one considers that Manson recently had an art showing of his work at his own gallery, that he is about to release his debut directed film (about the master wordplay humorist and fantasy writer Lewis Carroll), and that his latest album—*Eat Me, Drink Me*—was released in 2007, his status as a Renaissance man of rock remains beyond doubt. This range speaks to his (es)sense of humor, too, which can oscillate between the visual and the lyrical, the linguistic and the thematic, and the camp and the caustic. Whether within the rock (or metal) world or beyond, one suspects that Manson's provocative humor, with its intermingling of fantasy and reality, will show up in some form, somewhere, to shock some and to inspire others in future generations.

POP GOES THE PUNK

Like rap and heavy metal, punk rock came of commercial age during the 1990s. However, the form in which it came to the mainstream bore little relation to the fundamentalist oi and hardcore of the 1980s, nor to the sociopolitical protest punk of the late 1970s. Spearheaded by a California vanguard of Green Day, Rancid, and the Offspring, pop-punk penetrated the corporate rock world via the debris left after Nirvana blew up the alternative-mainstream divide in 1992. These three acts—and the many that followed in their trailblazing path—would become darlings of MTV and fixtures on the national charts throughout the decade and into the new millennium. The cry of "sellout" that greeted the pop-punk bands' arrival on the national stage was both a statement of fact and a gesture of concern over what had befallen rock's most proudly subterranean form. Punk, or what it had become, was clearly in flux.

Contrary to much conventional wisdom, the advent of pop-punk did not emerge with Green Day's ten-million-selling 1994 album, *Dookie*. Indeed, the subgenre's sound, form, and lyrical predilections date back to the very roots of punk rock on both sides of the Atlantic. The godfathers of pop-punk were, of course, the Ramones. Their minimalist three-chord assaults established the template for the pop-punk form and sound, and their parodies of teenage decadence established the limited thematic repertoire from which subsequent pop-punk would draw: girls, drugs, brats. Their faux-dumb humor was the prototypical pop-punk humor, though in the lyrics of many of their descendents the "faux" aspect was markedly absent. The foundations of pop-punk in the U.K. lay with Manchester's the Buzzcocks, whose tales of adolescent frustration over sex ("Orgasm Addict" [1977]) and puppy love ("Ever Fallen in Love with Someone (You Shouldn't Have Fallen in Love With)" [1978]) were the standard fare of the similarly depoliticized pop-punksters of the 1990s. With their simplistic but irresistible hooks and banal (pre)teen lyrics, both the Ramones and the Buzzcocks drew from the maligned bubblegum pop tradition more than from the revered folk and art rock genres. In the process, punk attracted a new and younger demographic—or at least immaturity level—after the AOR dominance of early-seventies music. Later, in the hands of bands like blink-182 and Sum 41, this pitch for a younger market encouraged some of the best and worst excesses of dumb humor as the genre descended into a world of eternal infantilism.

The fine-tuning of pop-punk's dumb humor took place through second-wave punk bands like the Dickies, the Vandals, and NOFX. Each consolidated the Ramones' bare-bones speed-guitar riffs while balancing adolescent silliness against punk credibility. Along with the Descendents, the Dickies and the Vandals established the so-called "SoCal" Los Angeles locus of American pop-punk. The Dickies struck early with "Banana Splits" (1979), a punk-meets-bubblegum cover of the theme of the children's TV show of the same name; the song rose to the top ten in the U.K. charts. The band's primary subversive strategy was to reduce "classics"—like Black Sabbath's "Paranoid" and Barry McGuire's "Eve of Destruction"—to zany pop-punk anthems. The Vandals similarly used cover songs as a way to destroy sacred cows and to elevate the elementary at the expense of the self-important. The *Grease* soundtrack's "Summer Lovin'" fell victim to their trash irony in 1995, while album titles like *Slippery When Ill* (1989) and *Fear of a Punk Planet* (1990) offered sly asides at the expense of Bon Jovi, the Beastie Boys, and Public Enemy, three of the hot-shot acts of the era. Perennial pranksters, the Vandals were not averse to "pissing in their own backyard" either. Many of their songs were insider tales exposing the more embarrassing incidents of L.A.'s punk subculture, while they provoked the more politically inclined socio-punks by performing a show for the College Young Republicans in 1984.

NOFX have been something of an aberration within the pop-punk fold in that they have married their catchy riffs and sing-along melodies to lyrics in the tradition of the Dead Kennedys and the Clash. After years of slogging in the trenches of underground punk culture, NOFX broke through to a broader constituency in the mid-nineties, thanks to the opportunities facilitated by Green Day's success. The NOFX sound is hardly ground-breaking, offering up the same brand of bass-melodic, guitar-riffing pop-punk played by their peers. Moreover, with their love of puns and wordplay, much of frontman Fat Mike's songwriting indulges in the subgenre's ubiquitous low humor. *Punk in Drublic* (1994), *Heavy Petting Zoo* (1996), *S&M Air Lines* (1989), and *The War on Errorism* (2003) are but a sampling of their clever/silly album titles. Where they differ from their pop-punk contemporaries is in the sociopolitical concerns of their lyrics. Their anti-conformist screeds root the band in the protest-anarchist traditions of punk, though even at their most outrageous, an underlying satirical humor drives the polemics and underscores the upbeat humor of their melodies. "USA-holes" (2006) and "The Idiots Are Taking Over" (2004) illustrate NOFX's forthright abuse-humor, the video for the latter featuring a montage of Bush-isms and administrative absurdities linked to a parade of tragicomic images that require no additional editorial comment. Fat Mike's satirical reach has extended beyond the Bush neo-Cons, too. Other targets have included working-class "Reagan Democrats," organized religion, conformist youth subcultures, and even the riot grrrl movement, which came in for a tongue-lashing in "Kill Rock Stars" (1997), a song that mocked (what NOFX regarded as) Kathleen Hanna's man-hating, negative postures.

The band deemed most responsible for the rise of pop-punk in the 1990s was Green Day. They have been historicized as the subgenre's equivalent of Nirvana, and their first label, Lookout! Records, has been regarded as being to pop-punk what Sub Pop was to grunge: the vehicle of transition. From Berkeley, California, the teenage Green Day lads started out ensconced in the punk subculture that located itself around the legendary 924 Gilman Street club. Their early work received positive plaudits, but when the band shifted to the major label Reprise Records for the release of *Dookie* in 1994, their roots-punk base was so appalled that the band were refused access to Gilman Street for years after. In the meantime, *Dookie* became the then-biggest-selling punk album of all time, while the band developed into critical darlings with the even bigger success of the Grammy-winning *American Idiot* album in 2004. Of course, as often befalls the success stories of once-underground rock, a constant backlash has hung heavy over the band. Johnny Rotten—never reticent and ever the curmudgeon—once wittily designated Green Day "plonk" rather than "punk," dismissing them as "phony" and "a wank outfit."[56]

Despite the perhaps envious critiques of their detractors, Green Day have become the most influential punk band of our times, spawning a pop-punk movement that has been dominant in commercial and underground rock since the release of *Dookie*. From that album came two trailblazing singles that underscored the snotty sarcasm underlying Green Day's humorous point of view. Both "Longview" and "Basket Case" were satirical salvos aimed at the slacker youths of the early nineties. Writing in a first-person narrative, songwriter Billie Joe Armstrong clearly intended to implicate himself and his subculture as parts of the pervasive condition of apathy, self-absorption, and entropy. Both songs are character sketches that employ (self-deprecating) caricature humor. "Basket Case" opens with the ironic rhetorical question, "Do you have the time to listen to me whine / About nothing and everything at once?" before postulating the narrator's social state in terms of a clinical-psychological condition.[57] As a "piss-take" of suburban slackers, even the work of the riot grrrls could not have been more pointed or sarcastic.

Hot on the heels of Green Day in the mid-nineties were fellow Californians the Offspring, who created a hybrid of pop-punk, metal, and rap that subsequent acts like Sum 41 and the Bloodhound Gang would replicate thereafter. Like Green Day, the Offspring used brattiness and catchy hooks to broaden punk's appeal to the (pre-)adolescent skate-punk crowd. Their biggest hit, "Pretty Fly (for a White Guy)" (1998), positioned the band's humor somewhere between Green Day's youth-fixated satire and "Weird Al" Yankovic's "White and Nerdy" loser jokes. The song focuses on the Middle American, middle-class, white suburban (pre)teens of their fan base, only to skewer them as self-deluding black wannabes (otherwise known as "wiggers"). Songwriter Dexter Holland provides humorous insight in his commentary on his subject "type": "He may not have a clue / And he may not have style / But everything he lacks / Well, he makes up in denial."[58]

Though the Ramones labored on the club circuit as their pop-punk "offspring" rose to national prominence, the Donnas were a constant reminder of that forerunner's enduring presence and influence. Rare female representatives within pop-punk's mostly male club, the Donnas were postmodern pariahs of the most calculating kind. Their pastiche of "bad girl" iconography was lifted straight from the Runaways' wardrobe, while their appropriation of "male" sexual assertiveness was a strategy L7 had been using for years. As with these bands, caricature humor and irreverence were foundations for the Donnas' delinquent group persona. "Get Rid of That Girl," "Teenage Runaway," and "Do You Wanna Go Out with Me?" were all songs from their eponymous 1998 album, offering stark evidence of the influence of the Ramones, while their adopted names of Donna A, Donna C, Donna F, and Donna R suggested the extent of that influence. For the Donnas and others, the Ramones' brand of caricature humor and cartoon bubble-punk had, by the 1990s, become a subgenre in its own right.

If Green Day and NOFX showed that there was a clever side to pop-punk dumb humor, bands like blink-182 and the Bloodhound Gang revealed that there were depths of dumb still left to plumb. The group blink-182—yet another California act (from San Diego)—specialized in toilet humor (e.g., *Enema of the State* [1999], "Dysentery Gary" [2001]) and in getting naked (e.g., *Take Off Your Pants and Jacket* [2001], the video for "What's My Name Again?" [2001]). With their proud commitment to arrested adolescence (e.g., "Dammit" [2001]), blink-182 reached deep into their collective id for the blissfully stupid world not yet colonized by adult responsibility. These boys would literally fight for their right to party, and if girlfriends or parents stood in the way of their immature endeavors, they became targets, too. "I'll never talk to you again / Unless your dad'll suck me off," the singer proclaims in "Happy Holidays (You Bastard)" (2001), drawing from their bottomless pit of childish comic abuse.[59] The rise of blink-182's brand of pop-punk humor at the end of the nineties was testament to how much the punk genre had changed since the raw social satire of its early years. Yet, for all its infantilism, blink-182 served to perpetuate rock's long-standing purpose of pissing parents off, the mission of its subversive youth humor since Chuck Berry and the Coasters released their generation gap anthems in the mid-1950s.

This dumb and dumber school has increasingly defined the pop-punk field. The Presidents of the United States of America and Bowling for Soup are contemporary successors to novelty punk acts like the Dickies and the Vandals. The Presidents' 1994 hits, "Lump" and "Peaches," were fun(ny), absurdist, and well suited for MTV accommodation, while Bowling for Soup have released a series of singles and videos showing that the dumbest ideas can often be both clever and engaging. Their Grammy-nominated "1985" (2004) refers to a time when there was "music still on MTV," while "Punk Rock 101" (2001) exposes the latent conformity of the modern punk subculture; the video for the latter hilariously casts its would-be rebel youths as regimented soldiers at a punk boot-camp. Bowling for Soup's goofball parodies, video dress-ups, and dorky image suggest that nowadays there is a fine line between pop-punk and Weird Al.

Within a subgenre that seems to give every band at least fifteen minutes of fame at some time, the Bloodhound Gang have remained in the margins since their formation in 1992. While this has perhaps preserved their punk credibility for some (should such a concept exist anymore), it might also be an indicator that even dumb humor has its limits of taste and tolerance. Despite pilfering liberally from the Beastie Boys' early period locker room humor and metal-rap rhythms, lyrically the Bloodhound Gang make the Beasties seem like highbrow intellectuals. *Use Your Fingers* (1995), *One Fierce Beer Coaster* (1996), and *Hooray for Boobies* (1997) are among the band's album titles that give some indication of their line in humor. Their biggest hit, "The Bad Touch" (1999), peaked at number fifty-two on the Billboard charts and included the raunchy couplet "You and me baby ain't nothin' but mammals / So let's do it like they do on the Discovery Channel."[60] Theirs is locker room humor run amuck, made for suburban adolescents hiding in the closet with their girly magazines. It is built to irritate conservative parents with its crass sexual innuendo, or conversely, liberal ones who might be concerned that the band's intrinsic (and proud) stupidity might rub off on little Johnny.

The recent hijacking of nineties pop-punk by such mainstream pop teens as Avril Lavigne and Ashlee Simpson has perhaps made the "punk" tag all but obsolete. Yet, the form continues—despite the cynics and naysayers—to doggedly persist into the 2000s. Punk continues to regenerate, spawning new generations of bands and fans, each new demographic seemingly younger than previous ones. Current pop-punkers Fall Out Boy, Panic! At the Disco, and Good Charlotte may not have the subversive rock humorist credentials of the Sex Pistols or the Ramones, but one might rhetorically ask in their defense: Would you rather have your ten-year-old son or daughter listen to these gender-bending pranksters, or would you rather have them buying into the creatively challenged mainstream alternatives (type)cast from the *American Idol* production line?

ROOTS REROUTED

Like the neo-hippy jam bands of the era (Phish, Blues Traveler, Widespread Panic), the return to roots music (country, bluegrass, folk, blues, etc. . . .) during the nineties signified a retro-yearning to escape from modern culture into an idealized "authentic" past. Like the jam bands, too, the neo-roots acts were rejecting more than culture; theirs was a dismissal of the content, production, representation, and marketing of contemporary music itself. Nevertheless (and again, like the jam bands in relation to their sixties antecedents), the nineties roots bands did not merely replicate their distant forerunners; rather, they merged the forms and spirit of old with present-day forces. The results were roots in flux, hybridized into contemporary musical manifestations via new constructions on recognizable foundations.

Besides showing inclinations toward nostalgia and escapism, new roots bands and jam bands also exuded a ubiquitous humor that was uplifting and positive, while simultaneously packing a satirical punch that underscored their distaste for modern trends. Alt-country acts like Robbie Fulks and the Waco Brothers offered caustic messages over the jaunty roots-rock veneers of their songs; their often biting satire was motivated by the state of modern country music as crafted by Nashville's corporate superstructure. They sought to revitalize the "good" humor of traditional country while chastising Nashville for rejecting its own roots. New roots bands were even more radically conservative than the neo-hippy acts; they projected a Luddite ideology that eschewed polished production and image-based marketing. With a sharp cynicism and biting wit molded by years of punk rock, alt-country artists went in search of the spirit of Hank Williams and Woody Guthrie. In these roots gurus they found the same working-class pride, lyrical humor, and "three chords and the truth" that punk had more recently provided.

As Nashville country morphed into an international pop genre during the nineties, alt-country set up a parallel universe based on a paradox: Its music was more authentically traditional than mainstream country, yet its constituent audience was drawn from college radio rather than rural roots. This schism was hardly a new phenomenon, though. Since the 1970s, certain acts had become disenchanted with the commercialization of the form, setting out to create their own alternative country club. Each time, the conservative country fan base had stayed behind, while new audiences drawn from counterculture rock circles had followed. The most renowned of these factions was the "outlaw" movement of the early seventies, which boasted such maverick Texans as Willie Nelson and Kinky Friedman. Friedman's fascination with America's Western heritage, coupled with his irreverent and biting wit, established the modern prototype for alt-country. His outlaw persona would be passed on to subsequent Texan rebels like Robert Earl Keen, Lyle Lovett, and Steve Earle. These new traditionalists spoke with reverence and reference to the deep roots of country music, as a result (and ironically) foregoing the riches a Nashville-based career may have brought them.

The city most responsible for fostering new roots music during the 1990s was Austin, Texas. With Austin's indigenous country traditions and a deep wellspring of innovative alternative rock bands, it is no coincidence that the merging of these forces would occur here. Home to the University of Texas and more live venues in a four-block radius than any other city in the nation, Austin has long been a home (or adopted home) for artists with independent *and* country inclinations. The irreverent wit of Austinite Kinky Friedman has insinuated itself into any number of local acts, while the proud independence of Austin's pride and joy, Willie Nelson, keeps the town's secessionist spirit alive. Their legacy has continued through tongue-in-cheek politicos like the Austin Lounge Lizards, whose tall tales and comedic skits have charmed and incited local crowds for decades.

More adventurous country roads have been traveled by Austin acts like the Bad Livers and the Gourds, both of whom have been audacious in their rerouting of roots styles. The Bad Livers were one of the first bands to bastardize the largely uncolonized and puristic bluegrass genre. Their incongruous introduction of the tuba to the form created humorous hybrids one could never have envisaged.

Audiences have been divided on the Livers, some hailing the band as pioneering innovators, others condemning them as irreverent, even sacrilegious. Indeed, one might wonder how Bill Monroe might have responded to hearing lead singer Danny Barnes apply his nasal country whine to the band's bluegrass rendition of the Butthole Surfers' "The Adventures of Pee Pee the Sailor."

The Gourds trumped even the Bad Livers in the unlikely covers stakes when they brought a hick-hop reading to Snoop Dogg's "Gin and Juice" in 1998. This brazen act of genre-fusing was amusing enough in itself, but the band's straight delivery—without hint of parody—made the version subversively humorous by provoking implicit audience questions: Are we laughing because we are not used to the narrow guidelines of country music being breached? Does the "natural" translation of Snoop's lyric from a hip-hop context to a country one suggest equally "natural" allegiances between black and white working-class cultures? Are the trite lyrics of the song better revealed for what they are (and thus laughed *at*) by virtue of being replanted outside the G-rap field? Elsewhere, the Gourds celebrate—without mocking, but with good humor—a romanticized country culture of drunken porch-party life, their loose-limbed, ragged beer-grass style p(l)aying tribute to their prioritizing of pursuits of fun over careerism.

The most radical humorists of the roots revival were Rob Miller, Nan Warshaw, and Eric Babcock, three country-loving ex-punks who set out to support the many label-less alt-country acts that populated Chicago's small nightclubs during the early years of the decade. These three amigos brought large doses of missionary zeal and rebellious humor to their Bloodshot Records label. Proclaiming their "insurgent country" identity, Bloodshot's founders used their website home page to launch some verbal guided missiles at Nashville's corporate country stronghold. "Help us fight the good fight," they declared in mock-revolutionary rhetoric. "Help us keep our steel-toed work boots firmly on the throats of the enemy." And if these statements did not adequately differentiate them from the majors, Bloodshot invoked H. L. Mencken with an epigrammatic mission statement: "There comes a time when every man feels the urge to spit on his hands, hoist the black flag and start slitting throats."[61] Such agitprop hyperbole may not have had the handlers of Shania Twain and Garth Brooks quaking in their boots, but it certainly established the label as riled-up antagonist-wits—rather than cowering defeatists—in the rough-and-tumble country game.

With a moral compass set for honesty and integrity, Bloodshot cast their net across the American Midwest (their financial limitations forced geographical limits, too) in pursuit of roots-based acts with an indie attitude. Like Stiff Records during the British punk insurgence, Bloodshot sought out humorous bands, but not novelty ones. They wanted to reestablish within roots music the kind of social satire that Woody Guthrie had once articulated, or the clever, colloquial wordplay that had once made Hank Williams the poet laureate of the working classes. And as Nashville country continued to consolidate the genre into limited "types," each further homogenized by cookie-cutter production, sound, and lyrical content, Bloodshot provided a counter-reaction to the prevailing trends, encouraging a raunchy spirit, unchecked adventurism, and down-home humor. By the time of their debut 1994 release, *For a Life of Sin: A Compilation of Insurgent Chicago Country*, Bloodshot Records' founders had brought the sounds of the windy plains to the dives of the Windy City, gathering a roster of like-minded artists with roots-country in their souls and subversion on their minds.

Though his tenure with Bloodshot would be a brief one, Robbie Fulks was one of the early trailblazers for the label. His Bakersfield honky-tonk style was retro, but his acerbic humor could be as stinging as any punk act. "Fuck This Town" (1997) became an insurgent anthem for both Fulks and Bloodshot, its shot-across-the-bow lyrics aimed squarely at Nashville. With un-PC vitriol, Robbie sent out a big "Fulks You" with these lines: "Nashville'll do just fine / As long as there's a moron market / And a faggot in a hat to sign."[62]

Bloodshot's signature band, the Waco Brothers, seconded Fulks's sentiments with their own song, "The Death of Country Music" (1997). "The bones of country music live there in the casket / Beneath the towers of Nashville in a black pool of neglect," spits singer Jon

Langford in mixed-metaphor mode.[63] Langford, a veteran of first-wave British punk band the Mekons, was a prototypical Bloodshot representative. His respect for working-class communitarianism and roots music humor was only surpassed by his disdain for big business's dilution and devastation of honest expression within the music industry and beyond. The Wacos have been to alt-country what Billy Bragg has been to modern folk, earning the band the descriptive country-punk sobriquet "half Cash, half Clash."

Besides these veterans, Bloodshot has also collected some of the more innovative young country acts of recent years. Though recently depleted by the death of singer-guitarist Kirk Rundstrom, Splitlip Rayfield—like the Bad Livers—have taken the bluegrass form into uncharted waters. Variously tagged as punk-grass, cow-punk, and y'allternative, Splitlip's mutation songs move at breakneck pace, satiating punks and country radicals alike. Tapping into a "rube" humor tradition dating back to Uncle Dave Macon and beyond, these Kansan boys inhabit a fantasy trailer park world, playing with—and celebrating—the stereotypes of this culture. "Drinkin' Around" (1999), "Drink Lotsa Whiskey" (2001), and "A Little More Cocaine Please" (2004) suggest their terrains of lyrical inspiration, while Jeff Eaton's one-string stand-up bass, built from the gas tank of a 1965 Ford Truck, provides an onstage gimmick to complement the band's party mayhem and earthy humor.

Label-mates the Meat Purveyors have been equally brash and rambunctious in their country explorations. If Splitlip Rayfield are the Ramones of cow-punk, then the Meat Purveyors have been its Talking Heads. Indeed, they even titled their 1999 album *More Songs about Buildings and Cows*. With cheeky wordplay and clever in-genre satire, the Meat Purveyors reveal a sly side to their hick affectations. They toy with country music's omnipresent themes, twisting tales of breakups and booze into ironic (self-)parodies. In "Thinking about Drinking" (2002), singer Jo Walston displays the band's warped wit with the clever/dumb lines "When I'm not drinking, I'm thinking about drinking. / And when I'm not thinking, I'm drinking about you."[64] Pointedly inverting the "born again" arrogance of much contemporary "inspirational" country music, the Meat Purveyors entitled their most recent album *Someday Soon Things Will Be Much Worse* (2006).

The return to roots by the many nineties alternative country and neo-hippy jam bands certainly indicates dissatisfaction and/or anxiety with the changes and developments the accelerated technological revolution has brought about. However, it would be simplistic just to dismiss these retro-seekers as mere escapists and sentimentalists. In their rerouting of roots forms lies the very essence of contemporary postmodern rock. Like other contemporary genres of rock—rap, punk, metal, pop—roots rockers plunder the past to invent a new future, one connected to, not severed from, that past. Rock's retro-instincts are part of the form's continuum, and its humor, likewise, forms links across history, often self-consciously speaking to, for, or against that history. In contemporary humorists lie the conscience and subconscious of rock music; they alert us to what is by connecting us to what was; and in their candid, uncensored (self-)reflections, they inquire (or cajole us) into what might be.

THE NAUGHTIES:
Post-irony and Identity Humor

THE EVENTS OF September 11, 2001, altered the character and trajectory not only of American popular culture but its expressions of humor, too. Humor scholar Giselinde Kuipers recalls the immediate aftermath of 9/11, when "laughter had become inappropriate," leading to an immediate-term "moratorium on humor." Soon thereafter, humor quietly crept back onto U.S. screens and stages in relief form, as "a means to cope."[1] At this stage, humor was embraced for its healing powers, used to encourage feelings of home solidarity (against the enemy), and employed to bind the nation during its time of grief.

Notably absent at this time—and for a few years hence—was the kind of satirical bite and subversive edge that had come to characterize much contemporary humor within rock culture and beyond. Comic commentators Bill Maher and Ann Coulter (representing markedly different political perspectives) became well-known casualties of the new national intolerance of subversive (or controversial) humor when they were unceremoniously fired from their respective jobs (Maher as host of the TV show *Politically Incorrect* and Coulter as a writer for *National Review*) for making statements deemed "inappropriate" in relation to 9/11.[2] The benefit of hindsight suggests that their silencing was significant, less for what they had actually said than for the fact that it marked a trend of media self-censorship at odds with America's vaunted freedom-of-speech ideals.

This "big chill" on subversive expression, alongside the media's apparent capitulation to the perspectives and "talking points" of the Bush administration, was to persist in the years following 9/11 and into the Iraq war buildup and execution. An Orwellian cloud appeared to descend over the nation, such that its humorists—so often its primary dissenters—toned down and tamed their material to fit the national climate of unqualified patriotism. With the notable exception of the libertarian-left's holy trinity of Michael Moore, Al Franken, and the aforementioned Maher, subversive humorists were few and far between during the early years of this decade.

Within rock culture, too, rebellion was missing in action, and it was soon apparent that a sixties-styled youth uprising would not be forthcoming. The Dixie Chicks illustrated the high price to be paid for dissent when, onstage in England ten days after the 2003 Iraq invasion, lead singer Natalie Maines admitted to the audience that she was "ashamed" of her fellow Texan, President Bush. The resulting backlash was immediate and sweeping within the country music community, with angry reactions emanating from "red state" (ex-)fans (some of whom conducted ceremonial Chicks-product burnings, reviving a practice previously exercised on the Beatles after John Lennon claimed the band were "bigger than Jesus"). Country radio stations blacklisted the band, and some fellow artists even reacted in kind, rabble-rouser Toby Keith hoisting up a stage backdrop featuring Maines's image alongside Saddam Hussein's. If off-the-cuff, flippant, and—let's face it—harmless remarks like

Maines's could elicit such extreme censure, record companies and media outlets were (perhaps understandably) reticent in encouraging any voices of political criticism, even (or especially) if they came in a humorous form.

By 2004, when it became clear that the Bush party line on Iraq had been built on faulty intelligence and manipulative propaganda—and that the media had been complicit in negligently accepting both—the tide began to change, not only in relation to expressions of dissent but, relatedly, to humor. Rediscovering their fundamental democratic right to free speech, critics and comics alike sought to compensate for the "moratorium" of the previous years. There was a sense of collective relief as years of pent-up frustration, anger, and guilt were spewed forth in an explosion of subversive comedy that some are now calling "the golden age of the satirical."[3] For their dereliction of duty, mainstream "news" outlets were mercilessly ridiculed by *The Daily Show* and later via its spin-off *The Colbert Report*. Outsider stand-up comics with sociopolitical agendas, like Lewis Black, Chris Rock, and Dave Chapelle, became central voices in the new rebellion, while stalwarts like Maher, Moore, and Franken gained inspired confidence and garnered vindication for their prior courage and commitment to the cause of comedic truth-telling.

Inspired by these developments, rock rebels emerged from their hibernation, too, with established acts like Eminem and the Beastie Boys targeting the Bush administration with theretofore unseen comedic venom.[4] Although waves of political humor have hardly followed in their wake, the comedic pulse within American rock has returned, such that today a tone and tenor of humor is ubiquitous within the national popular culture, making for an eclectic mix within and across multiple fields and for(u)ms.

The 1990s saw rock music styles mutate and hybridize more than they had at any other time in rock history. As a result, the collapse of conventional categories and images has led to reformulations more fluid than fixed, while the beneficiaries of rock's implosions have mostly been outsiders. A cursory survey of rock culture over the last decade reveals that white, male, heterosexual Americans are no longer at the center of rock identity as they were before. Indeed, that center has been erased as marginal cultures have flourished and multiplied and as new voices and identities have merged with, morphed into, or just circumvented the old models. The fruitful culmination of the struggles of generations of minority groups can now be witnessed in the panorama of subversive humor they are contributing to modern rock culture; indeed, the channels of comedic discourse today flow as much from female and gay culture as they do from males and straights. Furthermore, America's accustomed domination of rock developments is being increasingly challenged (artistically if not commercially) from beyond its borders, with bright young wits emerging with regularity from Britain, Scandinavia, Japan, and elsewhere.

If new identity humor has emerged as the decentered dominant of our times, post-irony is its prevalent tone and style. Like postmodernism (and other "posts"), post-irony is both intimately connected to and referential of the past, while being significantly separated from it. The post-ironic style of humor locates itself between the irony and the pastiche that have been the loci of modern humorist expression. In an age of rock where technology has enabled the downloading of past recordings (either literally or by way of influence) into current sounds, the post-ironist both concedes the act(s) of plagiarism/pastiche involved, while (implicitly or explicitly) commenting upon that recognition and act. The humor resides in the processes of *negotiation* between past and present: in the how, in the delivery, and in the reception. Whereas an ironist or parodist invokes the past in order to invert it, mock it, or resist it, and whereas the pastiche artist impassively duplicates the past, the post-ironist does both—differently. (S)he unapologetically pilfers a style or a sound-bite but does so without the slight of the parodist, instead showing reverence, delight, or perhaps complete indifference in the act. Tenacious D and Hank Williams III are quintessential post-ironic acts of our times. Their shameless dipping into the past conveys humor through an over-the-top enthusiasm and passion, *as well as* straight-faced reverence through those very same features. Paradoxically, there is no way to distinguish the two modes of expression for they inhere within each other. As such, post-irony both is and is not humorous, it might or might not be, or it can be but does not have to be. The post-ironists are essentially generation-hoppers in their downloading means of production, as well as in their modes of delivery and intended consumption. The Scissor Sisters and Andrew W.K., for example, offer certain perspectives and aspects of humor to one demographic that have wholly different significance to another. These acts exude a knowing nod and wink that we must all share (if differently) for the humor to register; the shared (non)revelation is that in the age of postmodernism nothing is new, but all is available for creative reconstitution and, ultimately, for comedic deconstruction.

CAMPING OUT

The history of rock has revealed gender and sexuality to be consistent issues for subversive humorists. From Little Richard in the 1950s to big Beth Ditto in the 2000s, sexually marginalized figures have represented their social positions through expressions of provocative and often contentious humor. Increasingly today, we are witnessing the coming out of these outsiders, as breakdowns in gender and sexual identities open spaces for these previously muted groups. Indeed, much of the most subversive humor to emerge in recent years has emanated from gays and/or gender and sexual provocateurs; their contributions are changing the face(s) of modern pop and rock, while reviving some of the oldest traditions of humor.

Like contemporary female humorists, homosexuals have developed their comedic expressions from stereotypes that have been thrust upon them in the past; as they cultivate these codes of language, aesthetics, and humor, they exaggerate identity distinctions in ways that are both critical and self-deprecating. If straight culture condemns homosexual behavior and gestures, gay humorists respond by acting them out with exaggerated pride. This preemptive process is not dissimilar to the rube humor employed within country culture, where a *play* on "dumb" stereotypes binds the community in comic self-defense against would-be oppressors while offering a larger exposé of the pomposity and hypocrisy of mainstream culture. Similarly, the flaunted effeminacy and theatrical affectations of camp have united the sexually ostracized community and offered resistance against heterosexual puritanism at a subcultural level. Camp style—as well as kitsch, its object-equivalent—operates via conventions that celebrate sexual "deviance." The result is a kind of sexual justice where straights become the new outsiders. Camp places performance, voice, and language in quotation marks, inviting you with a knowing wink to decode its theater and to face the realities of gender and sexual multiplicity. It is a comedic signal for sexual identities that have long been denied, vilified, and silenced, though its political component is largely implicit. Just as burlesque secretly mocked the aristocratic airs of the Victorian community and the cabaret of 1930s Germany celebrated life without restraint, so camp within recent rock bares a political consciousness, not through polemics, but by its very essence.

Peaches (a.k.a. Merrill Beth Nisker) has updated burlesque and cabaret for the modern age, using hilariously naughty provocations as her means to subvert mainstream mores of gender and sexuality. A one-woman crusader on behalf of shock, lewdness, and hypersexuality, Peaches makes Prince and Madonna seem positively PMRC-friendly. Working with the electropop dance styles favored by many from the new camp school, Peaches essentially uses music as a tool of convenience for her taboo-busting lyrical excursions. Her breakthrough album, *The Teaches of Peaches* (2000), established the bawdy wit that would be her calling card and included such raunchy electro-ditties as "Fuck the Pain Away," "Diddle My Skittle," and "Lovertits." A series of grunts and squeals punctuates this porn soundtrack, as the fruity one takes listeners on a camp trip through the sexy, the shocking, and the silly.

Initially, the surface-level sexual humor of Peaches seemed rather one-dimensional, but her next album demonstrated a desire to do more than just challenge the limits of our inhibitions or test the triggers of censorship. *Fatherfucker* (2003) portrayed Peaches in full beard for the cover shot, laying to rest charges that she was only and all about pornographic titillation. The album image and title—through incongruity humor—call attention to our "common sense" usage of language and imagery. Her acts of socio-sexual inversion transform parades into parody, sex into satire. We are forced to question gender roles and representations as well as obscenity and the representation of obscenity, as we are disturbed, or at least disrupted, by her gross antics. In "Two Guys (for Every Girl)" (2006), Peaches turns the ménage à trois concept upside down and inside out by making "the girl" the actor rather than the acted upon. "Slappin' those dicks all over the place," she coos with authoritative glee.[5]

Having established herself as an antidote to fundamentalists the world over, Peaches' latest album suggests that her irreverent instincts have not quelled. The pun-chline-titled *Impeach My Bush* (2006) again features our starlet on the cover, this time wearing a sequined burka. The songs she sings within are hardly those befitting a good Muslim girl, though, as the titles "Fuck or Kill," "Tent in Your Pants," and "Slippery Dick" might suggest. Whether Peaches manages to continue to raise her own bar on bawdy humor remains to be seen, but her creative capacity to out-shock all opposition has positioned her not only as one of the most controversial acts of our times but also as one who is leading with front-loaded humor in breaking down our self-constructed barriers to sexual and gender liberation.

Peaches may be forcing the frontiers of sexual identity, but a cast of other characters are following behind with similar body politics on their minds. Fischerspooner and Chilly Gonzales have also embraced the "electroclash" style—a camp mutation of Euro-disco and new wave—as the vehicle for their own campaigns of identity fluidity, while Har Mar Superstar, otherwise known as Sean Na Na (or Sean Tillman to his mother), has paraded his large frame in semi-naked form around the gay clubs of Europe and the United States. His ironic sexual boasting is matched only by that of Beth Ditto, the portly frontwoman of The Gossip. Like Sean, Beth calls attention to body image prejudices by strategically defrocking herself wherever the situation allows, be it onstage or on the cover of the *NME*. Unlike the above-mentioned electroclash gender shockers, Ditto represents a bawdy blues tradition that boasts such *big* and forceful characters as Big Mama Thornton, Etta James, and Candye Kane. Her outspokenness (such as on the pro-gay anthem "Standing in the Way of Control" [2005]) and shock poses are motivated by an activist agenda on behalf of female imaging and lesbian rights. *Ditto* her humor, which serves a cathartic role for the like-sized or like-sexual, as it ruptures the commonsense assumptions of body beauty and its socialization processes.

Britain's premier gay rock icons of recent years are Scissor Sisters—who are actually American. However, while in the land of Graham Norton and George Michael, the band reside comfortably as pop superstars; at home in New York they are little more than a cult act. Boasting a surrogate drag queen in Ana Matronic as well as three openly gay members in Jake Shears, Babydaddy, and Del Marquis, Scissor Sisters have revived mid-1970s rock, pop, and disco camp for a generation that was not around to profess their loathing for it first time around. Like most camp art, Scissor Sisters take prior kitsch product (once hated), highlight it as such (to designate irony), then reservice it (to comedic delight). In the retro-process we are all swept up in the nostalgia of it all, hearing Elton John and disco-period Bee Gees like we never did before. Guilty pleasures can now—via Scissor Sisters—be consumed (with a postmodern comedic wink) merely as pleasures.

Named in honor of a sex position for two women, Scissor Sisters was a softer version of their original moniker, Dead Lesbian and the Fibrillating Scissor Sisters. And although such songs as "Tits on the Radio" (2004) and "Hairbaby" (2006)—the latter of which addressed the topic of partially formed fetuses—got them banned from Wal-Mart (a fate befalling many who have outraged with less, as Sheryl Crow can testify), the band's output has been generally tame and their humor hardly Peaches-provocative. Scissor Sisters humor works by post-ironic association, alluding to homoerotic pop of the past (Elton John, Queen, George Michael) while staying wholly reverent to it in spirit. Theirs is the knowing theft of camp, with an unapologetic gravitation to a kitsch disco pop style that flies in the face of indie rock hip and macho-heterosexual guitar flailing.

A more innovative and aesthetically challenging form of rock camp has recently been produced by Rufus Wainwright, the openly homosexual son of musician parents Loudon Wainwright III and Kate McGarrigle. Rufus's articulate wit has drawn comparisons to such gay icons as Oscar Wilde and Morrissey. His musical style derives from opera and baroque as well as pop, while his soaring vocal delivery is as mock-heroic as the poetic lines he delivers. Like Morrissey, Wainwright conveys complex emotions through humor, his self-deprecating wit providing candor to his lyrical revelations. Both artists refer to private intimacies to reveal broader social observations, each employing linguistic details and a wry perspective to more-than-comedic effect. Like Morrissey, too, Wainwright's eccentric idiosyncrasies have endeared him to critics as much as to his rabid cult following.

In "Gay Messiah" (2004), Wainwright undermines traditional religious assumptions, but also laughs at the camp clichés of homosexuality with his opening slight, "He will be reborn from 1970s porn / Wearing tube socks with style." Employing Wilde-by-way-of-Morrissey dramatic overstatement, he discounts himself as a "Messiah" candidate, singing, "No, it will not be me / Rufus the Baptist I be."[6] "California" (2001) sees him following in the inspirational path of satirist Randy Newman with an update of the latter's "I Love L.A." Over the kind of ironically mock-jaunty musical backdrop for which Newman is renowned, Wainwright skewers the golden state, dismissing it as a "land of neon" and its populace as equally surface-shiny.[7]

Another recent band that have endeared themselves to the intellectual as well as the camp quarters of the gay community is the Dresden Dolls, a duo featuring Amanda Palmer on vocals and piano and Brian Viglione on drums. Performing the dark comedy of goth and burlesque, the Dolls' self-described "Brechtian punk cabaret" is rich in tradition, reinventing the costumes and theater of the Weimar Republic to complement Kurt Weill–informed—but contemporary-sounding—piano pieces. The bawdy roots of burlesque are embraced in "Coin-Operated Boy" (2002), a witty homage to sex toys, while "Girl Anachronism" (2002) brings a feminist twist to the band's gender musings. The Dresden Dolls, like contemporaries Gogol Bordello and Nellie McKay, show the malleability of the cabaret tradition in relation to alt-rock identity (the Dolls), national and ethnic identity (Bordello), or issues of gender and sexuality identity (McKay). The recent revivalist surge of cabaret within rebellious rock circles is not particularly surprising; its anarchist spirit and camp otherness are universally understood to lend themselves to music that is both comedic and subversive in intent.

ROCK ON!

The disintegration of social identity hierarchies has brought backlashes of many kinds. These reactions have been particularly pronounced within genres—like heavy metal and country—whose histories have relied upon certain expectations of race, gender, and sexuality, where the white, heterosexual male has been privileged and idolized. Recent heavy metal humor has acted much like country's rube humor in its defensive reflexes, comically exaggerating male fantasies, male sexual conquests (and other conquests), and male hedonistic gestures at a time when male primacy is losing much of its lust(er) and hip credibility. Like country's rubes, metal mockers reveal a twofold humor that, on the one hand, shows a nostalgic craving for the "good old days" of "cock rock," while on the other, recognizes the farce of such machismo in the modern age.

True, this polarity between heartfelt fantasy and (self-)parody has been a driving force in the ongoing saga that is heavy metal, but it has also been the source of its ever-present humor. The oscillation between the serious (or self-delusional) and the sarcastic (or knowing) has made hard rock an intriguing phenomenon that gives equal billing to its cravings and embarrassments. However, whereas past metal movements have been relatively clear in demarcating the parodists from the fantasists—the Spinal Taps from the Sabbaths—certain contemporary mock rockers have merged the two perspectives into a more ambiguous, post-ironic mode. Post-ironic rockers blur the lines between candor and camp; they recognize and caricature the clichés they *play* with, while still showing reverence to the genre's power by rocking out with earnest gusto. This facilitates different guitar strokes for different folks within the same music, as younger demographics might enjoy the same cathartic release in listening to Andrew W.K. as their parents once did to Led Zeppelin, while their parents, familiar with the signifiers being deployed and the knowing wink with which they are conveyed, might take pleasure in the cerebral cleverness of the dumb humorous construct.

Post-irony in hard rock—as elsewhere—is not a fixed determinant but a broad field with gradations of humor. Whereas Tenacious D accentuate the comical side of their identity, the Darkness sublimate their humor behind a more serious desire to be recognized as "rock gods." The distinction here is merely one of emphasis, not of essence.

What the recent metal humorists have in common, though, is more than likely a short shelf life. The nature of their referential humor is novelty, and most novelty involves a limited repertoire of one-dimensional jokes that soon run their course. The initial shock gestures may be powerful and affecting, but they can rarely be repeated anew; in some instances those gestures *are* the genre, leaving the artist no place to go and grow. This cruel fate is apparent among the new post-ironic rockers, most of whom are already old, dying, or dead. Tenacious D caused a stir with their eponymous 2001 album, but by their second disc (and accompanying movie) their lovable underdog myth had been erased by their own success; without an antagonist, they had no one to play "D" against.

Tenacious D may be the most self-consciously humorous—but also the most assertively subversive—of the recent metal school of rock. Moreover, their gestures are not just internal to the genre or the industry; sometimes they have a sociopolitical bent, at least as experienced by their target youth demographic. Speaking for the slacker masses in "The Government Totally Sucks" (2006), the D go to bat on behalf of their pet issue, the legalization of marijuana, skewering "the man" for his repression of the individual, while offering up this "potted" history for *critical* context: "Ben Franklin was a rebel indeed / He liked to get naked while he smoked on the weed. / He was a genius but if he was here today / The government would fuck him up his righteous A!"[8]

Tenacious D are a classic comedy tag team, Kyle Gass playing foil for Jack Black's frenetic antics. This self-proclaimed "greatest band on earth" provides sustenance for those who missed Spinal Tap the first time around. With willful self-delusion, the D *tap* into and echo their predecessors' "Stonehenge" period, evoking the grand myths and legends of yore. The central characters within their narrative tales are themselves, cast either as conquerors or warriors fending off demons and devils. The epic is their medium, and adventure is their mission. In "History" (2006) the legend is carved in rock: "We ride with kings on mighty steeds across the devil's plain / We've walked with Jesus and his cross / He did not die in vain—No!"[9]

The D's underlying satirical interest—like Spinal Tap's—is the inflated ego of the rock star who has lost touch with reality and resides in delusional perpetuity. The band's sexual powers—like their rock ones—are on frequent parade, with Black and Gass refusing to let their short, portly, balding statures stand in the way of self-mythologization. Faux machismo is given a hilarious twist of incongruity in "Fuck Her Gently" (2001), where the ball-busting "hard" rocker narrator turns out to be Mr. Sensitive. "I'm gonna hump you sweetly, I'm gonna ball you discreetly," Black sings with power ballad romanticism.[10] As with Spinal Tap's "Big Bottom," the laughter comes from the straight-faced delivery, while the subversion lies in us knowing how close the sentiments are to so many sentimental "power ballads" that have come before—but that were not intended for comedic reaction.

They may be high on novelty gestures (among other things), but Tenacious D possess musical features that are far from secondary to their purposes. The band clearly love the epic rock tradition that they so precisely parody, and tribute songs like "Dio" (2001) reflect as much, while still retaining a humorous perspective. Not content to be all lyrical boasts and no rock balls, The D hired the Dust Brothers to produce their debut album and gathered an all-star cast of backing musicians—including Dave Grohl on drums—to bring full realization to their ambitious rock anthems. The result is music that is as marked by quality as it is by humor.

Ensconced—like Tenacious D—in his own fantasy dreamworld creation, Andrew W.K. is one of the latest in a long line of rockin' party animals, a tradition that boasts such larger-than-life caricaturists as Ted Nugent and Kid Rock (both Motor City madmen like W.K.), Twisted Sister and Mötley Crüe, Billy Idol and Gary Glitter. W.K. writes for the party, lives for the party, and will no doubt artistically die for the party. Whereas prior party proponents like the Beastie Boys ultimately graduated from their "fight for the right to party" into pastures new, W.K. appears destined to flog his horse until they close the frat house down.

Arising seemingly out of nowhere at the start of the decade, Andrew W.K. satisfied the "Caucasian kitsch" demands of that segment of culture infatuated with *Maxim* magazine, *Jackass*, and World Wrestling Entertainment.[11] Like these phenomena, W.K. provided humor-proof machismo against the imposing forces of post-feminism and multiculturalism. Here was a white guy having traditional white guy fun, but without the whining and self-immolation of the period's nu metal narcissists. With lyrics dumbed down to the three-word, three-syllable slogans of their titles ("Girls Own Love," "Take It Off," "I Get Wet"), and guitars fully amped up and distorted, W.K. offered catharsis for the Beavis and Butthead and Wayne and Garth generation.

Establishing his manifesto with the independent release *Party Til You Puke* (2000), Andrew W.K. started the conveyor belt that would produce such adolescent directives as "Party Hard" and "It's Time to Party" (from *I Get Wet* [2001]), then "Long Live the Party" and "Make Sex" (from *The Wolf* [2003]). The song "Totally Stupid" (2003) reflected his cravings, not condemnations, while "Don't Stop Living in the Red" (2002) celebrated arrested adolescence, irresponsibility, and the freedom of the id(iot) life. His simple cartoon persona of the rock rebel unleashed pervades every drum crack, every fat guitar riff, and every dumb line that toes the party line. The jackass, mock-rock world that Andrew W.K. inhabits is one without compromise or subtlety; there, as with other contemporary metal post-ironists, the point is in the exclamation and the exclamation is the point!

COUNTRY'S CROSSROADS

The diversity of contemporary country music is reflective of developments beyond the genre. The technological revolution of recent decades has created a fast-moving, fast-changing culture; country music, traditionally the port in the storms of social upheaval, has not survived unaffected by these changes. Furthermore, multiculturalism and civil rights effects have trickled down into country culture, which has responded both in accord and in reaction to their consequences. For every progressive trend that has made country more amenable to new gender and class representations, there have been backlash artists who have resisted them. The ever-expanding alternative country scene straddles both trends, reflecting nostalgia for the genre's conservative past as well as an unwillingness to be encumbered by its less savory, discriminatory elements. Within mainstream Nashville country, the events of 9/11 created rifts within the culture, with progressive artists like the Dixie Chicks falling foul of reactionary forces seeking the comforts and certainties of a mythical past.

These dynamics and struggles have their correlative representations at the level of humor, too. Whereas Brad Paisley might showcase a new literacy and sophisticated humor aimed at a modern, bourgeois country base, Gretchen Wilson represents the remnants of rube humor, where working-class "redneck" stereotypes are as much celebrated as they are laughed at. As the rest of the rock world forges forth in establishing new identities for a dynamic world, country continues to struggle with its sense of self, inexorably torn between an idealized past and the anxieties of a present in flux.

The rube humor revival of recent years is both anachronistic and pertinent to our times. Although the "trailer trash" jokes of Larry the Cable Guy and Jeff Foxworthy have a flashback feel, as though they came from some old episode of *Hee Haw*, the huge popularity of these comedians suggests that their novelty values run much deeper than just revivalism. At a time when gender roles are uncertain, when class status is fluid and unstable, and when old nationalistic assumptions are being challenged, rural America has leaned on its neo-rube humorists for relief, escapism, and the optimistic sureties of nostalgia. Working-class rural culture—alongside its middle-class allies—has embraced "whiteness" with all the muscularity of its defense mechanisms, donning trucker hats and wife-beater shirts in ironic self-defense against any and all perceived change. By withdrawing into an imaginary 1950s—creating "symbolic authenticity" by "fabricating roots," as John Leland puts it—these nostalgics hope to laugh away the alarming issues and events sensationalized on their TV screens every hour of every day.[12]

The current darling of rube retro-activity is Gretchen Wilson. An ex-waitress single mother from a trailer park in rural Illinois, Wilson arrived in Nashville as the stereotypical "redneck woman" she would soon proclaim herself to be. Since, she has become a central icon of country traditionalism, with the feistiness of Loretta Lynn and the anti-modernism of Minnie Pearl. Wilson's emergence reestablished working-class female identity in the wake of the wave of prim and thin bourgeois beauties that had tweaked country's twang in mainstream pop directions. One was unlikely to hear Shania Twain or Faith Hill belting out "I'm here for the beer and the ball-bustin' band" as Gretchen Wilson did on "Redneck Woman" (2004).[13]

A plain looker by choice with a well-rehearsed honky-tonk attitude, Wilson serves as an every-gal for female fans and a real gal for the boys. Employing a compare-and-contrast rhetorical approach to draw clear lines of distinction, she rhetorically asks the "fellas" in "California Girls" (2005), "Ain't you glad there's a few of us left" who eat "fried chicken" and "dirty dance to Merle?"[14] For her and her "fundamentalist" demographic, the trendy Hollywood set is symbolic of modern pretensions and phoniness. By taking the back roads and the roads back, Wilson creates a fantasy-reality—in song—of the way things were and should be. "One Bud Wiser" (2005), Wilson puns in one of her titles, espousing the escapist philosophy inherent in her humor.

The more rabble-rousing side of rube humor has been best represented in recent years by Toby Keith, a figure seen by many as the Merle Haggard or Charlie Daniels of his generation. Envisioning himself as both outlaw and Western hero, Keith has assumed a "red state" populist position as the savior in the saddle (or on the microphone). With an image that requires an enemy to sustain itself, Keith brings the same put-down humor to the Dixie Chicks as he does to Saddam Hussein. Traitors and terrorists are the main targets of Keith's pun-filled diatribes, with rough justice the proposed course of action. In the parable "Beer for My Horses" (2002), he imagines himself as a Western hero bringing law and order to the land. In "Courtesy of the Red, White and Blue (The Angry American)" (2002), he helped fan the flames of anger and revenge within a nation still mourning the events of 9/11, pledging to put a "boot in the ass" of the enemy.[15] Capitalizing on the popularity of his macho posturing while diminishing the gravity of the ensuing wars, Keith brought new levels of insensitivity to his populist humor by titling his next release *Shock'n' Y'All* (2003).

When the Dixie Chicks' Natalie Maines expressed her shame that President Bush hailed from her home state of Texas, a firestorm of protest was set off in the country community, revealing schisms that had existed beneath the surface for some time. The subsequent Keith–Dixie Chicks "high noon" showdown symbolized the nation's ideological divide, as well as two strains of its humorous expression within modern country. Whereas Keith represented the "back" roads of conservative retreat and rube humor, the Dixie Chicks signaled progressive satire and liberal change. Early in their career the Chicks had enjoyed success with the feminist-fashioned murder fantasy song "Goodbye Earl" (1999), which, although controversial, had been embraced by a vast constituency of country's female fans. The band's humor had a spicy if apolitical edge at the time, though since Maines's infamous outburst and the subsequent backlash, they have grown more outspoken and cutting (as on the recent "Not Ready to Make Nice" [2006]), abandoning the Nashville mainstream just as that culture abandoned them. Today, the band receives considerable critical acclaim from the rock apparatus (recently winning five

Grammys), while a boycott of the band is still in effect within the country industry. The long-running drama of the Dixie Chicks may have its most profound conclusions in relation to issues of identity expression within country culture, where its humorist-spokespeople continue to struggle over the heart of the heartland.

If the Dixie Chicks signal departures into an assertive female country style, and Gretchen Wilson and Toby Keith are responsible for putting the grit(s) back into the genre, then Hank Williams III is the outlaw reborn. Williams III—or Hank III, or the Unholy III, or III, as he is variously called—has made it his mission to call up and cast forth the rabble-rousing spirits of his famous daddy and infamous granddaddy. If Wilson, Keith, and the Chicks have settled at the outskirts of Nashville, Hank III is the unwelcome troublemaker returning to the home of his forefathers after (self-)imposed exile. One of his songs even characterizes Nashville as "Trashville" (2002), while another, "Dick in Dixie" (2006), lays out his insurrectionary manifesto: "I'm here to put the dick in Dixie and the cunt in Country."[16] For all their irreverent wit and rebellious predilections, one cannot imagine Wilson or Keith or the Chicks going *there*.

Hank III–style country, though recognizably honky-tonk in sound, draws from punk humor for its effect. Whereas country rube humor has traditionally functioned as comic relief, its self-deprecating caricatures serving as preemptive defense mechanisms against a prejudicial outside world, Hank III puts those "types" on the attack as antagonists raging from the margins. *Risin' Outlaw* (1999) and *Lovesick, Broke and Driftin'* (2002) are the titles of his debut and sophomore albums, respectively; both suggest statements of intent as well as of artistic personality. Song topics have been equally brazen and unabashed, with "Pills I Took," "Smoke & Wine," and "My Drinking Problem" from *Straight to Hell* (2006) indicating that Hank III has been disinclined to the conservative values side of the country community. Indeed, his untamed lyrics and shock-attack wit on this album were such that his label, Curb Records, forced him to produce a clean version for Wal-Mart's shelves. Even then, it arrived with a Parental Advisory sticker, a first for a major-label country album. As combative with his record company as he has been with Nashville, Hank III once responded to his ongoing battles with Curb using prankster humor, selling "Fuck Curb" T-shirts through his official website.

Family ties may be what allow Hank III to remain as the thorn in the side of the country establishment, but, for his part, he has never rested on, relied upon, nor cashed in on this legacy. Indeed, onstage, his so-called "Jekyll and Hyde" shows mix hard-twang "hell"-billy sets with even less commercial punk-metal ones, the latter of which he performs with his stripped-down Assjack band. Here, he is able to fully release his hardcore demons and shock humor. Within a mainstream country culture decreasingly adventurous and increasingly turning its back on the rough-and-tumble roots of its rowdy past, Hank III reminds us—using boast and put-down humor—of a tradition beyond the controls of Nashville's corporate marketing, one that runs through Kinky Friedman, Johnny Cash, and the original "hick" humorist hell-raiser, Hank Williams Sr.

Despite its resistance to change, innovation, and its own history, Nashville has let a few other purveyors of "old school" creativity slip into its inner sanctums. One of these is Brad Paisley. His "new traditional" style has drawn him comparisons to George Jones, Randy Travis, and Alan Jackson, while his wise-cracking wordplay bears the intellectual hallmarks of Hank Williams Sr. Appealing to city and suburban country fans as well as rural ones, Paisley symbolically bridges the gap between Toby Keith and the Dixie Chicks. Inoffensive and engaging, Paisley lacks the provocative wit of country's "extremists," but his wry insights into the human condition and clever means of articulation are internally subversive, suggesting possible new roads for future country humor. "Alcohol" (2005) is one of Brad Paisley's more requested songs. Sung from the point of view of its subject matter, the song mixes literary references ("I helped Hemingway write like he did") with familiar ones ("I bet you a drink or two that I can make you put that lampshade on your head").[17] With topics traditional and a treatment clever and fresh, Brad Paisley may be the kind of country artist who can help unite rather than divide the genre's currently fragile and fractious factions.

INDIE INTELLECTUALS

One man's post-ironic humor is another man's plagiarism. As postmodernism threatens to reduce contemporary art to products of high-tech replication—with the attendant nod and wink—some dissenters have stepped up to cry that enough is enough; they are not amused. The major forces of the backlash to post-irony have come from within indie rock culture, nowadays a catchall term for alternative rock of many stripes. Rooted in the 1980s post-punk period, indie rock has expanded in a universe parallel to mainstream rock and pop, assuming its roles as innovator and/or keeper of the "authentic" rock faith. Indie rockers today constitute the avant-garde of the rock scene, preserving modernist ideals in the face of the postmodern onslaught. Though not necessarily elitist or pretentious, many indie rock acts privilege intelligence, creativity, and originality; they value high art forms as art rockers did in the 1970s, engaging them with purpose if not a little pomposity. In a decade where hipsters have deferred to the past as compensation for their own vacuums of creativity, the indie intellectuals have pursued the new, and when they have looked back for inspiration, it has been for an authentic spirit long lost, rather than for content to download.

If indie intellectuals provide a counter-reaction to the post-ironists of pastiche, their humor also reflects their defining identities. High-humored satire is more privileged by them than camp allusions, and eloquent narratives trump "cheap" puns and wordplay. These artists look to literary figures for sustenance rather than TV celebrities, and they are more likely to be inspired by the whimsical humor of baroque and Broadway than by disco and pop kitsch.

The Hold Steady are the quintessential indie rock traditionalists of the present. Staunch defenders of classic rock aesthetics, they set themselves unashamedly against the processed sounds, stylized images, and sound-bite lyrics of modern music. Rock realists, their pursuit of artistic truth and authenticity have elicited comparisons to Bruce Springsteen, the genre's most famous defender of the faith.

Like the Boss, the Hold Steady write story-songs about America with rousing rock anthems constructed to touch the heart rather than the hip. Unlike Springsteen, they use humor to bring pointed comment to their tales, as well as to reflect satirically upon the broad cultural trends of their nation in flux. As such, the band has as much in common with Warren Zevon and the Replacements as with Springsteen.

The Hold Steady's literate wit—not surprisingly—has been embraced with enthusiasm by a cognoscenti bored by the banalities in the current batch of conveyor-belt rock products. *Pitchfork* has celebrated the band as though they were the second coming, while *NME* are in the process of hyping them across the Atlantic. Plaudits for their recent *Boys and Girls in America* (2006) album have run deep, with many magazines rating it in their end-of-year top ten lists. *The Onion*—America's premier satirical publication—recognized it as their album of the year in 2006.

The lyrical wit prized by *The Onion* and others is provided by singer-songwriter Craig Finn. A thirtysomething stalwart of the indie rock scene, Finn has little time for the PBR-drinking cultural slummers of alternative kitsch, and even less for the retro-acts that coyly dust off superficial old pop ditties for a new generation. He may show tongue-in-cheek nostalgia for the "skater phase," "raver phase," and "razor blade phase" of his youth in "Positive Jam" (2004), but he has little patience for those who pilfer wholesale from the eighties as though it were the golden age of rock.[18] "The eighties almost killed me / Let's not recall them so fondly," Finn advises paternalistically in that song, his mind no doubt on the electroclash and Killers-pop brigades. In "Barfruit Blues" (2004) he takes aim again at the post-ironic scenesters, saying, "Clever kids are killing me / For one, they ain't that clever."[19]

The Hold Steady are artists in the Mark Twain tradition: their vision is grand and sweeping, their humor a tool of cultural comment, and their mission to capture the nation's spirit and elevate its sense(s). They flesh out characters into fully formed figures that have psychological depth and universal resonance. *Separation Sunday* (2005), for example, charts the character Holly across the album, bringing to life not only an individual but the culture of drugs, prostitution, and religious indoctrination that she inhabits. If rock poetry is an archaic concept today, the Hold Steady—as their moniker suggests—are refusing to let the more literate manifestations of rock humor fade without a fight.

Modest Mouse, the Shins, Sufjan Stevens, Bright Eyes, the Arcade Fire, and many others indicate that the Hold Steady have successful company within the new wave of intellectual indie rock; however, the Decemberists may be their closest allies in their expressions of humor. With their baroque, string-soaked folk-rock songs, the Decemberists have elevated literary rock to new levels of grandiloquence; their historical tall tales are whimsical and detailed, imaginative and fantastical. They show—by contrast—just how dumbed down our popular culture has become. An acquired taste within the larger rock culture, the band's adventure stories of the high seas have struck a chord with those seeking mind-stimulating wit; indeed, the listeners of National Public Radio recently voted the band's latest, *The Crane Wife* (2006), as their album of the year.

Equally stimulating and whimsical, and with a greater degree of musical dexterity, is Andrew Bird, an adept wordsmith and intrumentalist with a penchant for whistling. Bird's philosophical musings recall the wit of Kurt Vonnegut Jr., as the tongue-in-cheek, sophomoric questions of "Dark Matter" (2007) suggest: "Do you wonder where the self resides? / Is it in your head or between your sides? / Who will be the one who decides its true location?"[20] Like Elvis Costello, Andrew Bird luxuriates in words, enjoying their sounds and rhythms as well as their meanings. Imaginative humor infuses his language, which, in turn, transforms the everyday into the poetic and mystical, as in "Armchairs" (2007): "I dreamed you were a cosmonaut of the space between our chairs / And I was a cartographer of the tangles in your hair."[21] At face value, such romantic fantasies might not seem particularly subversive, but set against the larger context of a corporate entertainment culture determined to reduce the creative mind to a passive condition of blind (and bland) acceptance, Bird's reminders that the imagination can soar and that active humor is the gateway to freedom are revolutionary indeed.

From the less "in-crowd" quarters of the modern indie world, Nellie McKay has been busy transforming her Broadway training and classical music schooling into an independent career of intellectual songwriting on the outskirts of rock culture. Despite industry efforts to subsume her into the jazz-folk easy listening set inhabited by Norah Jones and others, McKay has always resisted, answering only to her own eccentric calling as an eclectic provocateur who likes to do things her own way. In response to her record company's attempts to categorize and package her, McKay titled her debut album *Get Away from Me* (2004), a sly inversion of Norah Jones's 2002 hit, *Come Away with Me*, with the added twist of its declaration of her artistic independence.

McKay started the decade as a stand-up comedian on New York's Manhattan and Greenwich Village circuits. Combining her comic with musical skills, she drifted into the city's anti-folk scene before being snapped up and signed by Columbia/Sony. Her sharp songwriting humor was apparent early, in songs like "I Wanna Get Married" (2004), which satirized the lives of submissive stay-at-home moms, and "Work Song" (2004), which mocked the bourgeois nine-to-five life. Here was an artist with nonconformist ways; her iconoclastic spirit set her in distinction from the malleable divas of her time, while her multistyled songs and theatrical quirkiness made niche-marketing a nightmare for her record company. The final straw came early for Columbia, who dropped McKay when she insisted that her second album—coming on the heels of her double debut—be sixty-five minutes long and include twenty-three tracks. McKay responded with practical humor, taking revenge by passing out the personal e-mail address of the label CEO to her fans. The album—*Pretty Little Head* (2006)—eventually came out on her own Hungry Mouse label, complete with a forty-four page accompanying booklet; as she had originally intended, the album included all twenty-three songs, thus still clocking in at sixty-five minutes in length.

With her "take-no-shit" attitude, comedian's eye for cultural insights, and accomplished and diverse skills of musicianship and songwriting, McKay continues her journey as a Renaissance woman of modern music, combining her assorted talents in unorthodox and innovative ways. Like her fellow indie intellectuals, Nellie McKay shines as a beacon to independence, creative energy, and critical comedy in an environment often less than encouraging of such traits.

BACK TO THE FUTURE

In the context of its history, rock music feels—in some respects—as if it has come full circle in the twenty-first century. Our postmodern era has created an eternal past-as-present where all existing styles, forms, and expressions are accessible at the touch of a button for consumption, appropriation, or inspiration. That same ubiquity exists for rock humor, too, where the targets, techniques, and practices of humor witnessed throughout the history of rock are still with us.

The most enlightened and subversive contemporary rock humorists have drawn from this past history (as well as other humor histories) without being wholly dependent upon it. John Leland sees their postmodern strategies as "hip" and forward-looking rather than retroactive, saying, "While [hip's] collective memory preserves the past, it also destroys it to begin anew."[22] The most progressive forces of contemporary rock humor have pushed forward on behalf of those who in the past have been pushed back or pushed aside. The post-ironists and identity humorists of the present may not have reinvented the wheel of humor, but they have propelled it forward on behalf of the rights and representations of women and homosexuals, ethnic and regional minorities, and other social groups new or rare to rock. Humor has served as the humanizing force in the mix, testing limits and taking risks.

Much has been written lately about the so-called "golden age of humor" we are currently living in. Positive critics have celebrated it as a mark of a healthy democracy after the comedy embargo and "big chill" of the immediate post-9/11 period. Others, however, have not been so welcoming of the orgy of humor that has befallen us. "Making fun of absolutely everything is defining a generation," critic Wyatt Mason recently moaned, before warning that humor administered in such large doses becomes an affectless placebo in an environment of universal self-congratulation rather than truth-seeking.[23] Michael Frayn, likewise, notes the "permanent sneer of everything," while Barry Humphries bemoans "an infuriating frivolity, cynicism and finally a vacuousness. Everyone's a satirist."[24] John Morreall offers a theoretical context for their concerns, explaining in *Taking Laughter Seriously* that too much humor is self-defeating and that contrast with an opposition is needed for comedy's essential incongruity to exist.[25] Certainly, these are concerns to heed. We should be aware that although humor may have subversive potential or even intent, it might not be consumed by the culture that way. The pervasive sarcastic demeanor that many critics have grown weary of in both rock and the broader culture may be a sign that we are overloading on humor bites while, in the process, negating their sting.

Perhaps the waning effects of modern humor will—like rock itself periodically does—spark a revolt into new expressions and energies. Although rock humor may never deploy the *same* subversives as Chuck Berry, Frank Zappa, and Warren Zevon again, it will produce new and different ones, adaptive to their times and adept with their own methods. Whatever its merits in the past or present, subversive rock humor is here to stay because its three elemental components—subversion, rock music, and humor—all relate to the same common human need and desire: freedom. John Morreall argues that you can never control a person who has humor, you can never brainwash or indoctrinate a person who has humor, and you can never create an institutional pawn out of a person who has humor.[26] In his/her drive to question with childlike curiosity, to resist rigidities, and to unite others in laughter, the humorist—like the fool or jester of old—steps outside, bringing an objectivity of truth and a perspective of freedom. Rock music—the most consistently subversive art form of the past century—would certainly have taken very different historical pathways without the monumental input and impact of its freedom-seeking humorists.

Notes

Introduction: Subversion, Rock, Humor

1. Charles Churchill. "The Ghost." *The Poetical Works of Charles Churchill—Volume Two*. Ed. W. Tooke. Boston: Little, Brown & Co., 1854. Book IV, lines 1,379–1,387.
2. Qtd. in Chris Powell and George E. C. Paton, eds. *Humour in Society: Resistance and Control*. New York: St. Martin's Press, 1988. p.207.
3. Charles E. Schutz. *Political Humor: From Aristophanes to Sam Ervin*. Rutherford, NJ: Fairleigh Dickenson University Press, 1977. p.32.
4. The Who. "My Generation." *My Generation*. Brunswick, 1965.
5. See John Morreall. *Taking Laughter Seriously*. Albany: State University of New York Press, 1983, for discussion of Freud and relief theory. pp.20–37.
6. Lester Bangs. "Bubblegum." *The Rolling Stone Illustrated History of Rock and Roll*. Ed. Jim Miller. New York: Random House, 1980. p.328.
7. See Roland Barthes. *Image/Music/Text*. Trans. Stephen Heath. New York: Noonday, 1977.

The Fifties: Revolution to Evolution

1. Big Joe, Turner. "Shake, Rattle, and Roll." *Big, Bad & Blue: The Big Joe Turner Anthology*. Rhino/WEA, 1994.
2. Chuck Berry. "Brown Eyed Handsome Man." *The Definitive Collection*. Chess, 2006.
3. —."Maybelline." *The Definitive Collection*.
4. —."Roll Over Beethoven." *The Definitive Collection*.
5. The Beastie Boys updated Berry's "drop" with their own hip-hop version in "The New Style" from *Licensed to Ill*. Def Jam, 1995. Here, instead of a coin dropping into the jukebox, a stylus needle dropping to the record ignites "the new style" of music.
6. Chuck Berry. "School Day." *The Definitive Collection*.
7. Langdon Winner. "Little Richard." *The Rolling Stone Illustrated History of Rock and Roll*. 1980. p.49.
8. Little Richard. "Tutti Frutti." *The Very Best of Little Richard*. Cleopatra, 2000.
9. Qtd. in Charles White. *The Life & Times of Little Richard: The Quasar of Rock*. New York; Harmony Books, 1984. p.68.
10. James Miller. *Flowers in the Dustbin: The Rise of Rock and Roll, 1947–1977*. New York: Simon & Schuster, 1999. p.112.
11. James Miller. *Flowers in the Dustbin*. p.112.
12. Little Richard. "Long Tall Sally." *The Very Best of Little Richard*.
13. —."Good Golly Miss Molly." *The Very Best of Little Richard*.
14. Qtd. in Charles White. *The Life & Times of Little Richard*. p.217.
15. Qtd. in Charles White. *The Life & Times of Little Richard*. p.218.

16. Qtd. in Charles White. *The Life & Times of Little Richard*. p.216.
17. Langdon Winner. "Little Richard." *The Rolling Stone Illustrated History of Rock and Roll*. p.48.
18. Little Richard. "Tutti Frutti." *The Very Best of Little Richard*.
19. Bo Diddley. "Bo Diddley." *The Essential Bo Diddley*. Universal, 2001.
20. —."I'm a Man." *The Essential Bo Diddley*.
21. —."Who Do You Love?" *The Essential Bo Diddley*.
22. —."Hey, Bo Diddley." *The Essential Bo Diddley*.
23. —."Say Man." *The Essential Bo Diddley*.
24. Qtd. in Ed Ward. *Rock of Ages: The Rolling Stone History of Rock and Roll*. Eds. Ed Ward et al. New York: Simon & Schuster, 1986. p.111.
25. Jerry Lee Lewis. "Whole Lotta Shakin' Goin' On." *The Definitive Collection*. Hip-O Records, 2006.
26. —."Great Balls of Fire." *The Definitive Collection*.
27. —."Breathless." *The Definitive Collection*.
28. —."Redneck." *Dueling Rock*. Direct Source, 2000.
29. Big Mama Thornton. "Hound Dog." *The Original Hound Dog*. Ace (UK), 1990.
30. Qtd. in Ray Topping. Sleeve notes to *The Original Hound Dog*.
31. Qtd. in Gillian G. Gaar. *She's a Rebel: The History of Women in Rock and Roll*. New York: Seal, 2002. p.2.
32. Gilbert, Joanne R. *Performing Marginality: Humor, Gender, and Cultural Critique*. Detroit: Wayne State University Press, 2004.
33. Wanda Jackson. "I Gotta Know." *Queen of Rockabilly*. Ace, 2004.
34. *David Halberstam's The Fifties*. Vol. 1: "The Fear and the Dream." VHS. A&E, 2006.
35. Wanda Jackson. "Cool Love." *Queen of Rockabilly*.
36. —."Fujiyama Mama." *Queen of Rockabilly*.
37. —."Hot Dog That Made Him Mad." *Queen of Rockabilly*.
38. David Seville. "Witch Doctor." Liberty, 1958.
39. Steve Otfinoski. *The Golden Age of Novelty Songs*. New York: Billboard, 2000. p.7.
40. Qtd. in Ed Ward. *Rock of Ages*. p.88.
41. The Coasters. "Yakety Yak." *The Very Best of the Coasters*. Elektra, 2004.
42. —."Charlie Brown." *The Very Best of the Coasters*.
43. —."That Is Rock & Roll." *The Very Best of the Coasters*.
44. —."Along Came Jones." *The Very Best of the Coasters*.
45. Qtd. in Nick Tosches. *Unsung Heroes of Rock and Roll*. New York: C. Scribner's Sons, 1984. p.127.
46. Screamin' Jay Hawkins. "I Put a Spell on You." *Spellbound! 1955–74*. Bear Family, 1994.
47. Qtd. in Ed Ward. *Rock of Ages*. p.143.
48. Qtd. in Nick Tosches. *Unsung Heroes of Rock and Roll*. p.124.
49. Screamin' Jay Hawkins. "Feast of the Mau Mau." *Spellbound! 1955–74*.
50. —."I'm Your Man." *Spellbound! 1955–74*.
51. Frankie Lymon & the Teenagers. "I Am Not a Juvenile Delinquent." Gee Records, 1957.

The Sixties: Humor Grows Up . . . and Away

1. Qtd. in Jonathan Eisen. *Age of Rock*. Ed. Jonathan Eisen. New York: Random House, 1969. p.4.
2. Qtd. in "Bob Dylan: The American Troubadour." *Biography*. DVD. A&E, 2000.
3. Janet Maslin. "Bob Dylan." *The Rolling Stone Illustrated History of Rock and Roll*. 1980. p.219.

4. Bob Dylan. "Talkin' New York." *Bob Dylan.* Sony, 2005.
5. See David R. Pichaske. *The Poetry of Rock: The Golden Years.* Peoria, IL.: Ellis, 1981. Pichaske explains Dylan's persona creation by claiming that he "arrived in New York City with no real personality of his own." p.122.
6. Qtd. in "Bob Dylan: The American Troubadour." *Biography.*
7. John Orman. *The Politics of Rock Music.* Chicago: Nelson Hall, 1984. p.86.
8. Bob Dylan. "Masters of War." *The Freewheelin' Bob Dylan.* Sony, 2004.
9. Geoffrey Stokes. *Rock of Ages.* p.312.
10. Janet Maslin. "Bob Dylan." *The Rolling Stone Illustrated History of Rock and Roll.* 1980. p.222.
11. Bob Dylan. "Talkin' World War Three Blues." *The Freewheelin' Bob Dylan.*
12. —."With God on Our Side." *The Times They Are a-Changin'.* Sony, 2005.
13. —."It Ain't Me Babe." *Another Side of Bob Dylan.* Sony, 2004.
14. Qtd. in David P. Szatmary. *Rockin' in Time: A Social History of Rock and Roll.* Upper Saddle River, N.J.: Prentice Hall, 2000. p.99.
15. Bob Dylan. "Maggie's Farm." *Bringing It All Back Home.* Sony, 2004.
16. —."Subterranean Homesick Blues." *Bringing It All Back Home.*
17. —."Rainy Day Women #12 & 35." *Blonde on Blonde.* Sony, 2004.
18. Phil Ochs. "Talking Vietnam Blues." *The Early Years.* Vanguard, 2000.
19. —."Draft Dodger Rag." *The Early Years.*
20. —."Love Me, I'm a Liberal." *Phil Ochs in Concert.* Elektra, 1995.
21. —."Outside a Small Circle of Friends." *20th Century Masters: Best of Phil Ochs.* A&M, 2002.
22. Susan J. Douglas. *Where the Girls Are: Growing Up Female with the Mass Media.* New York: Times, 1994. p.83.
23. Greil Marcus. "The Girl Groups." *The Rolling Stone Illustrated History of Rock and Roll.* 1980. p.160.
24. The Shangri-Las. "Leader of the Pack." *Best of the Shangri-Las.* Umvd, 1997.
25. Susan J. Douglas. *Where the Girls Are: Growing Up Female with the Mass Media.* p.98.
26. Ibid. p.92.
27. Country Joe & the Fish. "Superbird." *The Collected Country Joe & the Fish.* Vanguard, 1990.
28. —."I-Feel-Like-I'm-Fixin'-to-Die Rag." *The Collected Country Joe & the Fish.*
29. Ohio Express. "Yummy Yummy Yummy." *Golden Classics.* Collectables, 1994.
30. The Archies. "Sugar Sugar." *Archies—Greatest Hits.* Prime Cuts, 1995.
31. Qtd. in Jim DeRogatis. *Turn On Your Mind: Four Decades of Great Psychedelic Rock.* Milwaukee, WI: Hal Leonard, 2003. p.82.
32. Frank Zappa. "Who Needs the Peace Corps?" *We're Only in It for the Money/ Lumpy Gravy.* Rykodisc, 1990.
33. The Fugs. "C.I.A. Man." *The Fugs First Album.* Fantasy, 1994.
34. —."Kill for Peace." *The Fugs Second Album.* Fantasy, 1994.
35. —."New Amphetamine Shriek." *Virgin Fugs.* Esp, 2005.
36. —."Elm Fuck Poem." *The Fugs (Kill for Peace).* Esp, 1966.
37. Qtd. in Bruce Pollock. *When the Music Mattered: Rock in the 1960s.* Austin, TX: Holt, Reinhart, and Winston, 1983. p.183.
38. Qtd. in Legs McNeil and Gillian McCain. *Please Kill Me: The Uncensored Oral History of Punk.* New York: Penguin, 1996. p.18.
39. The Velvet Underground. "Waiting for the Man." *The Velvet Underground & Nico.* Polygram, 2002.
40. —."Heroin." *The Velvet Underground & Nico.*

41. —."Beginning to See the Light." *The Velvet Underground*. Polydor, 1996.

42. —."I'm Set Free." *The Velvet Underground*.

43. Lou Reed. "Vicious." *Transformer*. RCA, 2002.

44. —."I Believe in Love." *Rock and Roll Heart*. Buddha, 2000.

45. Qtd. in John Leland. *Hip: The History*. New York: Harper Perennial, 2004. p.270.

The Seventies: Radical Cynicism

1. Hunter S. Thompson. *Fear and Loathing in Las Vegas*. New York: Vintage, 1989. p.68.

2. Ibid. p.202.

3. See Legs McNeil and Gillian McCain, *Please Kill Me*. Various insiders here discuss the contrasts between the East and West Coast scenes of the late 1960s. pp. 3–24.

4. Janet Maslin. "Singer/Songwriters." *The Rolling Stone Illustrated History of Rock and Roll*. 1980. p.339.

5. Warren Zevon. "Frank and Jesse James." *Warren Zevon*. Elektra, 1992.

6. —."Desperados under the Eaves." *Warren Zevon*.

7. —."Join Me in L.A." *Warren Zevon*.

8. —."The French Inhaler." *Warren Zevon*.

9. —."Johnny Strikes Up the Band." *Excitable Boy*. Elektra, 1990.

10. —."Excitable Boy." *Excitable Boy*.

11. —."Werewolves of London." *Excitable Boy*.

12. —."Life'll Kill Ya." *Life'll Kill Ya*. Artemis, 2000.

13. Randy Newman. "Short People." *The Best of Randy Newman*. Rhino, 2001.

14. —."Rednecks." *The Best of Randy Newman*.

15. —."Louisiana 1927." *The Best of Randy Newman*.

16. —."Political Science." *The Best of Randy Newman*.

17. Geoffrey Stokes. *Rock of Ages*. p.312.

18. Qtd. in Joe McEwen. "Funk." *The Rolling Stone Illustrated History of Rock and Roll*. 1980. p.374.

19. Gil Scott-Heron. "The Revolution Will Not Be Televised." *The Revolution Will Not Be Televised*. RCA, 1990.

20. —."Brother." *The Revolution Will Not Be Televised*.

21. —."Whitey on the Moon." *The Revolution Will Not Be Televised*.

22. —."Pardon Our Analysis (We Beg Your Pardon)." *The First Minute of a New Day*. Tvt, 1998.

23. Qtd. in Philip Auslander. *Performing Glam Rock: Gender and Theatricality in Popular Music*. Ann Arbor, MI: University of Michigan Press, 2006. p.9.

24. Qtd. in Serene Dominic. "Alice Doesn't Live Here Anymore." *Metrotimes*. October 8, 2003. www.metrotimes.com/editorial/story.asp?id=5479.

25. Alice Cooper. "Go to Hell." *Go to Hell*. Warner Brothers, 1976.

26. —."Elected." *The Best of Alice Cooper: Mascara and Monsters*. Rhino, 2001.

27. —."Teenage Lament '74." *The Best of Alice Cooper*.

28. —."Wish I Were Born in Beverly Hills." *From the Inside*. WEA International, 1999.

29. Qtd. in Dave Laing. *One Chord Wonders—Power and Meaning in Punk Rock*. London: Open University, 1985. p.23.

30. Qtd. in Bill Martin. *Avant Rock: Experimental Music from the Beatles to Bjork*. Peru, IL: Open Court, 2002. p.4.

31. Qtd. in Legs McNeil and Gillian McCain. *Please Kill Me*. p.119.

32. Qtd. in Legs McNeil and Gillian McCain. *Please Kill Me*. p.115.

33. Qtd. in Legs McNeil and Gillian McCain. *Please Kill Me*. p.119.

34. Qtd. in Legs McNeil and Gillian McCain. *Please Kill Me*. p.190.

35. New York Dolls. "We're All in Love." *One Day It Will Please Us to Remember Even This*. Roadrunner, 2006.
36. The Modern Lovers. "Roadrunner." *The Modern Lovers*. Castle Music UK, 2003.
37. —."Hospital." *The Modern Lovers*.
38. —."I'm Straight." *The Modern Lovers*.
39. —."Dignified and Old." *The Modern Lovers*.
40. Ken Tucker. "New Wave: America." *The Rolling Stone Illustrated History of Rock and Roll*. 1980. p.441.
41. John Rockwell. "The Sound of Manhattan." *The Rolling Stone Illustrated History of Rock and Roll*. 1980. p.419.
42. Bernard Gendron. *Between Montmartre and the Mudd Club: Popular Music and the Avant-Garde*. Chicago: University of Chicago, 2002. p.249.
43. The Ramones. "Beat on the Brat." *The Ramones*. Rhino, 2001.
44. —."Havana Affair." *The Ramones*.
45. Jerome Davis. *Talking Heads*. New York: Omnibus, 1986. p.24.
46. Talking Heads. "Psycho Killer." *The Best of Talking Heads*. Rhino, 2004.
47. Jerome Davis. *Talking Heads*. p.xii.
48. Ibid. p.51.
49. Talking Heads. "Heaven." *The Best of Talking Heads*.
50. —."Air." *Fear of Music*. Warner Brothers, 1990.
51. —."Animals." *Fear of Music*.
52. —."The Big Country." *More Songs about Buildings and Food*. Warner Brothers, 1990.
53. —."Once in a Lifetime." *The Best of Talking Heads*.
54. —."Road to Nowhere." *The Best of Talking Heads*.
55. *Stop Making Sense*. Dir. Jonathan Demme. DVD. Extra Features. Palm Pictures, 1999.
56. Gillian G. Gaar. *She's a Rebel*. p.213.
57. Qtd. in Bernard Gendron. *Between Montmartre and the Mudd Club*. p.289.
58. Qtd. in Simon Reynolds and Joy Press. *The Sex Revolts: Gender, Rebellion, and Rock 'n' Roll*. Cambridge, MA: Harvard University Press, 1995. p.290.

The Eighties: Postmodern Regenerations

1. Ken Tucker. "Alternative Scenes: America." *The Rolling Stone Illustrated History of Rock and Roll*. Eds. Anthony DeCurtis et al. New York: Random House, 1992. p.659.
2. Ken Tucker. "Alternative Scenes: America." *The Rolling Stone Illustrated History of Rock and Roll*. 1992. p.614.
3. Qtd. in Claude Bessy et al. *Forming: The Early Days of L.A. Punk*. Santa Monica: Smart Art Press, 2000. p.91.
4. Qtd. in Claude Bessy et al. *Forming*. p.34.
5. Qtd. in Claude Bessy et al. *Forming*. p.31.
6. The Descendents. "Suburban Home." *Milo Goes to College*. New Alliance, 1982.
7. Steven Wells. *Punk: Young, Loud and Snotty*. New York: Thunder's Mountain Press, 2004. p.87.
8. Dead Kennedys. "California Über Alles." *Fresh Fruit for Rotting Vegetables*. Alternative Tentacles, 1980.
9. —."Kill the Poor." *Fresh Fruit for Rotting Vegetables*.
10. —."Nazi Punks Fuck Off!" *In God We Trust, Inc*. Alternative Tentacles, 1981.
11. Tricia Rose. *Black Noise: Rap Music and Black Culture in Contemporary America*. Hanover, NH: Wesleyan University Press, 1994. p.86.

12. Dick Hebdige qtd. in Tricia Rose. *Black Noise*. p.90.
13. Tricia Rose. *Black Noise*. p.99.
14. NWA. "Fuck tha Police." *Straight Outta Compton*. Ruthless, 1988.
15. John Leland. *Hip: The History*. p.173.
16. Tricia Rose. *Black Noise*. p.4.
17. Ibid. p.101.
18. Qtd. in John Leland. *Hip: The History*. p.107.
19. Qtd. in John Leland. *Hip: The History*. pp.91–92.
20. Tricia Rose. *Black Noise*. p.101.
21. Ice T. "Shut Up, Be Happy." *The Iceberg/Freedom of Speech . . . Just Watch What You Say*. Sire, 1989.
22. —."The Iceberg." *The Iceberg*.
23. —."The Girl Tried to Kill Me." *The Iceberg*.
24. —."Freedom of Speech." *The Iceberg*.
25. Beastie Boys. "Rhymin' and Stealin'." *Licensed to Ill*. Def Jam, 1986.
26. —."Fight for Your Right (to Party)." *Licensed to Ill*.
27. —."The New Style." *Licensed to Ill*.
28. —."In a World Gone Mad." Free download. 2003.
29. —."It Takes Time to Build." *To the 5 Boroughs*. Capitol Records, 2004.
30. *This Is Spinal Tap*. Dir. Rob Reiner. Videocassette. Embassy Pictures, 1984.
31. See John Fiske. "British Cultural Studies and Television" in *Channels of Discourse*. Ed. Robert C. Allen. Chapel Hill: The University of North Carolina Press, 1987. Includes a succinct and lucid summary of Stuart Hall's concepts of "dominant," "negotiated," and "oppositional" readings. pp.254–89.
32. Holly George-Warren qtd. in Ken Tucker. "Alternative Scenes: America." *The Rolling Stone Illustrated History of Rock and Roll*. 1992. p.612.
33. Tricia Rose. *Black Noise*. p.155.
34. Susan J. Douglas. *Where the Girls Are*. p.287.
35. Qtd. in John Fiske. "British Cultural Studies and Television" in *Channels of Discourse*. p.275.
36. Qtd. in Gillian G. Gaar. *She's a Rebel*. p.267.
37. Madonna. "Material Girl." *Like a Virgin*. Sire, 1984.
38. "Weird Al" Yankovic. "White and Nerdy." *Straight Outta Lynwood*. Volcano, 2006.
39. —."Smells Like Nirvana." *Off the Deep End*. Scotti Brothers, 1992.
40. —."A Message from Al." www.weirdal.com/msg.htm.
41. John Street. *Rebel Rock*. New York: Blackwell, 1986. p.94.
42. Qtd. in Michael Azerrad. *Our Band Could Be Your Life*. New York: Little, Brown & Co. 2001. p.196.
43. Michael Azerrad. *Our Band Could Be Your Life*. p.274.
44. Ibid. p.274.
45. Ibid. p.325.

The Nineties: Rock in Flux

1. John Leland. *Hip: The History*. p.257.
2. Pavement. "Range Life." *Crooked Rain, Crooked Rain*. Matador, 1994.
3. Michael Azerrad. *This Band Could Be Your Life*. p.499.
4. Pavement. "Cut Your Hair." *Crooked Rain, Crooked Rain*.
5. Weezer. "Buddy Holly." *Weezer*. Geffen, 1994.
6. —."Pink Triangle." *Pinkerton*. DGC, 1996.
7. Qtd. in Pieter Hofmann. "Waist Deep in Pianos and Buses." *Drop-D Magazine*. March 31, 1997. http://dropd.com/issue/46/BenFoldsFive/.

8. Qtd. in Sarah Thomas. "Ben Folds with the Sydney Symphony Orchestra." *Sydney Morning Herald*. August 25, 2006.

9. Ben Folds Five. "Underground." *Ben Folds Five*. Passenger, 1995.

10. —."Battle of Who Could Care Less." *Whatever and Ever Amen*. 550, 1997.

11. Nirvana. "Smells Like Teen Spirit." *Nevermind*. Geffen, 1991.

12. Qtd. in Paul Friedlander. *Rock & Roll: A Social History*. Boulder, CO: Westview Press, 1996. p.281.

13. Nirvana. "Stay Away." *Nevermind*.

14. —."In Bloom." *Nevermind*.

15. —."Serve the Servants." *In Utero*. Geffen, 1993.

16. —."Rape Me." *In Utero*.

17. —."Territorial Pissings." *Nevermind*.

18. Simon Reynolds and Joy Press. *The Sex Revolts*. p.385.

19. Neil Young. "My My, Hey Hey (Out of the Blue)." *Rust Never Sleeps*. Reprise, 1979.

20. Jason Cohen and Michael Krugman. *Generation Ecch!* New York: Simon & Schuster. 1994. p.142.

21. Beck. "Loser." *Mellow Gold*. DGC, 1994.

22. —."Get Real Paid." *Midnite Vultures*. DGC, 1999.

23. —."Debra." *Midnite Vultures*.

24. —."Hollywood Freaks." *Midnite Vultures*.

25. Liz Phair. "Flower." *Exile in Guyville*. Matador, 1993.

26. —."Fuck and Run." *Exile in Guyville*.

27. Qtd. in "Liz Phair." *Wikipedia*. http://en.wikipedia.org/wiki/Liz_Phair.

28. Ani DiFranco. "The Million You Never Made." *Not a Pretty Girl*. Righteous Babe Records, 1995.

29. Missy Elliott. "Wake Up." *This Is Not a Test!* Elektra, 2003.

30. —."She's a Bitch." *Da Real World*. Elektra, 1999.

31. —."Pump It Up." *This Is Not a Test!*

32. —."Toyz." *This Is Not a Test!*

33. —."Scream (a.k.a. Itchin')." *Miss E . . . So Addictive*. Elektra, 2001.

34. —."Work It." *Under Construction*. Elektra, 2002.

35. —."Meltdown." *The Cookbook*. Atlantic, 2005.

36. See John Leland. *Hip: The History*. pp.244–47.

37. Ibid. p.257.

38. Sonic Youth. "Kool Thing." *Goo*. DGC, 1990.

39. L7. "Fast and Frightening." *Smell the Magic*. Sub Pop, 1990.

40. The Notorious BIG. "Ready to Die." *Ready to Die*. Bad Boy Records, 1994.

41. Eminem. "White America." *The Eminem Show*. Aftermath, 2002.

42. John Leland. *Hip: The History*. p.9

43. Eminem. "White America." *The Eminem Show*.

44. —."Just Don't Give a Fuck." *The Slim Shady LP*. Aftermath, 1999.

45. —."Role Model." *The Slim Shady LP*.

46. —."Sing for a Moment." *The Eminem Show*.

47. —."Mosh." *Encore*. Aftermath, 2004.

48. —."The Real Slim Shady." *The Marshall Mathers LP*. Aftermath, 2000.

49. Marilyn Manson. "Irresponsible Hate Anthem." *Antichrist Superstar*. Interscope, 1996.

50. —."Mechanical Animals." *Mechanical Animals*. Interscope, 1998.

51. —."The Nobodies." *Holy Wood (In the Shadow of the Valley of Death)*. Interscope, 2000.

52. —."The Fight Song." *Holy Wood*.

53. —."The Golden Age of Grotesque." *The Golden Age of Grotesque*. Interscope, 2003.
54. —."The Bright Young Things." *The Golden Age of Grotesque*.
55. —."This Is the New Shit." *The Golden Age of Grotesque*.
56. Qtd. in "John Lydon Calls Green Day 'Plonk' Not 'Punk.'" *Gigwise.com*. www.gigwise.com/news.asp?contentid=13310.
57. Green Day. "Basket Case." *Dookie*. Reprise, 1994.
58. The Offspring. "Pretty Fly (for a White Guy)." *Smash*. Epitaph, 1994.
59. blink-182. "Happy Holidays (You Bastard)." *Take Off Your Pants and Jacket*. MCA, 2001.
60. The Bloodhound Gang. "The Bad Touch." *Hooray for Boobies*. Interscope, 2000.
61. See www.bloodshotrecords.com.
62. Robbie Fulks. "Fuck This Town." *South Mouth*. Bloodshot, 1997.
63. Waco Brothers. "The Death of Country Music." *Cowboy in Flames*. Bloodshot, 1997.
64. The Meat Purveyors. "Thinking about Drinking." *All Relationships Are Doomed to Fail*. Bloodshot, 2002.

The Naughties: Post-irony and Identity Humor

1. Giselinde Kuipers. "'Where Was King Kong When We Needed Him?' Public Discourse, Digital Disaster Jokes, and the Functions of Laughter After 9/11." *The Journal of American Culture*. March 2005. Vol. 28, Issue 1. p.71.
2. Victor Navisky. "Profiles in Cowardice." *The Nation*. November 5, 2001. Vol.273, Issue 14. pp.23–24. Maher got into trouble after saying that we (the United States) were more cowardly than the suicide bombers of 9/11, while Coulter was fired from the *National Review* after she suggested that we should invade the Muslim countries responsible for the 9/11 attacks and convert their citizens to Christianity.
3. Wyatt Mason. "My Satirical Self." *New York Times Magazine*. September 17, 2006. p.75.
4. Note, for example, Eminem's "Mosh" and the Beastie Boys' "In a World Gone Mad" single and *To the 5 Boroughs* album.
5. Peaches. "Two Guys (for Every Girl)." *Impeach My Bush*. Beggars XL, 2006.
6. Rufus Wainwright. "Gay Messiah." *Want Two*. Geffen, 2004.
7. —."California." *Poses*. DreamWorks, 2001.
8. Tenacious D. "The Government Totally Sucks." *The Pick of Destiny*. Epic, 2006.
9. —."History." *The Pick of Destiny*.
10. —."Fuck Her Gently." *Tenacious D*. Epic, 2001.
11. John Leland. *Hip: The History*. p.348
12. Ibid. p.350.
13. Gretchen Wilson. "Redneck Woman." *Here for the Party*. Epic, 2004.
14. —."California Girls." *All Jacked Up*. Epic, 2005.
15. Toby Keith. "Courtesy of the Red, White and Blue (The Angry American)." *Unleashed*. DreamWorks, 2002.
16. Hank Williams III. "Dick in Dixie." *Straight to Hell*. Bruc Records, 2006.
17. Brad Paisley. "Alcohol." *Time Well Wasted*. Arista, 2005.
18. The Hold Steady. "Positive Jam." *Almost Killed Me*. French Kiss, 2004.
19. —."Barfruit Blues." *Almost Killed Me*.
20. Andrew Bird. "Dark Matter." *Armchair Apocrypha*. Fat Possum, 2007.
21. —."Armchairs." *Armchair Apocrypha*.
22. John Leland. *Hip: The History*. p.338.

23. Wyatt Mason. "My Satirical Self." *New York Times Magazine*. p.72.
24. Both qtd. in Humphrey Carpenter. *That Was Satire That Was: The Satire Boom Of The 1960s*. London: Victor Gollancz, 2000. p.329.
25. John Morreall. *Taking Laughter Seriously*. p.83.
26. Ibid. pp.101–13.

INDEX